ALDOUS HUXLEY

GARLAND REFERENCE LIBRARY
OF THE HUMANITIES
(VOL. 198)

ALDOUS HUXLEY
An Annotated Bibliography of Criticism

Eben E. Bass

GARLAND PUBLISHING, INC. • NEW YORK & LONDON
1981

Library of Congress Cataloging in Publication Data

Bass, Eben E   1924–
  Aldous Huxley, an annotated bibliography of criticism.

  (Garland reference library of the humanities ; v. 198)
  Includes indexes.
  1. Huxley, Aldous Leonard, 1894–1963—Criticism and
interpretation—Bibliography.   I. Title.
Z8430.2.B37 [PR6015.U9]   016.823′912   79-7907
ISBN 0-8240-9525-1

Printed on acid-free, 250-year-life paper
Manufactured in the United States of America

This book is for Geri

CONTENTS

INTRODUCTION

A book of this sort depends on the research of others whose collective intent is to pay tribute to a great and notable author. The motive is not to tie unsuspecting Gulliver in place with Lilliputian ropes and pegs as if he were being subdued for the curious convenience of the little people, but rather to provide ways for Huxley's work to be read (as he would say) stereoptically, or from multiple perspectives. Some of the critical perspectives included in this bibliography give more insight than others, but even if the effect of those others is only that of the curved mirrors in a fun house, they may give us another, curious look, not unlike some of Huxley's own remarkable distortions.

The number of critical books and articles that comprise this bibliography should prove, for any who still doubt it, that Huxley continues to sustain the readership and critical attention that he commanded during a writing career of nearly fifty years. References that supplied lists of criticism are the *Annual Bibliography of English Language and Literature* (1920–1974); *Abstracts of English Studies* (1953–1978); and the *MLA Bibliography* (through 1978). Some contemporary reviews of Huxley's own works are listed and annotated, along with critical books and articles about Huxley. The most representative collection of current reviews, however, is that of Donald Watt: *Aldous Huxley: The Critical Heritage* (London: Routledge & Kegan Paul, 1975). This work should be consulted for the responses given Huxley's works at the time of their first publication.

This bibliography annotates critical books and articles in English, and many in French. The international appeal of Huxley's writing will also be apparent from the wide variety of languages represented by the unannotated critical books and articles. Further, more than 350 translations of Huxley's works have been made into 28 languages, with virtually all of his works having been translated into French, Italian, and Spanish (see Watt, Appendix II).

The most comprehensive journal article on Huxley criticism is that of Jerome Meckier, "Mysticism or Misty Schism? Huxley Studies since World War II" (370). Therein, Meckier states that "more than anything else, Huxley studies require an updated, annotated bibliography of works by and about Huxley." It is hoped that the present bibliography will serve this purpose.

The following list cites by number critical articles in this bibliography that relate to central topics in his works. The annotations for the articles listed here contain cross-references to other related items on:

39.	Huxley and French Literature
55.	Huxley and D.H. Lawrence
64.	Huxley and the Fine Arts
73.	Huxley as Essayist
79.	Huxley and Utopia
91.	Huxley's Poetry
99.	Huxley, Philosophy, and Religion
104.	Huxley, Literature, and Science
170.	Huxley and Music
197.	Huxley and Satire
211.	Huxley and Drugs
213.	Huxley and Mysticism
228.	Huxley and Shakespeare

As Meckier notes in his "Mysticism" essay, no full record of Huxley's book sales was kept before 1946, when the Huxley Collected Edition appeared, or for paperback editions published thereafter, but regular sales have averaged 13,000 volumes a year since 1946. Watt (Appendix III) records the top-ranking books of Huxley, according to their sales in the Collected Works, through 1972:

Brave New World	55,620
Point Counter Point	35,800
Ends and Means	26,170
Eyeless in Gaza	16,600
Crome Yellow	16,470

Limbo	16,170
Antic Hay	15,170
Those Barren Leaves	13,680
After Many a Summer	12,510

(Comparisons are not absolute because not all titles were available in this edition at the same time.)

Huxley's record of readership failed to impress critics during the 1950's, who ignored him in favor of such writers as Virginia Woolf, James Joyce, and D.H. Lawrence (before his death Lawrence was one of Huxley's closest friends and his writing was deeply admired by Huxley). In the late 1960's, a larger number of books and articles on Huxley appeared; these range in tone from adulation to disparagement, the chief reason for the differences of opinion being Huxley's own encyclopedic range of subject and attitude. Stated most simply (even simplistically), the complaint is that Huxley failed between two monuments, the "early" one of satire and the "late" one of mysticism; but as Meckier and other perceptive critics have shown, this anomaly troubled the unhappy critics more than it did Huxley. Like Emerson, Huxley saw foolish consistency as the hobgoblin of little minds. In fact, mysticism appears very early in Huxley's writings, and satire is found even in his latest works—indeed, even in the fragment of a novel he left at his death. The difficulty is not with Huxley himself, but rather with those readers of limited interest who are looking only for satire or only for soul-searching and who are chagrined when they discover the anti-type competing with their special concern. But the sense of Huxley's method is that it finds theology too doctrinaire, philosophy too abstract, literature too formalistic, and life, complex life, greatly to be cared about, marveled at, and deplored, all at once. It is easy enough when dealing with isolated evidence to make Huxley appear the dupe of practitioners in such curiosities as the Bates method, Sheldon's body types, Jung's archetypes, and a whole rash of topics variously related to parapsychology and extrasensory perception. But Huxley was a connoisseur of the curious, whether it was to be encountered among privileged eccentrics like the aristocratic Briton Sir George Sitwell, or equally eccentric, more impalpable beings like Aimee Semple McPherson, or the Hollywood types whom Huxley observed with growing interest and amusement during his California years. He did not live to see Jonestown, but he could easily have predicted it, just as the demise of Pala in his last novel, *Island*, foresaw the current international oil crisis.

Huxley died of cancer on the day of John Kennedy's assassination; the confusion caused by the one event tended to obscure even an awareness of the other. These coincidental events shared overtones that would have spoken to Huxley's own sense of life and the odd relations of matters unrelated. The man who raised his umbrella as the Kennedy motorcade approached the site of assassination did so to serve a symbolic and unpleasant reminder to John Kennedy of how his father, Joseph, had given diplomatic support to Neville Chamberlain's much-maligned peace policy. Chamberlain's umbrella became the universal symbol for appeasement, and the Dallas heckler used an umbrella to malign the Kennedy image. Huxley too labored hard as a pacifist for much of his lifetime, though some of his statements in the late thirties about making economic and territorial allowances to the "have-not" countries of Europe (Italy and Germany) seem naive now in terms of historical outcomes. Suspect too (nowadays) are Huxley's various anti-Semitic statements (some of which were used for Nazi propaganda during World War II); examples appear in *Do What You Will*. Aldous and Julian Huxley aided Jewish victims of the Nazis before 1939, and yet in a November 19, 1938, letter to Jacob Zeitlin, Aldous refused Zeitlin's request to write a public protest against atrocities committed by the Nazis against Jews. Huxley felt such a protest would not stem persecution, which was "immensely old" and an outgrowth of "traditional methods of social and economic organization." Clearly, Huxley was of two minds on the Jewish question. But to cite such objections is to judge Huxley severely for two of the weakest points in the galaxy of his ideas and interests.

While Aldous Huxley was a student at Balliol in 1914, his first publication appeared in *Climber's Club Journal*: "A Lunndon Mountaineering Essay." In 1915, studying French poetry, he composed his Mallarmé imitations; his Byronic poem on Glastonbury failed to win the Newdigate Prize for poetry; and he wrote "Mole," one of his more interesting early poems, which appeared first in 1916 in *The Palatine Review*. Also in 1916 he received a First in English Literature for his performance on the Schools Examinations (the performance consisted of extremely clever remarks ridiculing the questions themselves). In addition, he won the Stanhope Historical Essay Prize in that year, and, with W.R. Childe and T.W. Earp, edited *Oxford Poetry 1916*. August, 1916, saw the publication of three of Huxley's poems in the *Nation*, and September saw the publication of *The Burning Wheel*, his first book of poems. Also in 1916 Huxley began his eight-month stay at Garsington and his first non-academic association with important writers and thinkers: in effect, the year marked the beginning of a lifetime pattern to be continued in many other places, with many other friends, remarkable for their number and variety.

Huxley's journalistic career began early and is noteworthy for its range and productivity. In 1919, he reviewed 210 books, and in 1920, he reviewed 38 more, but he wrote only 9 reviews during the next 20 years, after which he wrote none. His feature articles for newspapers for 1932, 1933, and 1934 averaged nearly 50 items each year. Earlier, in 1920, he wrote 37 feature articles for newspapers, and 18 more in 1931. A few others appeared in other years, as late as 1935.

The separately published essays that appeared first in the *Athenaeum*, and later in such other magazines as *Vanity Fair* and *Vogue*, came early in Huxley's career and continued in reduced numbers until his death in 1963. These often, though not always, were republished in various series, like the early collection *The Olive Tree* or later in such collections as *Do What You Will*. In 1919, 28 such essays appeared in the *Athenaeum*; in 1920, ₁1 more appeared in the same publication, along with 26 "Marginalia" items signed "Autolycus." A smaller number of essays was published during the next three years, but in 1924, Huxley wrote 21 essays and in 1925, 24 more, for magazines like *Vanity Fair* and *Vogue*. Between 1926 and 1931, Huxley averaged between 10 and 20 published essays a year. Thereafter, the number is smaller, although 10 appeared in 1935 and 13 in 1956, but almost every year saw at least one published essay.

As for the forewords, introductions, and prefaces Huxley wrote for books by others, he averaged a long, evenly sustained performance; with a few exceptions, he wrote about one a year between 1925 and 1963, although he was busier with this sort of effort in the years 1937, 1938, and 1939, when he wrote introductions for 11 books. Having his choice about which books to sponsor contrasted greatly with the onerous book reviewing of Huxley's early journalism years, and the selection of topics he fostered by the introductions is interesting. Just as Huxley's identification with the Vedanta Society and related matters is indicated by the number of separate essays he wrote about them beginning in 1941, prefaces to books on Oriental mysticism are common with Huxley after 1947. After completing the "Autolycus" series for the *Athenaeum*, which ran from July 2, 1920, to February 4, 1921, Huxley generally signed his journal articles, whereas earlier they were mostly published anonymously. The use of a signature indicates his arrival as a known author, just as in a more sensational way the publication of *Limbo* and *Leda* (both 1920) and *Crome Yellow* (1921) made the world aware of his name.

By the time he was commissioned to do the Hearst newspaper series in 1931, Huxley was permitted his choice of topic, and although some of the essays were casually done on hotel stationery originating from wherever Huxley happened to be at the time, and bear other similar marks of haste, others have lasting value and found their way into the permanent essay collections. Huxley's record as a journalist shows that he learned very early to write with rapidity and skill on a great variety of subjects, but it is more important than the apprenticeship that much of what he wrote in this enterprise remains lively and interesting. In *Crome Yellow* Arnold Bennett is parodied as a methodical writer whose discipline produces a thousand words a day; his performance arouses the mixed admiration and resentment of Denis Stone, the young Huxley-like character who has written only "a slim volume of poetry." Though he berated himself as a slow worker, Huxley's own average was about 500 words a day, which he sustained with very few lapses for most of his career. He seldom took vacations, and these were brief; he worked on Sundays, and said that not to work every day made him physically ill.

Huxley's busiest spate of journalism arose from need, after he married Maria Nys in 1919, but poetry and short stories began to appear in 1917 and continued during the journalism years. In addition to the *Athenaeum* assignment, which paid little, Huxley wrote drama criticism for the *Westminster Gazette*, and beginning in 1920 he did other magazine articles for the Condé Nast publications. In the summer of 1921, *Crome Yellow* was written in two months, once the Huxleys had settled in Florence at Forte de Marmi. The Condé Nast work continued until the summer of 1923.

The many newspaper articles from 1932, 1933, and 1934 were produced during a crucial time in Huxley's career. In 1931, Huxley published *The World of Light* (and saw to its London stage production); he also published *The Cicadas*, a collection of poems, and *Music at Night*, a group of essays; *Brave New World* was written in that year. It was published in 1932, when the Hearst series began, a year that marked the publication of *T.H. Huxley as a Man of Letters*, *Rotunda*, *The Letters of D.H. Lawrence*, and *Texts and Pretexts*. In the same year Huxley also wrote his play *Now More Than Ever* and began work upon *Eyeless in Gaza*. Progress on this novel was interrupted by a trip to Central America and the beginning of an essay collection to be called *Beyond the Mexique Bay*; then Huxley did further work on *Eyeless in Gaza*. *Retrospect* appeared at the end of 1933. 1934 saw the publication of *Beyond the Mexique Bay*, after which Huxley developed insomnia, depression, and illness, but for these he was successfully treated by F.M. Alexander in 1935; not until then could he find his way to completing *Eyeless in Gaza*, generally recognized as the novel in which he turned decisively to mysticism.

Comparative sales figures for Huxley's works showed some decline during the 1950's from his popularity in the 1930's and 1940's, but the chief decline in the 1950's was in Huxley's favor among critics rather than readers. Still, his resilience brought recognized successes in the following decade. In 1959 the American Academy of Arts and Letters gave him its Award of Merit for the Novel, putting him in the company of such earlier recipients as Hemingway, Mann, and Dreiser. Huxley was nominated for, but did not receive, the Nobel Prize in Literature for 1960. In 1962, as the London *Times* reported (June 8), he was elected Companion of Literature by the Royal Society of Literature, to join the company of "10 living persons who had brought special distinction to English letters," others of whom were Winston Churchill, G.M. Trevelyan, Edmund Blunden, Somerset Maugham, John Masefield, and E.M. Forster. Proof of sales is provided by royalties which for the year 1962 totalled £6,496 in England and $26,646 in America.

Huxley worked at his writing for four or five hours daily, usually in the mornings, and kept his reading for evenings. In the Wickes and Frazer interview (581), he said that he rewrote everything many times, correcting or redoing each page more than once as he went along. He kept no notebooks, and only seldom and briefly diaries, calling himself "very lazy" for failing in these respects. The novels were planned a chapter at a time, with only a vague idea about general outcomes. On occasion he had to discard a great deal of what he wrote. Lacking a large, detailed plan to work from, he remarked, "Things come to me in driblets, and when the driblets come I have to work hard to make them into something coherent." But it is a Huxleyan kind of coherence achieved with rapid and surprising transitions between what often seem like unrelated topics.

Criticism seldom affected him, because he did not read it—although an exception was his concern about *Island*, his last completed novel, and the failure of many reviewers to recognize what he was trying to do.

Admitting to not being a congenital novelist, that is, lacking skill to invent plots, Huxley also said he was not very good at creating characters. He admired great plot-makers like Stevenson, Dumas, and his own aunt, Mrs. Humphry Ward, "a very sound writer who rolled off her plots like sections of macadamized road"—but clearly he thought no less of his own novels for being thin on narrative and repetitious in character types.

Queried about his less frequent use of satire in the late novels, Huxley responded that the reason was not his declining interest in it: "I'm all for sticking pins in episcopal behinds, and that sort of thing. It seems to me a most salutary proceeding." Nor did the late years indicate that he lost interest in the novel; he held that "fiction, biography and history, are *the* forms." Abstract ideas, he believed, could be best represented "in terms

of concrete characters and situations, whether fictional or real."
That is, "Dostoevski is six times as profound as Kierkegaard,
because he writes *fiction*. . . . In fiction you have the reconcilia-
tion of the absolute and the relative, so to speak, the expression
of the general in the particular."

Such traditional philosophers as C.E.M. Joad (275–279) have
deplored Huxley's philosophical method, just as such novelists as
Arnold Bennett (81) have applied wise strictures to Huxley's
novels, strictures admirable for what they say about Bennett and
his work, but having little to do with the manner in which Huxley visualized his own fiction. It makes much better sense to
employ what the New Critics used to call the intentional fallacy
and review Huxley's own statements about his purpose as a
novelist; these appear in the occasional interviews which he gave.
Clearly, Huxley did not care about Henry James's theories of
what a novel should be, and James's novels "left him cold." Walter Allen (56) very unfavorably remarked that Huxley "borrowed largely of the techniques and attitudes of other writers
and applied them to quite inappropriate material." But this is
judging Huxley by the standards of James or Forster, and not by
Huxley's own design and intent, which visualized the novel as a
much freer, more extemporaneous affair, one in which the narrative and essay forms were to become perfectly merged.

The avenues Huxley followed are many and surprising, and
the odd jumps to seeming irrelevancies reflect his personality
and method of work. Robert Baker's essay "The Fire of Prometheus" (64) on Huxley's use of the fine arts—Sir Christopher
Wren versus Romanticism and the Baroque—evokes one promising train of thought for understanding Huxley; this approach
is followed in a somewhat different manner by Dommergues
(175), who discusses the cultural atmosphere of Crome Manor
and the esthetics of its physical setting, or by LeGates (323) in an
effective analogy drawn between Huxley's essays and novels and
the paintings of Breughel. Huxley's interest in music, and his
"musicalization of fiction," are well presented in many of the
critical essays cited in this bibliography. Furthermore, Huxley's
curiosity about widely varying periods in history and cultural
settings gave rise to *Grey Eminence* and *The Devils of Loudun*. In
another interview (117) Huxley expressed a great fondness for

14th-century Italy, "its violence and picturesqueness ... that passage from extreme sanctity to extreme brutality—things we consider incompatible go in the same breath." The novel Huxley planned on Quattrocento Italy never materialized, but the contrast of sanctity and brutality that intrigued him has much to do with Huxley's dual mode of satire and mysticism.

Rather than judge Huxley for not being something or someone else, it is more productive to read him for what he is and intended to be. A fine example of the methodical unfolding of Huxley's ideas is King's essay (294) on Huxley's mysticism. Regardless of whether he is satirical or philosophical, Huxley stands at a distance from his characters and uses them to dramatize ideas; and these in turn he handles with an interested but clinical poise. Huxley's finest wish in *Island* was to unite the mysticism of the East and the technological skills of the West, and that stance is one that has struck many critics as odd. But Huxley always attempted odd achievements, building unlikely bridges between the unreconciled promontories and islands of the mind.

Much of the material cited here was obtained through the inter-library loan service at Slippery Rock State College; for this help I am grateful. Further material was acquired from Hillman Library, University of Pittsburgh; from the libraries of Carnegie-Mellon University and Duquesne University; from the Carnegie Library of Pittsburgh; from the Van Pelt Library, University of Pennsylvania; from The New York Public Library; and from the Yale University Library. I am indebted to Edward A. Kopper, Jr., for recommending to me the subject of this book and for recommending me to the publisher.

ALPHABETICAL LIST OF WORKS
BY AND EDITED BY HUXLEY

xix

ABBREVIATIONS

AH   Aldous Huxley
DA   *Dissertation Abstracts*
H   Aldous Huxley
PMLA   *Publications of the Modern Language Association*
TLS   *Times Literary Supplement*

ALDOUS HUXLEY

I
BOOKS AND PAMPHLETS

1. Atkins, John Alfred. *Aldous Huxley: A Literary Study*.
   London: Calder, 1953. 224 pp. New York: Roy Publishers,
   1957. New York: Orion Press, 1968 (new and revised
   edition).

   Reviews:
   McDowell, Frederick P.W. *Modern Fiction Studies*, 14
   (1968), 469-471.
   Meckier, Jerome. *Massachusetts Review*, 10 (1969), 820-
   823.

   This and Henderson's book (see 17) are the only ones on
   H until Bowering's and Meckier's books of the late 1960's
   (see 4 and 33). This literary biography considers the
   novels and other works against the background of his career.
   H's works are divided into topics. Atkins tends to review
   H's opinions, rather than his artistry. Topics include
   art, romantic passion, pacifism, and what Huxley called
   "the double crisis." "Takes Mr. Huxley with a seriousness
   and essential lack of comprehension which Huxley himself
   might satirize." *--Kirkus*, 25 (Sept. 15, 1957), 707. "On
   the whole a boring book, and the production is indescribably
   shoddy." --Maurice Cranston, *Manchester Guardian*, January
   8, 1957, p. 4.

2. Bedford, Sybille. *Aldous Huxley: A Biography*. Volume I:
   1894-1939. London: Chatto & Windus, 1973. 400 pp.
   Volume II: *1939-1962*. London: Chatto & Windus, 1974.
   378 pp.

   Reviews:
   Volume I: Meckier, Jerome. *Novel*, 8 (1974), 80-84.
   Volume II: Dinnage, Rosemary. *TLS*, September 20, 1974.

   Bedford met Aldous and Maria Huxley in 1930 and remained
   their close friend for many years. These volumes are based
   upon diaries, letters and interviews, as well as on H's

own publications. The account deals with both the public
and the private H, including his childhood, education,
his travels in Europe and America, his family and his many
friends, and how all these are expressed in his writing.
Remarkable for both the close and broad perspective on the
people involved; gives accounts of the day-to-day, being
born, getting married, dying, all mingled with debates on
art and truth, survival and independence. Does not analyze
H's work as literature, but has a keen eye for the autobiography it contains. The reader gets a thorough account
of H's ideas.

3. Birnbaum, Milton. *Aldous Huxley's Quest for Values.*
    Knoxville: University of Tennessee Press, 1971. 230 pp.

    Reviews:
        Cargill, Oscar. *CEA Critic,* 38 (March, 1972), 38.
        Dommergues, André. *Études Anglaises* (Vanves, France),
            26 (1972), 440–441.
        Meckier, Jerome. *Studies in the Novel,* 4 (1972), 527–
            530.
        Webster, Harvey Curtis. *Modern Fiction Studies,* 18
            (1972), 243–251.
        Wiebe, M.G. *Queen's Quarterly,* 79 (1972), 422–423.

    Discusses H's evolution from cynic to mystic, and
    analyzes the novels and nonfiction according to subject
    matter rather than separately. H considered his characters
    as states of being rather than what E.M. Forster would
    call "round characters." The characters are types; the
    novels, vehicles for ideas. The characters may be classed
    under various "humors": overdeveloped intellectuals, sar-
    donic cynics, promiscuous females, mystics. But not all
    of H's characters are so classifiable, especially the
    women. Birnbaum tends to overemphasize topics, rather than
    reading the novels as integral works; he tends to be over-
    analytical, whereas Huxley's approach was one of synthesis.
    Birnbaum also risks equating comments made by H's charac-
    ters with H's own remarks in essays. Allowance should be
    made for dramatic differences. The categories discussed
    in this book include education, the social self, love and
    nature, religion, science and technology. Though H used
    all of these as sources of values, religion came to be his
    main frame of reference for value judgments, but religion
    used in an eclectic sense. This study is based on Birn-
    baum's doctoral dissertation (see 606).

4. Bowering, Peter. *Aldous Huxley: A Study of the Major
    Novels.* London: Athlone Press, 1968. New York: Oxford
    University Press, 1969.

Reviews:

Firchow, Peter. *Journal of Modern Literature*, 1 (1969), 278-283.

Meckier, Jerome. *Mosaic*, 5 (1972), 165-177.

Roston, Murray. *Novel*, 4 (1969), 270-272.

Smith, Grover. *Modern Fiction Studies*, 17 (1971), 292-295.

Sees H as more than a twentieth-century Peacock. Not an original thinker, H was familiar with new advances in knowledge in a wide variety of fields, ranging from nuclear physics to the meditation practices of Cardinal Bérulle. His eclectic interests led him to attempt the synthesis expressed in his final novel, *Island*. Huxley is a supreme ironist comparable in power to Swift. Bowering gives one chapter each to the nine novels (*Crome Yellow* to *Island*); two introductory chapters on "The Novel of Ideas" and "The Moral Dilemma"; and a final chapter on "Moralist and Artist." The novels are seen as "exploratory vehicles for moral values" used by the author in "search for a more desirable way of life." But H's final concern is still more intellectual than moral because of the ideological breakdown of the modern world. This book is one of the best general introductions to H, stressing him as a major novelist. Bowering sees H resolving in his last works those dynamic differences that lent life to his best novels—to such an extent that H seems more like a saint and less like an artist.

5.   Brander, Laurence. *Aldous Huxley: A Critical Study*. London: Hart-Davis, 1969. Lewisburg, Pa.: Bucknell University Press, 1970. 244 pp.

Review:

Meckier, Jerome. *Mosaic*, 5 (1972), 165-177.

Treats the novels in two chapters, the short stories, the essays, the travel books, and the biographies each in separate chapters, with an additional chapter for each of the following: *Proper Studies*, *Ends and Means*, *The Perennial Philosophy*, and *Science, Liberty and Peace*. Another chapter deals with H's two books on hallucinogenic drugs. Brander sees H's books as embracing four of the most remarkable decades in Western history, when European traditions broke down, when technological knowledge exploded, and when Mass Man expected his share of materialistic bounty. H is seen as a committed intellectual with humanitarian motives. The accounts of the novels are thin and not very dependable, and the view of the earlier novels is condescending. Brander does not find the experiments in

technique very promising, but part of the reason is that
he does not really understand them. For example, he describes *Point Counter Point* as grossly mismanaged--it has
no plot and is pieced together simplistically and arbi-
trarily. Meckier, in his essay "Mysticism ..." (see
370), calls this a virtually useless book because it misunderstands the novels. It does do justice, he says, to
The Perennial Philosophy.

6. Bredsdorff, Morten. *Aldous Huxley* (Vor Tids Forfattere.
    Under Redaktion of Hakon Strangerup, No. 2). Copenhagen:
    Hirschsprung, 1938. 54 pp.

7. Brooke, Jocelyn. *Aldous Huxley* (Bibliographical series of
    supplements to *British Book News* on writers and their
    work, No. 55). London: Longmans, Green, 1954; revised
    1958. London: Longman Group, 1972. 34 pp.

    A pamphlet-essay, this groups H's works into three
    phases: (1) satirical debunking with a "surface gaiety"
    but an underlying pessimism; (2) H in role of teacher,
    philosopher: his need for political involvement, or for
    pacifism; (3) H's interest in religion, or mysticism--
    when the latter is empirically verifiable.

8. Brunius, Teddy. *Aldous Huxley: En Studie*. Stockholm:
    Wahlstrom and Widstrand, 1947. 216 pp.

9. Chatterjee, Sisar. *Aldous Huxley: A Study*. Calcutta:
    Firma K.L. Mukhopadhay, 1955; revised 1966.

    Follows "the evolution of a first-class mind ... through
    two decades of its development." Begins with the "point-
    lessness" of *Crome Yellow*, proceeds to the neo-Brahmanism
    of *After Many a Summer*, noting H "fumbling towards a syn-
    thesis of the variegated hotch-potch of his vast know-
    ledge." Synthesis is more particularly attempted in *Ends
    and Means*. But H "arrived at the startlingly unintellec-
    tual conclusion that 'progress must be progress by chari-
    ty.'" Early H, the Jesting Pilate, is the pyrrhonist,
    cynic and satirist, wallowing in the welter of pointless-
    ness. H as pyrrhonist sees life from every point of view
    save his own. He uses characters in his fiction as "ideas
    incarnate--animated spouts." *Point Counter Point* gives a
    new doctrine, via Rampion, of disparagement, but H is un-
    able to be a practicing convert of Lawrence's spontaneous
    living. *Eyeless in Gaza*, as well as and even more so
    After Many a Summer, "drifts toward mysticism and the
    intuition of suprahuman truths." *The Perennial Philosophy*

is a new kind of anthology, H choosing from the writings
of various mystics and including his own running commentary. H believed that if one were not a mystic, the next
best thing was to study the works of those who were.

10. Clark, Ronald W. *The Huxleys.* London: Heinemann, 1968.
    New York: McGraw-Hill, 1968.

    Reviews:
      Firchow, Peter. *Journal of Modern Literature*, 1 (1969),
        278-283.
      Roston, Murray. *Novel*, 4 (1971), 270-272.
      Smith, Grover. *Modern Fiction Studies*, 17 (1971), 292-
        295.

    In this biographical study of the Huxley family, the
    first half is given to Thomas Huxley. A short middle
    passage treats the next generation. The remainder of the
    book deals with Sir Julian and Aldous Huxley, with briefer
    accounts of several other members of the family. Given
    the complex subject, the book is well put together. The
    scientific half succeeds best, but even when dealing with
    Aldous Huxley the facts are balanced. Photographs of the
    family are included. There is less continuity to the book
    after the death of the family founder is passed. This is
    still not a complete family history; for example, little
    attention is given to Andrew Huxley, winner of the Nobel
    Prize in physiology. George Huxley, the eminent Greek
    historian, is scarcely mentioned. Many anecdotes are
    given about the "big three," but the philosophy of humanism
    of Sir Julian gets sketchy treatment. The book is a com-
    plex affair, listing about 120 names in all.

11. Day-Lewis, Cecil. *We're NOT Going to Do NOTHING: A Reply
    to Aldous Huxley's "What Are You Going to Do about It?"*
    London: Left Review [n.d.]. 31 pp.

    Day-Lewis accuses H of "a policy of final inactivity."
    H's argument that "means condition ends" is fallacious:
    duelling had to be prevented by threat of violent reprisal.
    H's argument doesn't indicate what should have been done
    to halt the Fascist powers, Italy and Germany. H admits
    that minimum force must be used in an emergency, but he
    fails to see economics as the basic cause of war. H's
    passive resistance won't work in technological warfare.
    His pamphlet overgeneralizes and uses false analogy. Day-
    Lewis's argument turns part way through to a defense of
    communism as a peaceable transformation of a democratic
    society. He himself loses track of the argument. (See
    also 503.)

12. Fietz, Lothar. *Menschenbild und Romanstruktur in Aldous
     Huxleys Ideenromane* (Studien zur Englischen Philologie,
     13). Tubingen: Niemeyer, 1969. 212 pp.

     Review:
       Goetsch, Paul. *English Studies* (Amsterdam), 54 (1969),
         300-302 (see 219).

     Attacks the view that H is merely an "essayist in fic-
     tion" who failed as a true novelist. A common theme ap-
     pears in the novels: multiplicity and identity come with
     a variety of resolutions. H belongs to the tradition of
     English empiricism. A clear development exists from H's
     early aspirations to the "perfect personality" to the
     final attempt at detachment and self-transcendence that
     allowed freedom from time and personality.

13. Firchow, Peter. *Aldous Huxley, Satirist and Novelist*.
     Minneapolis: University of Minnesota Press, 1972.

     Reviews:
       Dooley, D.J. *Queen's Quarterly*, 79 (1972), 652-653.
       Meckier, Jerome. *Modern Fiction Studies*, 19 (1972),
         620-625.

     Isolates and analyzes the main techniques and victims
     of H's satire, but does not attempt to place H in the
     English and continental satiric tradition. Identifies H
     as an extracurricular rather than a congenital novelist.
     Of the great satirists, Swift is the closest to H, es-
     pecially to H's earlier works, but H's later efforts do
     not express the intense misanthropy of Swift. Firchow
     assumes H is always a satirist, but he discusses only the
     novels; hence, the pervasiveness of H's satire is not
     demonstrated. The chapter on *Brave New World* is the best.
     It holds that this novel is H's comment on America; H's
     essay "America and the Future" was written shortly after
     his first visit to this country; it originally appeared
     in *Harper's* as "The Outlook for American Culture." Also
     of interest is the contention that in the Spandrell-
     Rampion contest in *Point Counter Point* H is at least
     partly on Spandrell's side, advocating his unflattering,
     black view of humanity.

14. Gérard, Albert. *À la rencontre de Aldous Huxley*. Liège:
     La Sixaine, 1947. 47 pp.

     Cites several critical pronouncements on H--by Swinner-
     ton (H's affinity for the *Encyclopedia Britannica*), Edgar
     (H as the Voltaire of his own epoch), Desonay, Weidle,

Mallinson, Connolly. *Crome Yellow* and *Those Barren Leaves* are modeled on the same pattern, lively satire. Yet H's later expanded philosophy is implied in the early books. Chelifer and Calamy are later spokesmen. The ideal is a kind of resignation without enthusiasm, but also a courage to face reality. *Point Counter Point* attempts a synthesis. A novel with a thesis, of ideas, experimental, documentary, fantasy, serious, but still not a great novel. *Point Counter Point* has four central themes which are modulated, harmonized, varied, according to the manner of musical themes. But the book lacks internal harmony, the quality of a great book. *Brave New World* satirizes the pursuit of the Renaissance spirit, followed to its extreme: science produces an inhuman stability. *Eyeless in Gaza*, like the works of Faulkner and Proust, narrates simultaneously five periods from the life of a man. But Beavis, the hero, re-capitulates earlier H heroes. *Ends and Means* provides further explanation of the same themes. H mirrors the perception of English novelists between two wars. He has personal detachment which is yet not negative and sterile. Love and intelligence free the individual. God is seen as an impersonal conscience. H's voice is the reformer's; he suffers from the intolerance that is the proper malady of all Savonarolas.

15. Ghose, Sisirkumar. *Aldous Huxley: A Cynical Salvationist.* New York: Asia Publishing House, 1962.

    Expresses adulation for H's discovery of the Vedanta. But Ghose notes that H remained skeptical about his own sense of infallibility, or about mankind's readiness to accept utopias or promises of immortality.

16. Heintz-Friedrich, Suzanne. *Aldous Huxley: Entwicklung seiner Metaphysik.* Lugano: Feldani, 1948.

    Based on her Zurich dissertation (see 619).

17. Henderson, Alexander J. *Aldous Huxley.* London: Chatto & Windus, 1935. 258 pp. New York: Harper & Brothers, 1936. New York: Russell & Russell, 1964.

    Review:
    Hoops, R. *Englische Studien*, 72 (1938), 300–302.

    The only book in English on H until Atkins' study in 1958 (see 1); this in spite of the fact that many books were being written in the 1950's on Lawrence, Woolf, and Joyce. Henderson examines H as a novelist, poet, essayist, critic, and philosopher. The opening chapter contains a

brief biography. Although thorough, the book is not convincing in its attempt to show consistency in H as a
philosopher. It is best for its appreciation of H's
style, and for its analysis of *Point Counter Point*. Intended for the casual reader rather than for the expert
in H studies, it provides an introductory guide to the
fiction. Not profound, it nevertheless gives an earnest,
careful reading of H.

18. Hines, Father Bede. *The Social World of Aldous Huxley*.
     Loretto, Pa.: The Seraphic Press, 1957. 104 pp.

     Published version of his doctoral dissertation (see
     622).

19. Holmes, Charles M. *Aldous Huxley and the Way to Reality*.
     Bloomington: Indiana University Press, 1970.

     Reviews:
       Dommergues, André. *Études Anglaises* (Vanves, France),
         26 (1972), 440.
       Meckier, Jerome. *Mosaic*, 5 (1972), 165-177.
       Smith, Grover. *Modern Fiction Studies*, 17 (1971), 292-
         295.
       Webster, Harvey Curtis. *Modern Fiction Studies*, 18
         (1972), 243-251.

     Presents the intellectual and spiritual account of the
     novelist, poet, essayist; it begins with the early poems
     and ends with *Island* and *Literature and Science*. The
     writing is seen as an expression of H's inner life. The
     assumption, however, that H "clearly found personal salva-
     tion" at the end of his life is stated, not proven. Holmes
     is better at dealing with the essays than with the fiction.
     Nevertheless, because this study traces the evolution of
     H's ideas through all of his works, it is a competent
     survey. The weakness is that Holmes puts H's art on the
     level of autobiography, and then faults H's irony when it
     seems to become an impediment to self-revelation. Holmes
     tends to praise the saint and underrate the satirist in H.
     The emphasis is spiritual rather than esthetic.

20. Hori, Masato. *Shintei Aldous Huxley Keuku*. Tokyo:
     Eihosha, 1974.

21. Hull, J. *Huxley: The Growth of a Personality*. Zurich,
     1955.

22. Huxley, Sir Julian Sorrell. *Memories*. New York: Harper
     & Row, 1970.

This semi-autobiographical book has surprisingly little to say of Sir Julian's humanist brother.

23. Huxley, Sir Julian Sorell, ed. *Aldous Huxley, 1894-1963: A Memorial Volume*. London: Chatto & Windus, 1965. New York: Harper & Row, 1965.

    Review:
    Meckier, Jerome. *Massachusetts Review*, 10 (1969), 820-823.

    Twenty-seven tributes by friends, relatives, associates, and admirers of H. Also included is H's final essay, "Shakespeare and Religion." The authors include T.S. Eliot, Victoria Ocampo, Leonard Woolf, Stephen Spender, Robert M. Hutchins, Christopher Isherwood, Anita Loos, Yehudi Menuhin. Sir Julian saw his brother as taking "all knowledge for his province and seeking to achieve self-transcendence while yet remaining a committed social being." Much of the book is given to marginalia, trivia.

24. Huxley, Laura Achera. *This Timeless Moment: A Personal View of Aldous Huxley*. London: Chatto & Windus, 1968. New York: Farrar, Straus & Giroux, 1968.

    Reviews:
    Firchow, Peter. *Journal of Modern Literature*, 1 (1969), 278-283.
    Meckier, Jerome. *Massachusetts Review*, 10 (1969), 820-823.

    Written by H's second wife, this book covers the years 1948-1963; it explores his character via conversations, personal letters, and excerpts from H's writings. The title comes from the hypnotic refrain H used to ease his first wife through her dying hours. An entirely sympathetic account is given of H and his wife of 35 years, Maria. The chapters on LSD and H's death are vividly done. Humor, emotion, frankness, openness, characterize the approach. H is shown in his endless pursuit of The Answer, which included his flirtation with "Hollywood type preoccupations like psychedelic drugs, amateur hypnotism, including magnetic passes of the hands."

25. Jackson, Gertrude. *Norman Douglas und Aldous Huxleys "House-Party Novels"* (Wiener Beiträge zur Englischen Philologie, 76). Vienna: Braumuller, 1975. 169 pp.

26. Jog, D.V. *Huxley the Novelist*. Folcroft, Pa.: The Folcroft Press, 1963.

    "The novels indicate a preference for the intellectual

scepticism of the 18th century, they reflect the intellectual aristocrat's distrust for the common man, they
reveal a concern about the soul-killing scientific utopia
to come, they suggest the superiority of spiritual meditation over meaningless pleasure-hunting." In *Island* "the
chapters exclusively devoted to discussion are rather dull
and heavy.... And yet, in view of the author's special
approach to the utopian novel, the uniformly positive
manner of its narrative, the attempt at delineating the
normal feelings of men, the work can be regarded as a
peak achievement in the career of this great novelist."
A good deal of Jog's book pays heavy attention to the
views of other critics; it doesn't really form a coherent
argument of its own about H, other than to praise him.

27.   Jouguelet, Pierre. *Aldous Huxley*. Paris: Edition du
      Temps Present, 1948.

Topics include "Profiles of Huxley," "Author of *Point
Counter Point*," "Towards the Perennial Philosophy,"
"Provisionary Conclusions." H noted that Flaubert avoided
floating images. Yet H himself could not resist such rich
advantages. Brilliant digressions, monstrous excrescences,
ludicrous parallels, pedantic or bizarre or discordant
allusions, such are the variegated devices that pollute
his writing. *Point Counter Point* shows that one can't
live without values, and one can't live with arbitrary
values. By the time he wrote *Point Counter Point*, H found
the peace that passes understanding outside of, not within,
life. How to control the mystical experience is the problem
of its validity. How to express it is the problem of its
content. How to develop it within an order of ethics is
the problem of its radiance. To go beyond global humanism
in a religious view of the world, to find a model of
spiritual life in the quest of mysticism, to call these
vows an order of contemplative and free men: these are
the major goals of H. A French critic, familiar with
Flaubert, has an easier time with H's technical virtuosity
and pessimistic outlook than do English critics. The chapters on Marx and Catholicism call too much attention to
these topics, which are but two of H's innumerable interests.

28.   Kirsh, Robert B.; Lawrence C. Powell; *et al. Aldous
      Huxley, 1894-1963: Addresses at a Memorial Meeting Held
      in the School of Library Service, February 27, 1964*.
      Los Angeles: University of California, 1964. 10 pp.

29. Krishnan, Bharathi. *Aspects of Structure, Technique and Quest in Aldous Huxley's Major Novels.* Stockholm: Almqvist & Wiksell, 1977. 181 pp.

This version of Krishnan's doctoral dissertation (see 627) was published by the University of Uppsala. A beginning chapter discusses the "House-Party" novels-- *Crome Yellow*, *Those Barren Leaves*, and *After Many a Summer*. Some of the techniques noted from these novels include the use of digressions through such devices as notebooks or journals, family history. The presence of a questing guest is exemplified by Denis in *Crome Yellow*. Another chapter discusses the novels of counterpoint and multiplicity: these include *Antic Hay* and *Point Counter Point*. Some of their characteristic techniques include the novelist within the novel, and Quarles's notebooks and his interest in zoology as an analogy to human behavior. The uncertain quest is personified through Gumbril Senior (*Antic Hay*) and Rampion (*Point Counter Point*). A third class of novels is identified as Conversion: they include *Eyeless in Gaza* and *Time Must Have a Stop*. Techniques employed in them include the familiar devices of notebooks and diary, as well as bookish characters who constantly and introspectively review their lives. Also, H is more strongly present as a moralist in these novels. A hero on a quest is typified by Anthony Beavis. The final division of novels is the Utopian, including *Brave New World* and *Island*, the former negative, the latter positive. Technique used is the recurring counterpoint, as well as names chosen for irony or verisimilitude. Quests are made by nonutopian heroes: Farnaby in *Island* and Savage in *Brave New World*. Krishnan's study is competent, methodical, and not very imaginative. The treatment is much too systematic for a writer and thinker as various as Huxley.

30. Kuehn, Robert E., ed. *Aldous Huxley: A Collection of Critical Essays.* Englewood Cliffs, N.J.: Prentice-Hall, Inc., 1974.

Includes: Robert E. Kuehn, "Introduction" (see 309); Frederick J. Hoffman, "Aldous Huxley and the Novel of Ideas" (see 254); "A Critical Symposium on Aldous Huxley" (see 573); Sanford E. Marovitz, "Aldous Huxley's Intellectual Zoo" (see 350); Milton Birnbaum, "Aldous Huxley's Quest for Values: A Study of Religious Syncretism" (see 99); Charles M. Holmes, "The Early Poetry of Aldous Huxley" (see 257); Jerome Meckier, "The Counterpoint of Flight:

Huxley's Early Novels" (see 33, Ch. 3); Peter Firchow,
"The Music of Humanity: *Point Counter Point*" (see 13,
Ch. 4); Peter Bowering, "*Eyeless in Gaza*" (see 4, Ch. 8);
Joseph Bentley, "The Later Novels of Huxley" (see 84);
Harold H. Watts, "Huxley as Biographer: *Grey Eminence*
and *The Devils of Loudun*" (see 47, Ch. 6); Donald J. Watt,
"Vision and Symbol in Aldous Huxley's *Island*" (see 569).

31.   Lloyd, Roger B. *The Undisciplined Life: An Examination
      of Aldous Huxley's Recent Works*. London: Society for
      Promoting Christian Knowledge, 1931. 32 pp.

      Following the spectacle of human folly in *Antic Hay* and
      Crome Yellow, H becomes a moralist in *Jesting Pilate*.
      His code is the Balanced Excess; Life is the deity, value
      consists in the accumulation of experience. H attacks
      those religions which prevent the worship of life. *Do
      What You Will* recommends worship of a multitude of gods
      and devils. Following Blake, H deplores the search for
      unity and universality in meaning. Human life, not the
      search for infinity, is the only criterion for reality.
      Yet H does admit a unity underlying diversity, even though
      only the diversity is knowable. H cites great leaders who
      lack Balanced Excess (St. Francis, Pascal)--but he ignores
      Jesus. Rampion in *Point Counter Point* is the paragon of
      Balanced Excess. But, says Lloyd, Rampion like Huxley is
      blinded: both lack humility. "Life worship ... depends
      for its existence upon the toil of millions who can never
      partake of its alleged joys."

32.   May, Keith M. *Aldous Huxley*. London: Elek, 1972.

      Reviews:
        Ashley, Robert. *Criticism*, 16 (1973), 90-92.
        Dommergues, André. *Études Anglaises* (Vanves, France),
          26 (1972), 441-442.
        Meckier, Jerome. *Modern Fiction Studies*, 19 (1972),
          620-625.

      Eleven of H's novels are grouped in two categories:
      Novels of Exploration (1921-1936) and Novels of Certainty
      (1939-1962). May sees comparisons between H and Swift as
      misleading, because Swift was more indignant than H, and
      Voltaire was more passionate in his attacks on clericalism
      and injustice. Though interested in mysticism after the
      mid-thirties, H complemented this experience with the
      most recent developments in psychology. He was the com-
      plete liberal. The chief value of this book consists in
      its showing how meaning relates to structure and the tech-
      nical problems of the novels.

33. Meckier, Jerome. *Aldous Huxley: Satire and Structure.*
London: Chatto & Windus, 1969. New York: Barnes &
Noble, 1969.

    Reviews:
    Gindin, James. *Studies in the Novel*, 4 (1972), 119-122.
    Smith, Grover. *Modern Fiction Studies*, 17 (1971), 292-
    295.
    Wiegner, Kathleen. *Modern Language Journal*, 55 (1969),
    330.

    Identifies H's major satiric themes, which are expressed
    by way of egoistic and eccentric characters. Then the
    themes are related to the forms the novels take to express
    these themes. *Point Counter Point* is the best, struc-
    turally, of H's 11 novels; Meckier makes a thorough study
    of this book. The contrapuntal method of *Point Counter
    Point* is used to build characters and incidents in H's
    other novels as well, in order to create the sense of
    balance that H perceived as the best objective in life.
    This book contains a good discussion of the relationship
    between H and D.H. Lawrence. Meckier's chief theme is
    the contrapuntal structure of the novels, which is
    strongly apparent in *Eyeless in Gaza*, and others of H's
    novels, as well as in *Point Counter Point.*

34. Morand, Carlos. *Los adolescentes en la obra narrativa de
    Aldous Huxley.* Santiago de Chile: Edit. Universitaria,
    1963.

35. Narita, Shigehisa. *Aldous Huxley.* Tokyo: Kenkyusha, 1956.
    209 pp.

36. Nordhjem, Bent. *Aldous Huxley. Udvikling og Stilling i
    Samtiden.* Copenhagen: Munksgaard, 1948. 182 pp.

37. Plesner, Knud F. *En kynish idealist--Aldous Huxley.*
    (Kulturbaerere Tidskritiske Studier). Copenhagen:
    Aschehoug, 1938. 118 pp.

38. Savage, David S. *Mysticism and Aldous Huxley: An Examina-
    tion of the Heard-Huxley Theories.* Yonkers, N.Y.:
    Baradinsky, 1947. 21 pp.

    Faults H for his virtually a priori assumption that
    physical unity of the universe (demonstrated by science)
    is paralleled by spiritual unity--an ultimate reality
    behind appearances. But H doesn't want to use faith as
    the basis for accepting spiritual unity. H passed
    directly from the philosophy of meaninglessness, existence

solely on the level of matter, to the contrary state, de-
materialized spirit. Justification for the spiritual
unity is derived from arguments based on analogy whereby
the physical world is the evidence. Savage faults H for
putting the individual as separate from, and outside of,
the "whole" universe, whether physical or spiritual.
H hasn't resolved the split between "individual mysticism
and collective, coercive politics." *Grey Eminence* presents Father Joseph as an example of mysticism and political pragmatism working together--but Savage deplores the
inconsistency. "Neither Heard nor Huxley seems to be
able to conceive any form of mediation between the individual and society apart from an individualistic withdrawal on the one side and a fanatical power-wielding on
the other."

   Meckier (369) attacks Savage's assumptions, as follows:
that there ever was a Huxley-Heard philosophy; that H
borrowed enormously from Heard; that H was always being
influenced by some thinker or other (Lawrence, Sheldon,
et al.). Meckier believes that H's debts to thinkers,
philosophers, are very complex, and not a simple matter
of borrowing and imitation. The fictionalized versions
of Heard in H's novels are Miller and Propter, but the
fictional characters are not the same as Heard.

39.   Scales, Derek P. *Aldous Huxley and French Literature.*
      Sydney: Sydney University Press, 1969.

   Scales gives a competent survey of the French influences
on H, who was cosmopolitan enough to have borrowed from
the French intellectual world of the 1920's even if he
wasn't a part of it. Scales notes H's dislike, as a young
man, of Bergson's philosophy. H's real love was for
Balzac, and he later grew more tolerant of Bergson. The
facts about possible relationships between *Point Counter
Point* and the novel it was modeled after, Gide's *The
Counterfeiters*, are summarized. H's changing views of
Pascal are carefully shown, from earlier rejection to
later acceptance. Maurois said H was as much a man of
French, as of English, culture. H discovered French
literature during his first year at Balliol; while at
Oxford he wrote several reviews on French authors; he
spoke fluent French as an undergraduate, married a French-
speaking Belgian wife, owned a Mediterranean French villa:
French became his daily spoken and written language. He
admired French classical drama, but preferred Shakespeare.
H imitated the style of La Rochefoucauld, whom he said
anticipated Freud. For H, 18th-century France was the

most civilized period of history. Crebillon's and de
Nerciat's erotica are often admiringly alluded to in H's
fiction. H despised Rolland's novels; he admired Stendhal,
Balzac, Flaubert, the most. He said Montaigne and Pascal
are basic to understanding modern European culture.
Praising Rabelais' scatological gusto, H never successfully
imitated it. Though admiring Voltaire on occasion, he
deplored Voltaire's anger. (See also 70, 189, 241, 440,
521.)

40. Shelvankar, Krishnaro S. *Ends Are Means: A Critique of
     Social Values*. London: Drummond, 1938. 146 pp.

     Summarizes H's views in *Ends and Means*: the causes of
war are ultimately psychological. But to Shelvankar, this
view unrealistically detaches psychology from the social
milieu. H's pseudo-religious formula to end war is inadequate. H's philosophical categories are unanalyzed
and unexamined, except in terms of each other (spirit,
matter, mind, free-will, etc.). Supposedly, good leads
to unity of being, which leads to love, which leads to
virtue. No real relation is shown between these abstract
terms and what H seeks to demonstrate about pacifism.
"So engrossed is Huxley in preparing the blue prints for
Utopia that he completely forgets to tell us the ways and
means by which actual evils and injustices can be overcome." H believes in a common, ideal end for all, to be
achieved by a diversity of means, some ideal and some
nonideal.

41. Strangerup, Hakon. *Aldous Huxley*. Kobenhevn: Aschehoug,
     1961. 73 pp.

42. Svobòda, Fedor. *Aldous Huxley i njegor 'kinktrapunkt
     života*. Zagreb: [n.p.], 1958. 21 pp.

43. Thody, Philip. *Aldous Huxley: A Biographical Introduction*
     (Leaders of Modern Thought). London: Studio Vista, 1973.
     New York: Scribner's, 1973. 144 pp.

     "Statements of ideas from Huxley's letters, essays, and
novels are mixed to show the relationship between Huxley's
fiction and his personal attitudes and beliefs, and to
point up the autobiographical elements in the novels."
This is really a biography of H's thought. It makes good
use of H's nonfiction as well as of the novels in discussing
H's ideas. This book is valid for its emphasis on H as a
personality and a thinker, rather than simply as an artist,
especially given that H himself did not see his role as

being limited to that of an artist, even though he freely
used the devices of artistic expression. "Huxley was an
attractive if enigmatic personality who lived through and
expressed some of the representative crises of a 20th
century intellectual."

44.   Ueda, Tsutomu. *A Study of Huxley.* Tokyo: Elihosha, 1955.
      256 pp. Revised 1967.

45.   Vann, Gerald, O.P. *On Being Human: St. Thomas and Mr.
      Aldous Huxley.* London: Sheed & Ward, 1934. 110 pp.

      Most of this essay, which originally appeared as a
      series of articles in *Blackfriars*, is devoted to the
      humanism of St. Thomas. Gracefully ornamented with quota-
      tions from and allusions to St. Thomas, other church
      fathers, and literary classics, the essay cites H a half-
      dozen times before presenting him more directly in the
      Appendix, "The Polytheism of Mr. Aldous Huxley." There-
      fore, the essay is really an exposition of the Saint,
      with only an afterthought on H rather than an overall con-
      trast, as the essay's title would seem to imply. The
      essay's urbanity tries to supersede H's iconoclasm as
      illustrated from *Proper Studies* and *Do What You Will*.
      But that is only Vann's illusion; H would never have ac-
      cepted a harmonious system-builder's incorporating arti-
      facts from his works into the great cathedral, as Vann
      calls it, of St. Thomas's *Summa Theologica*.

46.   Watt, Donald, ed. *Aldous Huxley: The Critical Heritage.*
      London: Routledge & Kegan Paul, 1975.

      A comprehensive selection of the major critical responses
      to H's development throughout his lifetime. Most of the
      commentary refers to H's fiction, but some is about the
      nonfiction as well. Common faults found with H's fiction
      include his cavalier attitude toward the art of fiction,
      his indecency, his heartlessness, and his overproduction.
      The Introduction by Watt (pp. 1-36) provides an excellent
      overview of criticism on H. The Appendix lists transla-
      tions of H's works and collected works sales.

47.   Watts, Harold H. *Aldous Huxley* (Twayne English Authors
      Series, 79). New York: Twayne Publishers, 1969.

      Reviews:
      Firchow, Peter. *Journal of Modern Literature*, 1 (1969),
          278-283.
      Meckier, Jerome. *Mosaic*, 5 (1972), 165-177.

Smith, Grover. *Modern Fiction Studies*, 17 (1969), 292-295.

Emphasizes the second half of H's career. In the 1920's, H saw man as not worth saving; man's "animality" was the reason. The cultural achievements of man are only pallia- tive. This early satire of dismissal is never entirely absent even from the later works. But despite his contempt for mankind, H wished to serve it. From the 1930's on, H creates singular characters who transcend the limits of personality, concern about death, limitations of time and place. "Both novel and essay, as Huxley elaborates these forms, are inescapably didactic, as are the two biographies in which the history of the past is set to work milling the grain of the present and near future."

48. Woodcock, George. *Dawn and the Darkest Hour: A Study of Aldous Huxley.* New York: Viking, 1971. 299 pp.

Reviews:

Dommergues, André. *Études Anglaises* (Vanves, France), 26 (1972), 442.

Grosskurth, Phyllis. *Canadian Literature* (University of British Columbia), 56 (1972), 117-119.

King, Carlyle. *University of Toronto Quarterly*, 42 (1972), 417-418.

Despite its claim, this is not really the first book to see H's life and work as integrated. Woodcock depends a good deal on the insights of other critics. He succeeds best with H's short fiction, but the chronological approach to H's career creates problems because H rode so many different horses at the same time. Woodcock does give a more convincing account of the literary value of H's writing than do Atkins or Birnbaum (see 1 and 3). The emphasis is biographical: Woodcock recognizes H as a pacifist, decentralist, and political libertarian, aware of the perils of the misuse of scientific discoveries. Woodcock argues that H's changed view of art and the artist's function, after 1936, was a false direction that had negative effects on his work.

II

ARTICLES AND PARTS OF BOOKS

49. "A. Huxley: un portrait." *Le Mois*, August, 1936, pp. 150-152.

    H was born into a distinguished family. He has confided little about his formative years, but clearly he is a cosmopolitan. One of the most remarkable writers of his time, and not simply because of *Point Counter Point*, at 42 years of age he has scarcely completed an all-embracing philosophy of life, but an important component of his philosophy is the passive resistance of Gandhi. H is intellectually at home with French postwar writers, and physically at home in Italy and southern France.

50. "About the Author." *Theatre Arts*, 36 (May, 1951), 52; includes the play *The Gioconda Smile*.

    H did an enormous amount of work for the *Athenaeum*, which he joined in 1919: drama, art, and music criticism; articles on interior decoration and architecture; reviews of novels; and bibliographical notes. He showed himself to be a prolific writer with encyclopedic knowledge.

51. Adcock, Arthur St. John. "Aldous Huxley," in his *The Glory That Was Grub Street: Impressions of Contemporary Authors*. New York: Stokes, 1928. Pp. 135-145.

    H wrote 12 books in 10 years, all before he was 33. *Antic Hay* is a more mature book than *Crome Yellow*, but it also lapses more often into primitive sexuality. Sex is used for its own sake, whereas in some H stories it has thematic value--as in "The Gioconda Smile," with its psychological analysis of Mr. Hutton.

52. "After Ten Years." *The New Yorker*, 23 (Oct. 25, 1947), 26-27.

    A New York interview with H after he had spent 10 years at Wrightwood, California (50 miles from Los Angeles), in

the mountains. H tells of his work on the film version of
"The Gioconda Smile"--his only murder story. He gives
his impressions of his work on a new novel (*Ape and Essence*), set in California, in an imagined setting after an
atomic war. He is depressed by the lack of stability in
the world and says that novelists depend on some sense of
social stability. He thinks that present insecurity is
responsible for the abundance of historical novels.

53. Aldington, Richard. "Aldous Huxley." *Sunday Referee*
    (London), Dec. 15, 1929; reprinted in *Richard Aldington,
    Selected Critical Writings*. Carbondale: Southern Illinois
    University Press, 1970. Pp. 19-23.

    Commenting on H's essays in *Do What You Will*, Aldington
    admires H's attempt to be positive, "to set up a sanction
    for life." This is an antidote to Eliot's whimper. H is
    a "life worshipper." Aldington praises H's "admirable
    analysis of monotheism, his exposition of the diversity
    of the human being, his ruthless exposure ... of Francis
    of Assisi, his twenty-six rounds with Pascal...."

54. Alexander, Claudia. "Bach, Beethoven, and Point Counter
    Point." *Innisfree*, 2 (1975), 17-21.

55. Alexander, Henry. "Lawrence and Huxley." *Queen's Quarter-
    ly*, 42 (Spring, 1935), 96-108.

    H was reared from and trained to greatness; Lawrence's
    upbringing was obscure. H easily won fame; Lawrence, only
    with difficulty. Their subjects and settings are in con-
    trast. Both depict relationships of the sexes--Lawrence
    in a deeply emotional, sincere, outspoken manner that is
    highly autobiographical. H is much more light-hearted, in
    the manner of Restoration comedy; he is amoral, but with
    an element of disillusionment underneath. Lawrence's set-
    tings depict industrial encroachment upon the countryside.
    H's settings are less symbolic--a gathering place for in-
    tellectual talk, but with little descriptive setting.
    Note the intellectual cross section of London in *Point
    Counter Point*. Both H and Lawrence criticize the substi-
    tution of intellect and ideas for life itself. H was
    influenced by H.G. Wells in the futuristic novels. Law-
    rence is virtually nonderivative, though there is a bit
    of Gissing in his account of industrial poverty, and his
    intensely human figures are sometimes like Hardy's. The
    works of Lawrence seem to have more permanent qualities
    than do those of H. (See also 72, 83, 157, 199, 319, 320,
    390, 457, 469, 525, 543, 551, 615, 616.)

56. Allen, Walter. *The English Novel: A Short Critical History.* New York: Dutton, 1954. P. 168.

    Bulwer-Lytton, like H, had "an ambitious talent, but that of the popularizer rather than that of the creator.... Like Huxley, he had little sense of literary tact; he borrowed largely of the techniques and attitudes of other writers and applied them to quite inappropriate material. In his own time he seemed an original novelist; he was in fact a profoundly derivative one...."

57. ————. "*Point Counter Point* Revisited." *Studies in the Novel*, 9 (Winter, 1977), 373-377.

    H appears as at least two characters in *Point Counter Point*: Walter Bidlake is H as he was about ten years before *Point Counter Point* was published, the young man just finished with Balliol who worked for Murry on the *Athenaeum*; and Philip Quarles the novelist is H at the time he wrote *Point Counter Point*. H also imaginatively identifies with Spandrell in order to provide Rampion with a worthy rival. H apparently entertained a subversive love for his victims such as Spandrell. As a personal expression, *Point Counter Point* is a failure, but it is not necessarily a failure as art. The brilliance outweighs the flaws. The great satirical caricatures give a sense of life viewed as a multiverse, and they give the sense of H's courage.

58. Allentuck, Marcia. "Aldous Huxley on Mark Gertler: An Unremarked Essay." *Papers of the Bibliographical Society of America*, 68 (1974), 180-183.

    H wrote an introduction (not cited in the bibliographies) to the 1937 exhibition catalog of Gertler's paintings. The introduction is reprinted.

59. Ament, William S. "Jesting Huxley Waiting For an Answer." *The Personalist*, 18 (Summer, 1937), 254-266.

    Summarizes the changes in H's views to date. *Proper Studies* (1927) rejects current substitutes for religion: Unitarianism of science, of democracy, of international capitalism; or other, political, ritualistic, artistic, substitutes. H defends a Polytheism--"the value element in uncorrelated drives for self-fulfillment." The assumption is that freeing all of these drives will produce balance among the extremes.

60. Arnheim, Rudolf. "Psychological Notes on the Poetical Process," in his and others' *Poets at Work*. New York:

Harcourt, 1948. Pp. 144–146.

Arnheim follows the revisions in a H poem about animals
suddenly seen in the dark by headlights. The changes
move from objective correctness to a subjective truth:
"momentary gleam" becomes "momentary eyes." There is a
deviation from the practically reasonable in order to intensify an experience that the reader is meant to share,
the author's "truth."

61. Arnold, Edwin T. III. "Faulkner and Huxley: A Note on
     Mosquitoes and *Crome Yellow*." *Mississippi Quarterly*,
     30 (Summer, 1977), 433–436.

Faulkner's debt to H may be shown by comparing *Mosquitoes*
and *Crome Yellow*. Both novels deal with a brief period in
the lives of a disparate group of people isolated from the
outside world. Denis Stone is like Ernest Talliafero;
Gombauld is like Gordon; Mr. Barbecue-Smith is like Mr.
Hooper; and Henry Wimbush is like Josh Robyn. Similar
topics are discussed in both books—sex, words, freedom,
war, art, and emotion. Also, both novels tell stories
within their main story.

62. Baker, Howard. "In Praise of the Novel: The Fiction of
     Huxley, Steinbeck and Others." *Southern Review*, 5
     (1940), 778–800.

The relationship of intellect and emotion is acute in a
novel; greatest success lies in fusion of the divergent
functions. H's *After Many a Summer* and Steinbeck's *The
Grapes of Wrath* are complementary. Intellect predominates
in H: brilliant ideas, formed from intellect alone, become
shapeless and arid. H seizes upon mysticism in an intellectual manner—doesn't recognize that it should begin
as a spontaneous and emotional experience. H knows what
he says only intellectually, not emotionally.

63. Baker, Robert S. "Aldous Huxley." *Contemporary Litera-
     ture*, 16 (1975), 492–499.

Review of Sybille Bedford, *Aldous Huxley: A Biography*.
Bedford is ill at ease with literary scholarship—and with
the formidable intellectual history of H; hence, she
becomes a biographer-scribe. She tries to separate the
books from the man. Her account of the novels, in
separate chapters, is perfunctory. She does not consider
H as a satirist. This is not a definitive biography, but
rather a memoir. Highly fragmented (divided into 98 short
chapters), it depends on excessive quotation. It lacks an

underlying conception. Though containing much new source
material, it is not well edited. It explains (faultily)
H's friendship with D.H. Lawrence solely in terms of Mark
Rampion in *Point Counter Point*. This biography is best
for its extensive, valid account of H's California years:
use of LSD, para-psychology, mysticism, international
economics--the endless parade of fads that occupied H.
Bedford believes that H's "transcendental pragmatism" is
expressed in *Island*--religious orientation in a materialist universe.

64. ————. "The Fire of Prometheus: Romanticism and the
     Baroque in Huxley's *Antic Hay* and *Those Barren Leaves*."
     Texas Studies in Literature and Language, 19 (Spring,
     1977), 60-82.

Romanticism and the baroque, H believed, were aberrations
from the norm established by Sir Christopher Wren. H's
early novels contain many references to Romanticism and
the arts. He saw the roots of postwar problems in the
Romantic Revival. *Those Barren Leaves*, often criticized
as a loose novel, has the unifying element of H's criticism
of baroque art. The characters are all Promethean types.
H saw many weaknesses in Shelley, Wordsworth; Piranesi is
the antithesis of Wren; so is Veronese. *Antic Hay* celebrates Wren's bicentenary. Benjamin Haydon is another
faulty Promethean. *Those Barren Leaves* is filled with
Promethean aspirations that fail. Mrs. Aldwinkle is a
connoisseur of such trumpery. However, mysticism in H's
view is not part of the Promethean apocalypse. This is
a valuable article. (See also 116, 323, 349, 630.)

65. ————. "Spandrell's 'Lydian Heaven': Moral Masochism and
     the Centrality of Spandrell in Huxley's *Point Counter
     Point*." *Criticism*, 16 (1974), 120-135.

Spandrell's mother fixation has distorted his view of
women in general. His hatred of them, his search for
God, his obsession with Calvinism and Augustine's theology
can be explained by Freud's theory of the prostitute complex. H achieves "Gothic intensity" when Spandrell plays
a Lydian melody, the A minor Quartet of Beethoven, to
accompany his own death scene. Spandrell remains devoted
to a poetic ideal as he listens to the music; the ideal
has made him helpless in the face of reality.

66. ————. "A Tour of Brighton Pavilion and Gog's Court:
     The Romantic Context of *Point Counter Point* and *Eyeless
     in Gaza*." *Studies in the Novel*, 9 (Winter, 1977), 537-
     563.

H developed a carefully detailed and dialectically composed theory of romanticism with elements rejected from,
as well as retained from, Blake, Wordsworth, Shelley, and
Keats. He applies these ideas from 17th-century baroque
esthetics to 20th-century cubism, but romanticism is their
central source. Shelley and Wordsworth on one side, Wren
and Chaucer on the other, represent the contending attitudes. Wren is restrained, dignified; Chaucer avoids
"vision-inducing" histrionics. Baroque art fails for H
not only for esthetic reasons, but also for ethical ones:
the sham facades are analogues for the moral failure of
Sidney Quarles. "Wagner and Bernini are artists who can
turn what is false and theatrical into something almost
sublime." Blake achieves the "third essence" by his
theory of contraries, the assimilation of antagonistic
values into a richer, more vital integrity. Three compo-
nents comprise H's view of romanticism, the first two
being related: (1) Promethean (following Shelley), but
also a monastic evasion of life's diversity; (2) Collective
Man (following the Bolshevik millennium), but neglectful
of man's individuality; (3) Impersonal Self, a collection
of ideas from Wordsworth, Blake, and Lawrence. The
Promethean view is rejected because it is ungovernable,
irrational, and egoistic. The view of Collective Man lacks
meaning because history too is a gathering of selfish greed
and violence. "By defining the self in negative, sharply
circumscribed terms H avoids the inflated egoism of the
baroque-romantic and the equally egocentric self-pity of
the reverse romantic." Blake's prophecies, Wordsworth's
criticism, Keats's letters, and Shelley's poems furnish H
with his theory of romanticism, which is highly eclectic,
and may be summarized as follows: "H begins by attacking
Wordsworth and Shelley only to gradually alter his assess-
ment, choosing specific ideas or theories like Wordsworth's
associational theory of memory and Blake's doctrine of
the states as the cornerstones of his own theory of selfhood while the mystical experience of Anthony Beavis owes
much to Shelley's *Adonais*, a poem increasingly important
to Huxley."

67. Bald, R.C. "Aldous Huxley as Borrower." *College English*,
    11 (Jan., 1950), 183-187.

Bald discusses "Huxley's too acute literary awareness,
with its consequent attenuation of literary power."
Ulysses and *The Counterfeiters* deeply influenced H's own
works--Joyce in *Time Must Have a Stop* and *Brave New World*,
Chapter 3; Gide in *Point Counter Point* and *Eyeless in Gaza*.

Lypiatt, the painter in *Antic Hay*, is much like the artist
Benjamin Robert Haydon. H doesn't simply use these
references as literary allusions; he follows the originals
in considerable detail. When he borrows, he does something worse, rather than something better, than the original. Meckier ("Mysticism or Misty Schism?" 370) calls
these accusations a crude misrepresentation; by the same
logic, one could "prove" that *The Waste Land* was largely
written by other poets.

68.   Baldanza, Frank. "Huxley and Hearst." *Essays on California
      Writers* (Itinerary 7), ed. Charles L. Crow. Bowling
      Green, Ohio: Bowling Green University Press, 1978. Pp.
      35-47.

69.   ————. "*Point Counter Point*: Aldous Huxley on 'The Human
      Fugue.'" *South Atlantic Quarterly*, 58 (1959), 248-257.

This, with King's article (293), is the most thorough
study of "the musicalization of fiction" and the episode
of the Bach B minor suite in chapter 2. Quarles's
journal contains notes on the suitability of musical structure for the novel of ideas. Primarily, Beethoven's
quartets are used for the "musicalization of fiction."
Cue taken from abrupt transitions in music ("majesty alter-
nating with a joke"): "While Jones is murdering a wife,
Smith is wheeling the perambulator in the park." Just as
there are modulations and subtle variations of music, so
in fiction one can have similar characters perform dissimilar acts; or dissimilar characters caught in parallel
situations. Elinor is the balance-character between Rampion (intellect) and Webley (emotion). The basic structure
unit of the novel is "scene": a group of contrasting
characters gather for conversation. At its musical opening
the novel introduces Illidge, the Communist, who is introduced to reactionary militarists, and finally to the
Fascist Webley. H uses the "'hour-glass' pattern in which
each character at the end of the scene holds the position
occupied by the opposing character at the opening of the
scene." The end of the novel consists of variations on
the theme of death.

70.   Baldensperger, F. "Les petits illogismes d'un grand
      romancier: une hypothèse historique d'Aldous Huxley," in
      Essays in Honor of Albert Feuillerat, ed. Henri M. Peyre.
      New Haven: Yale University Press, 1943; originally in
      Yale Romantic Studies, 22.

Sees H's versions of French history as extraordinary

oversimplifications; he is a friend of France who doesn't
understand France. For example, H says that Richelieu's
policies resulted in Napoleonic imperialism, the reaction
of the Prussian empire, and "the disasters of the twentieth century."

71. Barensfeld, Thomas. "Aldous Huxley's Seven Years in
     America." *New York Times Book Review*, June 27, 1943,
     p. 2.

     H predicted it would take at least five more generations
     before America achieved any kind of homogeneity in popula-
     tion. He found America remarkable for its hopefulness.
     His work in 1938 for MGM on the story of Mme. Curie with
     Garbo was shelved: "Who's going to go for a dame who goes
     for chemistry?" Now, H felt he had become more proficient
     at embodying his ideas in his fiction, but he disliked
     looking back on his earlier works. He cited Lawrence on
     the advantage of using fiction as a vehicle for ideas:
     they penetrate better, they're carried on an emotional
     wave. Fiction has a wider range than essays, though essays
     have more accuracy. The artist himself has trouble re-
     lating to the "good man" (e.g., Propter in *After Many a
     Summer*) because the artist "is not of the highest himself."
     H denied that he and Heard were developing a "new reli-
     gion."

72. Bartlett, Norman. "Aldous Huxley and D.H. Lawrence."
     Australian Quarterly, 36 (March, 1964), 76-84.

     H tried to rejoin flesh and spirit by evolving a theory
     of knowledge that would replace the one destroyed by the
     Industrial Revolution. He tried to incorporate Lawrence's
     beliefs in sensuality but he couldn't relate to Lawrence's
     theory of intuitive knowledge; H depended on reason. Both
     H and Lawrence omit the awareness that all human traditions
     must be accepted with reservations because man has an in-
     herent element of evil. Like all intellectual/philosophi-
     cal solutions, H's and Lawrence's answers seek the unusual
     for its own sake or else simply retreat to sterile contem-
     plation when the standard traditions fail. H's earlier
     works were influenced by Lawrence, but after *Eyeless in
     Gaza* H turned to his own attempt to discover mysticism
     through rational means. H and Lawrence mistakenly assumed
     that traditions vanish if they do not satisfy or if they
     lack vitality.

73. Barzun, Jacques. "The Anti-Modern Essays of Aldous Huxley."
     London Magazine, 4 (Aug., 1957), 51-55.

Praises H's intelligent versatility with the arts, philosophy, and science. Reviews *Adonis and the Alphabet*, which aspires both to science and to mysticism. H's "anti-modernism is thus suggestive and symbolic rather than substantial and thorough." (See also 93, 114, 232, 339, 455, 533, 604.)

74. Bataller Ferrándiz, José. "Aldous Huxley y la novela." *Revista de Literatura*, 16 (July-Dec., 1959; pub. 1960), 57-89.

75. Baugh, Albert C., *et al*. *A Literary History of England*. New York: Appleton-Century-Crofts, 1948. Pp. 1565-1566.

H, as he acknowledged in drawing his self-portrait as Quarles in *Point Counter Point*, is not a "congenital novelist" but a thinker using fiction as a platform for presenting ideas. His are "discussion novels" with little or no plot, the only action being the clash of opposing attitudes. Comparable are Peacock's novels, or Norman Douglas's *South Wind*.

76. Beach, Joseph Warren. "Counterpoint: Aldous Huxley," Chapter 36 in his *Twentieth Century Novel: Studies in Technique*. New York: Appleton-Century-Crofts, 1932. Pp. 458-469.

Gide's influence on H may be seen in the following: characters who are experimental biologists and who gather odd facts about natural history, as seen in Gide's *Les Caves du Vatican*, H's *Antic Hay*; also, Lord Edward in *Point Counter Point*. The novelist in Gide's *The Counterfeiters* uses many ideas from a young marine biologist. In *Point Counter Point* Quarles puts in his notebook curious habits about certain parasitic male fish which he sees paralleling human behavior. The unmotivated crime in *Les Caves* parallels Spandrell's lack of reason to kill Webley in *Point Counter Point*. Most important, *The Counterfeiters* and *Point Counter Point* both have a major novel-writing character who resembles the author of the novel. Both author-characters write novels of ideas. The difference is that H made the novel of ideas his large objective; Gide simply leaves this as Edouard's objective within the novel. Both Edouard and Philip Quarles favor the analogy between the novel and a musical composition, and both defend this "rather too queer" approach as "the more it will be like life." H aims for a "multiplicity of eyes and aspects seen." He alternates groups of characters to give ironic contrasts, to demonstrate relativity

rather than absolute values. Beach objects that a character's ideas don't really constitute the character. Rampion talks like an integral character, but he doesn't act
like one. This is a lucid comparison of the two major
novels.

77. Bedford, Sybille. "A Living Death." *Decision*, 1 (Jan.-
Feb., 1942), 73-77.

Review of *Grey Eminence*. H sees "reality" in a transcendent and immanent God; hence, he warns against "merely
behaving like human beings." Bedford notes the irony of
H's sharp change in religious views—but H has always been
emotionally distant from humanity. He was boisterously at
ease, though, when talking about art, music, architecture.
None of H's characters enjoy what they do. Father Joseph
is a superb Huxleyan monster: an odd way for H to advertise
the benefits of mysticism, in which of course he really believes.

78. Bedoyère, Michael de la. "Aldous Huxley's Challenge."
Dublin Review, 202 (Jan., 1938), 13-26.

H attempts to build a constructive philosophy, but he's
still satirizing the absurdities of the day, including
ones found in religion. On the level of human action, H
is a pacifist; his moral idea is "nonattachment";
religiously, he worships a nonpersonal Deity. The ideal
of nonattachment means intelligence and love. H bases
his philosophy upon a purely empirical induction as to
what constitutes the ideal man and upon a personal faith
in nonviolence. "A refusal to believe in the Incarnation
leads Huxley to underestimate the individuality and worth
of the human person."

79. ————. "Huxley Decries 'Social Engineering.'" *Catholic
World*, 189 (May, 1959), 148-152.

Brave New World Revisited does not question Julian Huxley's concerns about overpopulation. H doesn't mention
birth control in *Brave New World Revisited*. Dictators
take over in underdeveloped nations with fast population
growth, according to H, and this event will be followed
by democracies being taken over by dictatorships. (See
also 110, 112, 120, 121, 182, 184, 280, 305, 306, 311, 321,
324, 353, 385, 389, 467, 523, 556.)

80. Beerman, Hans. "An Interview with Aldous Huxley."
Midwest Quarterly, 5 (Spring, 1964), 223-230.

Contains questions and answers on human values, Western
education, Eastern thought, made during an interview at
Topeka, Kansas, in 1960.

81. Bennett, Arnold. "The Progress of the Novel." *The Realist*,
1 (April, 1929), 3-11.

"Scratch a serious novelist, and you will find a preacher
with a moral message." But if the preacher is laid bare
without a deep scratch, the author has made a story from a
message, not vice versa. Serious novelists may be limited
in scope (Austen) or all-embracing (Balzac). Wells
created societies first, and individuals second; but utopias exist best in the mind. Image-making novelists include Disraeli, Galsworthy, Wells; image-breaking ones include Dreiser, Lewis. Compassion for characters is shown
by Dostoevski, Balzac, Hardy, Galsworthy. Proust deals
with psychological minutiae, but is not innovative. Joyce
began a new method and new field of psychology. H, prolific, promises much; *Point Counter Point* is his one sound
and complete novel so far. He knows social structure, has
acute intelligence, usually employs a scientific approach,
has taste and erudition, power and style, and is courageous.
He has less sociological breadth than Balzac. Almost entirely destructive, he is usually hostile toward his characters. His censure of them can be justified only by
original sin, not by anything they do in the novels. *Point
Counter Point* is a valid corrective to the sentimentalism
of the British novel, but it's a reactionary book, both in
a spiritual and technical sense.

82. Benterud, Aagot. "Aldous Huxleys erkjennelsesvei."
Spektrum, 1948, pp. 71-84.

83. Bentley, Joseph Goldridge. "Aldous Huxley's Ambivalent
Responses to the Ideas of D.H. Lawrence." *Twentieth
Century Literature*, 13 (Oct., 1967), 139-153.

H's satirical approach uses a dual consciousness to
show the inconsistencies of flesh and spirit with each
other; Lawrence, however, tries to unify the personality
that is divided along these lines. H's essays in *Do What
You Will* intellectually embrace Lawrence's ideas, even
though H has trouble doing so emotionally. The portrait
of Lawrence in *Point Counter Point* (Rampion) presents
these ideas with deep admiration. But Lawrence himself
disliked *Point Counter Point* because it still showed that
H was a Manichean, and hence by temperament opposed to
Lawrence.

84. ———. "The Later Novels of Huxley." *Yale Review*, 59
    (1970), 507-519; reprinted in *Aldous Huxley: A Collec-
    tion of Critical Essays*, ed. Robert E. Kuehn (see 30),
    pp. 142-153.

    H's late novels tried to merge, unify divergent areas
    of experience; created a formal discontinuity that was an
    esthetic disaster. Physiological and scatological details
    are used for a repugnant end, but not with the satirical
    effectiveness of Swift, who was always sure of his victim.
    H's late novels have a specific character use this sort
    of invective, which boomerangs against him. The enlightened
    person cannot accept despair, negativism, which derive
    from the dislocation of man's flesh from his spirit.
    When H in the later novels sets out to explore the physio-
    logical correlates of spiritual experience, he creates,
    against his will, satiric or derisive overtones. *Island*
    is purged of the dualistic irony characteristic of his
    best novels; his efforts to be entirely positive in this
    utopian antithesis to *Brave New World* render the book
    almost entirely devoid of esthetic value. *Brave New World*
    marks the end of H's career as a satirical novelist. H
    couldn't be satirically outrageous and morally affirmative
    at the same time.

85. ———. "Semantic Gravitation: An Essay on Satiric Reduc-
    tion." *Modern Language Quarterly*, 30 (March, 1969),
    3-19.

    Criticizes Maugham, Bald, Savage, for misunderstanding
    H's mode as a satirist: the dualism of mind versus matter.
    The presence of elements of low connotation creates a
    gravitational pressure pulling the high elements downward
    and thereby functioning satirically. (To some extent,
    this overlaps Bentley's article "The Later Novels of
    Huxley"; see 84.)

86. Bentley, Phyllis. "The Structure of 'Eyeless in Gaza.'"
    English Journal, 26 (Feb., 1937), 127-132. Appeared
    first in *London Mercury*, 34 (Sept., 1936), 434-437.

    Beavis regards his memories as a shuffled pack of snap-
    shots in the hands of a lunatic. Each chapter is a dated
    snapshot, but the chapters can be chronologically rear-
    ranged by the reader, a process making clear that:
    (1) there are four dated periods in Beavis's life;
    (2) reading the chapters chronologically gives a closely-
    knit narrative; (3) not only Beavis's memories, but those
    of other characters, are given; (4) within each of the four

sequences, there is no sequence; in fact, the order is
jumbled. Conclusions: the novel doesn't exist only within
Beavis's mind, but the only complete mind-portrait is
that of Beavis. The "other" incidents are included to
make the overall story clear. Relevant incidents are
summoned to mind as present ones call them. H used dis-
ordered chronology, despite problems to the reader, to
show how the memory works: it forgets the present mission,
and it recalls things simultaneously. For Beavis, then,
there are four levels of recall. Also, the juxtapositions
of nonchronological events give subtle associations of
character, theme, and place. "Unconscious but artful
selectivity governs our memories and lives."

87. Bergonzi, Bernard. "Essays in Fiction." *New Society*
   (Nov. 12, 1970), 874-875.

   H's novels through *Point Counter Point* pale in comparison
   with the great novels of Lawrence, Joyce, Fitzgerald,
   Hemingway, Forster, Woolf. H's "essays in fiction" have
   "sunk to about the right level of modest public esteem."
   Every novel has a character who is a mouthpiece for H.
   H's personal separations--thought and action, mind and
   body, sense and art--trouble the novels too much; he can't
   resolve them. Bergonzi gives Brander's book on H (see 5)
   a poor rating: it gives little critical insight, fails to
   appreciate why H's ideas are often contradictory.

88. ————. "Life's Divisions." *Encounter*, 41 (July, 1973),
   65-68.

   Thody's book on H stresses biography--e.g., Lawrence
   implied that the account of Little Phil's death by meningitis in *Point Counter Point* brought on an estrangement
   between H and his first wife, Maria. Thody, Woodcock, and
   Firchow are all interested in the total literary personality
   of H--life, ideas, fiction. May tries to treat H solely
   as a novelist--but the result is pedestrian because H's
   work doesn't respond to orthodox modes of explication.
   Woodcock's book is the best. (See 13, 32, 43, 48.)

89. Beringause, Arthur F. "Debate Between Body and Soul."
   CEA Critic, 26 (June, 1964), 4.

   "The Gioconda Smile" shows H's understanding of Freudian
   theory. Hutton, self-absorbed, callous, conceited, can't
   perceive the significance of the poems he remembers tag
   lines from: Arnold's sonnet on Shakespeare and Wordsworth's
   sonnet on Milton. The themes of both sonnets relate to

Hutton's dilemma; gratification of his physical desire
doesn't bring him Shakespeare's freedom or Milton's happiness.

90. "Best of Bad Times." *Newsweek*, 56 (Oct. 3, 1960), 80.

At 66, H is as active as ever; he discusses plans for a
new utopian novel, the reverse of *Brave New World* (*Island*).
The problems of today are the population explosion, traffic
and smog in the Los Angeles area, living space, and quality
of living. "Why does mental arteriosclerosis set in 45
years before physical arteriosclerosis?" Most people, H
believes, are lazy--want the Pill to do everything for
them--like Soma, in *Brave New World*. His new novel is to
be a fantasy about "a society in which real efforts are
made to realize human potentialities." Democracy is the
best society because it makes outlets for all human diversity possible.

91. Bethell, Philip. "The Philosophy in the Poetry of Aldous
     Huxley." *Poetry Review*, 24 (Sept., 1933), 359-368.

H's poems show "an unusual combination of 18th century
sentimentalism with speculative post-war free-thinking.
An essentially old-fashioned heart working with the aid of
the most up-to-date intellectual instruments has produced
this nicely balanced compendium of emotion, aestheticism,
spirituality and intellect ... a mind which prides itself
on its all round balance and poise." (See also 164, 190,
203, 221, 274, 342, 468, 549, 552, 564, 567.)

92. Bienvenu, R. "Le voyage dans l'oeuvre d'Aldous Huxley."
     Études Anglaises, 24 (1971), 22-40.

H has never been attached to one place. He lived in
Italy (1923-28), France (1928-37), the U.S. (after 1937).
Other "voyages" took him to Tunisia, Spain, Germany,
Antilles, Cypress, Greece, Brazil, Denmark, Peru, Sweden.
Italy is the setting for *Time Must Have a Stop*, but most
of the novels feature characters who are restless travelers,
like H himself. H wrote several essay travel books--
e.g., *Along the Road*--but he also satirizes inveterate
travelers who so engage because the best people do it.
H deplores the Baedeker approach to travel. He chooses
his own literary and painterly allusions to illuminate
his perceptions of places visited. In *Along the Road* and
Jesting Pilate, H's mode of synthesis is like that which
he later develops in *The Perennial Philosophy*.

93. "Biographical Note." *Saturday Review of Literature*, 17
     (Nov. 20, 1937), 21.

     Review of *Ends and Means*. An entire proposal for re-
     organizing society, an alternative to the laxness of
     democracy, and the forcibleness of dictatorships. Salva-
     tion exists in the detached mind--which holds that all
     formulas are unacceptable, that truth is elusive. *Ends
     and Means* tries to show the working of the detached mind
     in all areas of life.

94. "Biographical Note." *Saturday Review of Literature*, 31
     (Aug. 21, 1948), 8.

     Review of *Ape and Essence*. The novel begins on the day
     of Gandhi's assassination; text of *Ape and Essence* spills
     off a rubbish truck carrying rejected Hollywood scripts.
     "Ends are ape-chosen; only the means are man's." A world
     of apes, aping men, is at war with itself; there is mutual
     annihilation in a world largely devastated by a nuclear
     war. Only small land areas--New Zealand, central Africa--
     have survived. *Ape and Essence* is a somewhat thinner,
     more labored effort than *Brave New World*.

95. Birnbaum, Milton. "Aldous Huxley," in *Politics of Twentieth
     Century Novelists*, ed. George A. Panichas. New York:
     Hawthorn, 1971. Pp. 65-84.

     Governments and wars fill H with horror; absolute power
     in government produces absolute corruption. He opposes
     benevolent despotism (*Brave New World*). Socialism is
     fatally committed to centralization and standardized
     urban production. Communism is "organized hatred," as
     is Fascism. H accepts democracy, but with reservations:
     its citizens are lethargic about government; the press
     becomes too powerful; charlatans get into office; still,
     citizens have a degree of freedom. H deplores nationalism,
     the chief cause of war. Only Western religions provide
     a moral rationale for war (Calvinist "righteous indigna-
     tion"). War also derives from economic greed; small
     localized communities could counter this feeling. Political
     power should also be decentralized, as well as industry.
     An aristocracy of minds and character is desirable, but
     no form of government can be completely trusted. H is
     less interested in a world government than he is in solving
     the demographic and ecological crisis. Yet H also sati-
     rizes attempts to ameliorate society. Even Pala of *Island*
     is not finally ideal, though H tried to make it so.

96.   ————. "Aldous Huxley: An Aristocrat's Comments on
      Popular Culture." *Journal of Popular Culture*, 2 (Sum-
      mer, 1968), 106-112.

      H feared that more leisure time for the masses would
      produce a flood of trashy "entertainment." Movies prevent
      people from viewing life with a sense of reality. The
      media encourage consumerism, a life style which still
      leaves people bored. Work and entertainment are both
      mechanized. H deplored popular music; he alludes to or
      describes with love the music of Mozart, Beethoven--but
      he hates Romantic composers (Berlioz, *et al*.). Music
      shouldn't be a matter of emotional intoxication. In
      popular culture in general, H saw a lack of values; the
      arts should criticize, interpret life, not be idolatrous
      ends in themselves.

97.   ————. "Aldous Huxley's Animadversions Upon Sexual Love."
      Texas Studies in Literature and Language, 8 (Summer,
      1966), 285-296.

      Unlike Lawrence, H seldom found sexual love worshipful
      or mysterious, either in fiction or non-fiction. Only
      the artificially "happy" marriages in *Island* are satis-
      fyingly consummated. Frustration, or guilt, is commonly
      associated with the sexual act by H's male lovers; the
      women are sometimes driven (Lucy Tantamount) to abasement.
      The person in love becomes obsessed with an idealized un-
      reality, or gives in to debauchery--H presented only the
      extremes. H tried to use J.D. Unwin's theories on
      channeling sex drives into constructive areas. But H
      never clearly formulated these principles. He was never
      able to divorce himself from a Swiftian hatred of the act
      of copulation. Sexual love was to him a delusion.

98.   ————. "Aldous Huxley's Conception of the Nature of
      Reality." *The Personalist*, 47 (July, 1966), 297-314.

      (1) Until the mid-30's H dealt with the world of tradi-
      tional values: Judeo-Christian, patriotic scientific
      progress; he was disillusioned with these. (2) *Eyeless
      in Gaza* (1936) and *The Perennial Philosophy* (1945) are
      H's attempts at mysticism, especially Buddhist thought.
      (3) H finally tried to incorporate Buddhism and Western
      science. For H, science gives a very limited view of
      reality. Philosophy, unless aided by self-transcendence,
      is inadequate. Heredity, environment, free will, collec-
      tively control our lives. The ultimate reality is the
      mysticism of self-transcendence. This and the loss of

personality are the only ways the world can overcome
idolatry, stupidity, cruelty. H experimented with drugs
as a means whereby people could approach mysticism, since
most lack the will to do so unaided.

99.   ———. "Aldous Huxley's Quest for Values: A Study in
    Religious Syncretism." *Comparative Literature Studies*,
    3 (1966), 169–182; reprinted in *Mansions of the Spirit*,
    ed. George A. Panichas. New York: Hawthorn, 1967. Pp.
    239–258; also reprinted in *Aldous Huxley: A Collection
    of Critical Essays*, ed. Robert E. Kuehn (see 30), pp.
    46–63.

H's earliest comments on religion are contemptuous,
but Lawrence's vitalism influenced a change in him. H's
anti-Jewish remarks were sometimes quoted by the Nazis.
Because he found many historical instances of cruelty
committed by Catholics and Puritans, H often presented
ministers and priests satirically in his fiction. But
H sought to retain the mystic experience of Christianity.
He called his book *The Perennial Philosophy* (not Perennial
Religion). *Eyeless in Gaza* was his first complete en-
dorsement of mysticism, though he had always expressed
an interest in it. In *After Many a Summer*, Mr. Propter
more specifically defines mysticism. *The Perennial Philosophy* is H's most complete statement of it: contemplation, intuitive awareness of God. Love will then emanate,
man won't ravage the earth, creativity will return to
his work, he'll be freed from selfhood. But H also depended on science to alleviate overpopulation, economic
problems. Unfortunately, in H's view, East and West had
exchanged their worst features; H wanted them to exchange
their best. H's solution was synthetic, and part of it
depended on drugs: mescalin or, in Pala (*Island*), the
moksha-medicine. (See also 128, 130, 131, 144, 146, 153,
156, 172, 233, 235, 246, 279, 294, 341, 351, 384, 401,
459, 474, 485, 519, 529, 550, 561, 619, 620.)

100.   ———. "Aldous Huxley's Treatment of Nature." *Hibbert
    Journal*, 64 (Summer, 1966), 150–152.

Nature is never conspicuous in H's novels; he seems an
urban novelist. He attacks the Romantics, who see Nature
as a source of beneficence. *Jesting Pilate* (1920)
imagines Wordsworth contemplating Nature in Borneo. But
H does warn against the careless exploitation of natural
resources. "Wordsworth in the Tropics" from *Do What You
Will* attacks Wordsworth's view of nature as false, anthro-
pomorphic. H seldom looks to nature for solace, but he

does express concern about ecology, planned use of
natural resources. Nature is "not a source of value,
but a valuable means to an end."

101.   ———. "Aldous Huxley's Views on Education." *Xavier
       University Studies*, 6 (May, 1967), 81-91.

H had little faith in education for most people. *The
Perennial Philosophy* deprecates culture and education as
ends in themselves. H's educated characters fail to live
harmonious, integrated lives. H's evaluation of the educational system: kindergartens do well, but from then on,
teaching becomes prescriptive. Educators should suit
preparation to students' needs, abilities. Privately
controlled schools should supplement state-aided ones.
Lectures are virtually anachronistic. Research should
be original. Academic study should alternate with periods
of practical, physical labor. H has little trust or admiration for teachers, professors. In *Island* children
are trained to become well-adjusted individuals, not
forcibly standardized. H doesn't clearly distinguish between English and American educational systems, and he
doesn't recognize the variety of systems within the U.S.
As with other topics, H is inconsistent; sometimes he is
almost pessimistic and feels that education does no good;
when more optimistic, he offers constructive criticisms
for improvement.

102.   ———. "Aldous Huxley's Views on Language." *Etc.: A
       Review of General Semantics*, 26 (March, 1969), 141-144.

Inadequacy of language is the source of many of the
world's difficulties. Literature itself lies between the
extremes of the language of science and the language of
magic (Woolf, Joyce). "Magic" is more likely to be in
Greek and Romance languages than in Germanic ones. Outside of literature, language inadequacies become much
greater. Emotions conveyed in words are often stronger
than responses to the objects that the words stand for.
Euphemistic use of language can be the most dangerous
of all, as in the politics of war. Words are even less
adequate to account for ultimate reality.

103.   ———. "Politics and Character in *Point Counter Point*."
       Studies in the Novel, 9 (Winter, 1977), 468-487.

Only male characters express political views in *Point
Counter Point*. Walter Bidlake has a "delightful hatred
for Capitalists and Reactionaries," but he also feels

squeamish in the presence of working-class people. Like his weak moral scruples (conscience-stricken about deserting Marjorie Carling, his pregnant mistress, he yet pursues the lusty Lucy Tantamount), Walter's socialism is an ineffectual flutter. Frank Illidge strongly defends Communism in theory, but in fact he vacillates between personal insecurity and hatred of capitalists, the real bases for his politics. Spandrell is not the object of mockery, but rather the expression of it. He mocks the war poetry of Rupert Brooke, as he mocks everything else. Deprived as he thinks he is of the heaven of innocence (his love for his mother before she remarried), he feels obliged to seek out absolute evil. The weakness in this characterization is that we are asked to believe Spandrell consciously and deliberately chose his Satanism because of his mother's second marriage. "In his descent into diabolical nihilism, he perverts his interest in politics into another source for satisfying his desire for malevolent mischief." Everard Webley, victim of Spandrell's hatred, is simply the mouthpiece for the fascist-like Brotherhood of British Freemen. Webley's purpose is to keep all classes strong; their "hostile symbiosis" will make society better able to survive. Only when he falls in love with Elinor Quarles does Webley become somewhat humanized, and his being assassinated while on the way to meet her makes him more than just the "Tinpot Mussolini" he was to begin with. Mark Rampion scolds all politicians: they are all "equally anxious to take us to hell." Philip Quarles also deplores demagoguery, but he prefers only to burrow inside himself or inside of a book. Other characters in the novel have less, if any, concern about politics. H himself at the time of writing *Point Counter Point* was not enthusiastic about politics. He detested both Fascism and Communism, but more particularly Communism because he felt it was more efficient at curtailing human liberty. He tolerated democracy, but doubted its ameliorative potential as much as that of any other system. He strongly supported the pacifist movement between the World Wars, but felt that politics alone were inadequate to deal with world problems.

104. Black, Max. "Aldous Huxley, 'Literature and Science.'" *Scientific American*, 210 (March, 1964), 141-144.

H is unfair in accusing Snow and Leavis of extremities; his own works are filled with juxtaposed opposites. He sought to reconcile the opposites by searching out the "something whose dwelling is everywhere, the essential

Suchness of the world, which is at once immanent and
transcendent." H assumes that both science and literature concern themselves with expressing "experiences."
Hence, they should be partners, not competitors. Science
deals with the more public of human experiences, literature, with those that are more private. Science is
"sharable," literature less so. But H fails to discriminate between the received impression and the conceptualized
response when he uses the generic term "experience."
Fortunately, he doesn't stick with his metaphysical
model; he recognizes that people can respond to the "en-
lightening truth" of Shakespeare; hence, literature isn't
"strictly private." H's chapter on the necessity for
poets to know ornithological data about nightingales is
absurd in its implications. (See also 135, 198, 490,
514.)

105.   Blocker, Günther. "Huxley und die Gnade." *Merkur*, 10
       (Nov., 1956), 1120–1121.

106.   Blom, E. "The Musician in Aldous Huxley." *Chesterian*,
       17 (Nov., 1936), 37–45.

       H is both a craftsman and an artist in his use of
       music. In his essays he writes music criticism, but
       never music journalism. He always shows originality.
       "After silence, that which comes nearest to expressing
       the inexpressible is music"; this statement typifies H's
       wisdom about music. He prefers Beethoven and Mozart to
       Wagner because Wagner doesn't know how to use musical
       silences. H knows how to balance a lyrical description
       of music against something matter of fact or something
       cynical. He noted that Browning and Milton were the two
       English poets who best understood music, but he takes
       Browning to task for overdoing this skill. *Point Counter
       Point* is H's most musical novel because of its form.
       Brave New World is notable for its satire on the misuse
       of music, as is *Antic Hay*. *Those Barren Leaves* sati-
       rizes the effects of a jazz band; H had no use for jazz.

107.   Bloomfield, Paul. *Uncommon People: A Study of England's
       Elite*. London: Hamish Hamilton, 1955.

       H is "one of the few capable makers of a cultural syn-
       thesis in our time." His function has been comparable to
       that of his great-uncle Matthew Arnold. This book de-
       scribes the important descendants of George Villiers,
       1st Duke of Buckingham.

108. Blotner, Joseph I. "Aldous Huxley and George Orwell:
     The Future in Perspective," in his *The Political Novel*.
     Garden City, N.Y.: Doubleday, 1955. P. 23.

     H and Orwell use their novels as political instruments
     to warn believers in the democratic tradition against
     the threats that endanger democracy: H shows the dangers
     of godlessness, immorality; Orwell shows those of
     totalitarian government.

109. Bode, Helmut. "Die Wandlung Aldous Huxleys." *Literarische
     Revue* (München), 4 (1949), 181.

110. Bonicelli, Elena. "Libertà dell'Utopia, Utopia della
     libertà in Aldous Huxley." *Revista di letterature
     moderne e comparate* (Firenze), 26 (1973), 307–314.

     Brave New World catalogues the frightening, inhuman
     prospects for the future world. H uses the format of
     the traditional utopia, but his purpose is to win a wider
     audience for this kind of literature. Many aspects of
     the book anticipate science fiction. But H's strong
     emphasis on an underlying thesis prevents *Brave New World*
     from really becoming this new form. His involvement with
     ideology prevents him from being as innovative and percep-
     tive as he might otherwise have been, and the creative
     approaches to his problem that are suggested or implied
     in the novel are quickly dropped.

111. Borelius, Alex. "Die Wandlung des Aldous Huxley."
     Wirtschafts-Zeitung (Stuttgart), 4 (1949), 10.

112. Borinski, Ludwig. "Wells, Huxley und die Utopia."
     *Literatur-Kultur-Gesellschaft in England und Amerika:
     Aspekte und Forschungsbeitrage Friedrich Schubel zum
     60 Geburtstag*, ed. G. Muller-Schwefe and K. Tuzinski.
     Frankfurt, 1966. Pp. 257–277.

113. Bortolon, Liana. "I diavoli di Loudun." *Vita e Pensiero*,
     37 (Feb., 1954), 110–115.

114. Bowen, Elizabeth. "Huxley's Essays" (1936) in her *Col-
     lected Impressions*. New York: Alfred Knopf, 1950.
     Pp. 146–148.

     "As a novelist, he still has a touch of the prodigy:
     in a great glare of intellectual hilarity his characters
     dangle rather too jerkily; they are morality characters

with horrified puppet faces." But the novels are better
in one respect than the essays--"they are continuous."
H is remarkable for "the transitions he makes, the posi-
tions he abandons, the connexions he underlines." In
The Olive Tree H is a superb stylist.

115. Bowen, Zack. "Allusions to Musical Works in *Point Counter
      Point*." *Studies in the Novel*, 9 (Winter, 1977), 488-
      508.

The major thematic weight of *Point Counter Point* is
borne by the classical music in which H was especially
interested. Most obviously, the counterpoint method of
the Bach suite determines the structure of the novel.
Yet if H was bold enough to represent and sometimes
parody himself as the novel-writing Philip Quarles, it
is equally possible he was being less than idealistic in
his presumed analogy between music and the eternal truths.
"Huxley uses the art of music as a contrapuntal variation
on his own art and the art of Philip Quarles." On occasion, H attributes so heavy a meaning to music that the
effect can only be absurd (e.g., Bach's Sarabande sugges-
ting "a young girl singing to herself under clouds").
This unlikely and overliteral interpretation of Bach
anticipates the later "verbose and impassioned construction of the proof of God with which Spandrell burdens
the Beethoven." The Bach suite is "the metaphor against
which all flux can be measured." Lady Edward's conversation with General Knoyle about Handel's *Water Music*
illustrates "the attempt to aggrandize already great
music by associating false legends and stories with it."
This is still another example of reading false meanings
into musical compositions. The real point of the exchange between Spandrell and Rampion about Beethoven is
the comic absurdity of it all. Everard's musical confrontation in the park with the anti-vivisectionist parade
is another parody of the assumption that God is to be
elicited through any such abstracts as mathematics or
music. Further satire is seen in the Queen's Hall concert in which an absurd Satie composition (symphony of
rumbling noises in the intestines) precedes Beethoven's
Coriolanus, a "programmable" work with an ascertainable
story line. Such parodies of music as "meaningful" accompany similar parodies on scientific experimentation
and literary realism. After the bravura scene of Beethoven, Spandrell, and Rampion, H gives us the ridiculous
Burlap inspired by Mendelssohn's "On Wings of Song."
Not knowing of his mistress's death, but glad to be rid

of Ethel Cobbett, he whistles the "Wings" melody, in
preparation for the evening scene in which he and Bea-
trice romp like children in a big, old-fashioned bath.
"At best a healthy cynicism constitutes the proper mood
for entering the Kingdom."

116. Bowering, Peter. "'The Source of Light': Pictorial
      Imagery and Symbolism in *Point Counter Point*." *Studies
      in the Novel*, 9 (Winter, 1977), 389-405.

Kenneth Clark praised H as "one of the most discerning
lookers of our time," in contrast to most novelists, who
write poor stuff about painting. H rarely goes past the
late 19th century with his pictorial imagery. He used
paintings to express symbolic truths; thus Stoyte's
failure to appreciate Vermeer (in *After Many a Summer*)
shows Stoyte's spiritual inadequacy. *Point Counter Point*
contains the highest concentration of allusions to the
arts to be found among H's works. As a novel of ideas,
this work expects its characters to have a breadth of
knowledge in the arts. *Point Counter Point* is framed by
motifs taken from science, music, and art; it begins with
biological notations about Marjorie's pregnancy, and
accounts of the Bach suite and of Bidlake's "Bathers,"
and it closes with biological notations on Webley's
corpse, Bidlake's failure to paint the gardens at Gatten-
den, and an account of the A minor Quartet. An account
of the pictures in Bidlake's rooms gives us the ethos of
this Edwardian artist's life: his friends, his life as a
student in Rome, the London scene in which he prospered,
his love affairs and models, are all given in ways that
remind the reader that Bidlake's fatal illness makes all
of these past associations meaningless. Bidlake's "The
Bathers" is opposed to both Shelley's romanticism and
Bach's spirituality. Like the painter, it ignores half
of life's experience and is therefore only one more abstraction of reality. The paintings of Mark Rampion help
strengthen what is otherwise a somewhat weak characterization of Lawrence, the life model for the character. In
one of these pictures an embracing nude couple is the
source of light in the midst of an exotic landscape in
which plants and animals forego their predatory habits.
The painting in the novel goes much beyond Lawrence's
own real paintings. H's symbolic painting by Rampion
depicts an ideal denied the other characters. But a
final painting in H's last novel, *Island*, portrays a landscape without figures, "a proof of man's capacity to
accept all the deaths in life."

117.   Breit, Harvey.   "Talk with Aldous Huxley." *New York
       Times Book Review*, May 21, 1950, p. 28; reprinted in
       his *Writer Observed*.   Cleveland: World Publishing Co.,
       1956.

       H recalled his desperation while working for the
       Athenaeum as a reviewer when confronted by floods of
       books.   People who run literary reviews think they're
       much more important than authors.   H had plans to do a
       historical novel on 14th-century Italy, because "It's
       really human nature with the lid off.   The violence and
       picturesqueness ... that passage from extreme sanctity
       to extreme brutality--things we consider incompatible go
       on in the same breath."   H is fascinated by the California
       and New Mexico desert--"I imagine no one except some ex-
       traordinary, eccentric genius like Turner could paint
       it."

118.   Brkic, Svetozar.   *"Setni Kroum*: 'Kubisticki' roman Oldesa
       Akslija."   *Letopis Matice Srpske* (Novi Sad), 414 (1974),
       340-352.

       This essay discusses *Crome Yellow.*

119.   Brooke, Jocelyn.   "The Wicked Uncle: An Appreciation of
       Aldous Huxley." *Listener*, 70 (December 12, 1963), 99.

       To schoolboys used to Galsworthy and Bennett, H's
       novels were a revelation.   But he wore thin after *Point
       Counter Point*, with his successive preoccupation with
       utopias, pacifism, and Yoga, and with the compulsive
       repetition of his mannerisms.   *Time Must Have a Stop* is
       virtually unreadable because of its style.   The late
       novels are labored and repetitive, with only occasional
       flashes of the old brilliance.   Yet his intelligence
       never failed.   In pursuit of religion, he strove for ob-
       jectivity; blind faith was not enough.   H's best fiction
       was written during his first period, and "Two or Three
       Graces" is one of his best stories, with its malicious
       portrait of Lawrence.   But thereafter he is best with
       the writing of essays.

120.   Brown, Edward James.   *"Brave New World," "1984," and "We"*:
       *An Essay on Anti-Utopia: Zamyatin and English Litera-
       ture* (Ardis Essay Series 4).   Ann Arbor: Ardis, 1976.
       61 pp.

       Similarities between *Brave New World* and *We* include:
       Zamyatin's benevolent dictator and H's World Controller;
       the "mephi" outside the wall in *We* and the reservation of

savages in *Brave New World*. Both books assume that the more complex the society, the less individual freedom it allows. H in particular assumes that at a lower, less organized level of life the individual, love, honor, and poetry are "somehow" preserved, whereas these tend to disappear at higher levels. H makes naive use of the "noble savage." Utilitarianism dominates *Brave New World*, a book which seems heavy-handed and obvious when compared to *We*.

121. Browning, William Gordon. "Toward a Set of Standards for [Evaluating] Anti-Utopian Fiction." *Cithara*, 10 (1970), 18-32.

(1) As a warning to the future, the author projects onto an imaginary society those traits of contemporary society that he dislikes most. (2) Author uses a setting that is distant either in time or place. (3) The techniques used are those of Menippean satire (see Northrop Frye). (4) Characteristic weaknesses are described to produce a nightmare society. Zamyatin's *We*, H's *Brave New World*, Orwell's *1984*, are in this genre. H's humor confuses the reader as to the seriousness of *Brave New World*; H confessed to being an "amused, Pyrrhonic aesthete" when he wrote the book. Still, *Brave New World* arouses the reader's indignation. H's solutions are vague; a clear statement is delayed until *The Perennial Philosophy* (1944). The social flaw in the *Brave New World* society is the desire to have complete happiness at any cost--even the cost of relinquishing free will. *Brave New World* makes creative use of detail; it has obvious but effective symbols. It is a clever book, but it lacks the sincerity, intensity of *We* and *1984*. The four-point criterion above is from Irving Howe, "The Fiction of Anti-Utopia" (see 262).

122. Buck, Philo M., Jr. "Sight to the Blind: Aldous Huxley," in his *Directions in Contemporary Literature*. New York: Oxford University Press, 1942. Pp. 169-191.

In *Brave New World*, "'Soma' and 'Feelies' compensate for the instinctive striving for unique self-expression." Poetry is one of the ways out of the perfect comfort in *Brave New World*. H's thought dominates his imagination --he is the virtuoso rather than the creator. The essays in *Ends and Means* are a gloss on the novel *Eyeless in Gaza*--but a great novel needs no gloss. *After Many a Summer* has too many Hollywood echoes.

123.   Bullough, Geoffrey.   "Aspects of Aldous Huxley."   *English
        Studies*, 30 (Oct., 1949), 233-243.

        H's best novels were written during his relativist
        phase. Before *Brave New World*, his novels imitate Pea-
        cock, or Norman Douglas's *South Wind* (1917). This is an
        intellectualist method, which allows interaction among
        odd characters. H used the concepts of Freud and Pavlov
        to help him probe the weaknesses of humanity. *Those
        Barren Leaves* presents Calamy, whose interest in mystics
        anticipates H's later, more formulated, *The Perennial
        Philosophy*. In *Point Counter Point* the characters are
        less like caricatures, are more individualized. Quarles
        expresses much of H's own purpose on the "musicalization
        of fiction." *Point Counter Point* is not true tragedy--
        it expresses saddened irony at determinism, determinism
        expressed by making the characters victims of their own
        and others' selves. *Brave New World* is the first book
        to find H sharply critical of science. This is H's most
        successful book; the novels after it are inferior. *The
        Perennial Philosophy* no longer depends on the capricious
        development of all sides of one's nature, or on a balance
        of excesses; its purpose is to see "behind the phenomenal
        Mask of the unknown God." "The aesthetic implications of
        The Perennial Philosophy would be to stress the positive
        rather than the negative in human behavior, to blend the
        fragmentary...."

124.   Burgum, Edwin Berry.   "Aldous Huxley and His Dying Swan."
        Antioch Review, 2 (Spring, 1942), 62-75. Reprinted in
        his *The Novel and the World's Dilemma*. New York:
        Oxford University Press, 1947. Pp. 140-156.

        H became two people, two opposite personalities that
        couldn't be reconciled. Burgum assumes that H, who by
        temperament withdrew from what offended him, became a
        mystic as an alternative to suicide. H blames the "born
        novelist" for accepting the world at its own self-valua-
        tion, but he himself lacked the moral strength to do so.
        Grey Eminence shows H's flagging creative powers--the
        book is a retreat into journalism. H was forced to go to
        Hindu mysticism because of the contradictions in Western
        mysticism--Father Joseph, a mystic, was nevertheless
        Richelieu's agent. (Burgum reviews H's writing career,
        with generally negative comments.) H was part of the
        Puritan tradition, but he lacks part of its reticence.
        His difference from Proust and Joyce was his refusal to
        penetrate the surface. Despite the counterpoint method
        used in *Point Counter Point*, H doesn't clarify the social

meanings in the novel. If good results, it's the ironic accident of two evils canceling each other. There is no real attempt to weave the contrapuntal themes into a central fugue. Gide succeeded better with the central "counterfeiter" theme of his novel. *After Many a Summer* doesn't resolve the dilemma of mystic withdrawal because Mr. Propter depends on the despicable Mr. Stoyte for financial support. *After Many a Summer* does not mark the demise of H's vitality; this was already apparent in "Leda," which H wrote 20 years earlier. H had many defects in social vision and concern for politics.

125.   Burton, Katherine. "Aldous Huxley and Other Moderns." *Catholic World*, 139 (Aug., 1934), 552-556.

Point Counter Point expresses an exceeding weariness and uselessness of life. *Brave New World* has a much higher tone--at least the idealist doesn't commit suicide the way Spandrell does. (Burton also writes about O'Neill and Sinclair Lewis.) H deplored private faiths--"Religion provides a public faith in values so fundamental that men and women can believe and so obtain an accession of power."

126.   Busch, G. "Herausfordung des Zeitalters." *Die Anregung*, 1 (Jan. 13, 1961), 4-5.

127.   Butts, Mary. "Aldous Huxley," in *Scrutinies*, ed. Edgell Rickword. London: Wishart, 1931. Vol. 2, pp. 74-98.

H is the perfect writer or stylist; he has enormous knowledge; but "what is it for?" *Antic Hay* is patterned after a masque. "While his chief work as a critic is an analysis and appreciation of how superb things get done, his work as an inventor is often monotonous, showing why things cannot be done: are undone: or, if done, produce incalculable and pernicious results."

128.   ———. "Heresy Game." *Spectator*, 158 (March 12, 1937), 466-467.

Butts responds to H's *Texts and Pretexts*, in which H calls into question George Herbert's faith in God as expressed in "The Collar." "The voice that calls the poet ... is a voice from the depths of his own nature.... a projection of his most real, his essential self," says H. H is completely wrong-headed in his gloss of Herbert's poem; the gloss is "as pure a specimen of wish-fulfillment as one could hope to find."

129.   Buzura, Augustin.   "Tentatia echilibrului" (The tempta-
       tion of the equilibrium).   *Tribune*, 11, no. 20, May 18,
       1967, p. 8; no. 21, May 25, 1967, p. 8; no. 22, June 1,
       1967, p. 8; no. 23, June 8, 1967, p. 8.

130.   Cairns, David.   "Huxley: Cosmology and Ethic."   *Expository
       Times*, 50 (Nov., 1938), 55-60.

       In his novels, H excels as an essayist and philosopher,
       but not as an artist.   He recognizes what professional
       philosophers know--that in a world in which reality is
       space-time, morality or beauty or truth has no meaning:
       a materialist cosmology produces ennui.   Even Spandrell's
       criminality in *Point Counter Point* lacks moral signifi-
       cance.   *Ends and Means* seeks to establish an ethic and a
       cosmology; the ethic is a high value placed on disinter-
       estedness in love, on nonattachment to craving for power
       or personal urges.   His cosmology accepts an impersonal
       Absolute, with whom we gain union through mystical ex-
       perience, which we prepare for through goodness.   But H's
       cosmology and ethic do not harmonize; "goodness" for him
       is unity of amoral reality.   H's pantheist mysticism will
       not solve his problems.

131.   ————.   "Why Mr. Aldous Huxley Is Not a Christian."
       Expository Times, 50 (Jan., 1939), 155-159.

       H rejects Christianity by asserting the following:
       (1) God is not personal, not good, not love.   H assumes
       that the mystical experience in which this knowledge is
       gained is "reality."   (2) Person-worship in Christianity
       always leads to intolerance, as can be shown by the many
       persecutions committed in the history of the Christian
       church.   (3) Christ's character shows faults of commission
       and omission: commission, his violence in the Temple;
       omission, his accepting human limitations of knowledge
       and power.   (4) A personal God demands the curtailment
       of personal freedom.   Cairns asserts that H's pantheistic
       cosmology will prove incapable of any of the things he
       expects of it.

132.   Cajumi, Arrigo.   "Il nuovo romanzo inglese: A. Huxley."
       La Cultura, (Aug., 1929), 480-489.

133.   Cary, Richard.   "Aldous Huxley, Vernon Lee and the *Genius
       Loci*."   *Colby Library Quarterly*, 5 (June, 1960), 128-
       141.

       The beauty of H's amplitude of knowledge is its un-
       pedantic quality.   In the 1920's, the travel essay was

one of his specialties; at that time, he wrote Vernon
Lee, praising her *Golden Keys* (1925), which describes
the area of Bologna and Siena. Replying to an inquiry
from Cary, H said he first met Lee at Garsington, then
saw her often when he and his wife lived in Florence.
Both he and Lee were great conversationalists, both were
prolific writers, both had versatile interests. By 1925,
Lee had written seven travel books, which were praised
for their style. "Genius loci" is her sense of the
presence of a place. Cary gives several examples of
places she enshrined in her books. H is more facetious
in his travel books--he ridicules fashionable travelers
in search of "sensations." Lee wrote about "the sacred
fury of travel"--and though H saw beauty in scenes and
places, he noted incongruities too: he referred to "the
vice of travel."

134. Castier, J. "Aldous Huxley, sociologue." *Revue Bleue,*
      Revue Politique et Littéraire, 76 (Nov., 1938), 410-413.

135. ————. "De la culture scientifique d'Aldous Huxley."
      Revue Bleue, Revue Politique et Littéraire, 74 (Aug. 15,
      1936), 550-558.

      Castier notes the role of the sciences throughout H's
works. There are many allusions to mathematics. Geometry
appears in *Along the Road*, when he remarks that his love
for it prepared him to love Holland. "Young Archimedes"
tells of the child prodigy Guido and his feeling for the
harmony of numbers. *Point Counter Point* uses physics
(the flotation of icebergs), chemistry (the political
impact of exhausting supplies of coal, petroleum),
biology and the study of intestinal cancer by way of X
rays, or the symptoms of meningitis, in the death of
little Phil. *Brave New World* is full of science, including the test-tube babies. H found beauty, harmony,
in natural laws. Also, H shows wide interest in the
arts: architecture (e.g., the essay in *Along the Road* on
Alberti and Brunelleschi, or another essay, on the vulgarity of the Taj Mahal), painting (many characters in
the novels are painters, e.g., Bidlake and Rampion in
Point Counter Point; or elsewhere, the fictionalized portrait of Benjamin Haydon). Music is a subject in *Along
the Road*, which has an essay on the growth of popular
music, like the waltz. *Point Counter Point* is full of
ideas about musical appreciation. H was also familiar
with an extraordinary range of English writers, as well
as with many French ones: Anatole France, Voltaire,
Baudelaire, Rimbaud, Mallarmé, and others. H's interests
included all human activities.

136.   ————. "Les heroines d'Aldous Huxley et son évolution
        psychologique." *Revue Bleue, Revue Politique et
        Littéraire*, 75 (May 15, 1937), 342-346.

        Eyeless in Gaza shows H abandoning his earlier neutral,
        impassive view of life to preach a moral lesson. He
        began, in *Crome Yellow*, as an amused spectator of the
        human comedy. Aside from those in *Brave New World*, the
        heroines are grouped in opposite pairs with geometrical
        precision to show H's moral commitment in human affairs.
        At zero value, without moral character, is Grace Peddley
        ("Two or Three Graces"), the "naive young girl." Her
        extreme opposites are Lucy Tantamount and Rachel Quarles
        of *Point Counter Point*. Lucy is the complete egotist,
        given to the search for personal pleasure. Rachel finds
        her refuge in a religion of doing good. In *Eyeless in
        Gaza*, Mary Amberley and Mrs. Foxe form the same opposites:
        Mary is, like Lucy, a pleasure seeker. Mrs. Foxe gives
        herself to mistaken altruism in rearing her son Brian;
        her impossible idealism causes his suicide. Also opposites
        are Beatrice Gilray of *Point Counter Point*, and Pamela
        Tarn ("After the Fireworks"): Beatrice has overwhelming
        disgust for men, and Pamela welcomes them with open arms.
        Another pair are Mrs. Aldwinkle (*Those Barren Leaves*) and
        Mary Rampion (*Point Counter Point*)—both wealthy bour-
        geois. Mrs. Aldwinkle acquires splendid palaces, rules
        like a despot; Mary gives up the glittering world,
        marries penniless Mark Rampion, whom she deeply admires
        but doesn't understand. The "positive" region includes
        sentiment, altruism; the "negative," egotism, lack of
        scruples. Aside from some abstract or conventional
        characters in *Brave New World*, H's women can be classed
        as positive or negative. (Castier has translated H's
        novels into French.)

137.   Cecil, David. "Santayana." *Times Literary Supplement*,
        Jan. 15, 1970, p. 58.

        Cecil takes H to task for his December 18, 1969, *Times*
        essay on Santayana, in which H describes Santayana's
        style as "exquisitely good writing ... that is only
        another name for bad writing." H is indulging in meaning-
        less paradox, revealing his own imperfect taste.

138.   Cerf, Bennett. [Untitled]. *Saturday Review* (New York),
        35 (April 12, 1952), 6; reply, *Saturday Review*, 35
        (May 24, 1952), 6.

        Anecdote of H's giving an address on his system of
        eye-exercise to replace the use of glasses; but H had

memorized the address, wasn't reading it--as was proven
when he forgot a passage and had to use a magnifying
glass to make it out on his script. H replied that the
spotlights made it hard for him to read at the Screen
Writers' Banquet--that the Bates method of caring for
eyestrain had enabled him to end his use of increasingly
thick glasses.

139.   Chakoo, Bansai Lal. "Aldous Huxley: *The Perennial
       Philosophy*." *Aryan Path*, 42, no. 7 (Sept., 1971),
       304-308.

       H compiled this anthology of mysticism and planned it
       as a minimal outline of beliefs for those who don't belong
       to a formal church, but who need more than a humanistic
       belief. *Perennial Philosophy* seeks to define the nature
       of the one Reality that can't be immediately known save
       by those who meet certain spiritual requirements: to be
       loving, pure in heart, poor in spirit, and to define that
       self which is separate from body, mind, senses, thoughts.
       H endorses Buddha's Eightfold Path as the proper means to
       meditation.

140.   Champness, H.M. "Aldous Huxley at Sixty." *Spectator*,
       193 (July 23, 1954), 109.

       Describes a *Punch* caricature of H's head: "It talked
       as it wrote, with a deft informal rhetoric of alternate
       pedantry and satire and a vocabulary derived at will,
       with indulgent patronage, from the classics, the psychia-
       trist's casebook, the stinks-lab and the Paris studio."
       In the novels following *Eyeless in Gaza* didacticism has
       often blunted the satire that was so successful in the
       earlier works; nonattachment has replaced the earlier
       scorn and anger. H is sometimes painfully sanctimonious
       in his later writing on mysticism.

141.   Chapman, J.B. *Genealogy of Aldous Huxley and Some Others*.
       Foreword by Aldous Huxley. Limited edition (50 copies).
       London: Rapley, 1931. 11 pp.

142.   Chapman, Mary Lewis. [Literary Figures Derived from
       Real People]. *Literary Sketches* (Williamsburg), 16
       (1976), 1-5.

143.   Charques, Richard D. "The Bourgeois Novel," in his *Con-
       temporary Literature and Social Revolution*. London:
       Secker, 1933. Pp. 99-107.

       What has art to do with social conditions? H gives
       several answers in *Those Barren Leaves* (satirical,

rational, humanitarian, mystical), which add up to his
not being sure of any one answer. Calamy holds that the
highest reality consists of the deepest contemplation of
itself. Many of H's answers have to do with the past.
He has many admirable qualities as a writer, but he lacks
major ones--kindness or sympathy or deep emotion. H
"cannot help loving those he chastens. For all its
spiritual imperfections, English middle-class society is
in a sense his spiritual home." "His lack of sympathy
is wide enough to embrace the better part of humanity."

144.   Chase, Richard V. "The Huxley-Heard Paradise." *Partisan
        Review*, 10 (March-April, 1943), 143-158.

        Mysticism is implicit in *Brave New World*: "the intensi-
        fication and the refining of consciousness" which the
        "utopia" opposes. H is again an ingenious, but unoriginal,
        writer in advancing the theories of Heard. Heard assumes
        that materialism is evil, that science is the means to
        advance materialism. Human evolution, according to both
        H and Heard, is mental, not biological, proceeding from
        mutations. It is achieved by the answers provided from
        religious mystics. H and Heard's utopia could not exist
        in any highly civilized society. The Zuñi Indian culture
        is similar to their objective, but such a society wouldn't
        allow outlets for active, assertive, or creative individ-
        uals. The works of H and Heard are a retreat from human
        reality.

145.   Chesterton, Gilbert K. "The End of the Moderns." *London
        Mercury*, 27 (Jan., 1933), 228-233; reprinted in his
        The Common Man. New York: Sheed & Ward, 1950.

        Brave New World shows that H has only grim hopes for
        the future. Lawrence, touted by the "moderns," was
        totally opposed to progressive science, education, in-
        dustrialism. H asks too much of man, to walk a tightrope
        and avoid being either animal or angel. Lawrence and H
        are the last figures of a defeated anarchist army. Law-
        rence groped grandly but blindly in the dark; H is ideally
        witty, but at his wit's end. H gives the best advice he
        can, in conditions of converging impossibility.

146.   ————. "The Huxley Heritage." *American Review*, 8 (Feb.,
        1937), 484-487.

        H is a wit at his wit's end. He is summed up in the
        biblical statement, "The Fathers have eaten sour grapes;
        and the children's teeth are set on edge." T.H. Huxley

and his agnostic friends assured the world that science would be strictly ethical, and that losing its creeds wouldn't hurt the world. His grandson Aldous's teeth are set on edge by way of seeking a disclaimer to this assertion. Dickens's form of satire made people more monstrous than they are, but enjoyed the monstrosities. H's type of satire describes normal people as they are, then reacts against them in abnormal irritation.

147. Choudhary, Nora S. "The Huxley-Hero." *Rajasthau University Studies in English*, 6 (1972), 70-84.

148. ————. "*Island*: Huxley's Attempt at Practical Philosophy." *Literature East & West*, 16 (1972), 1155-1167.

H said that *Island* was to be read not as a novel, but as a manual on the art of living in which Tautric Philosophy is daily applied. Oriental mysticism was to have the upper hand over Western science, which had only an instrumental status in Pala.

149. Church, Margaret. "Aldous Huxley's Attitude Toward Duration." *College English*, 17 (April, 1956), 388-391.

In the early novels, H rejects Bergson's ideas on time and Proust's attempts to recover the past, which is "discontinuous." He moved from the philosophic extreme of time and object as real, to mysticism, which divorces body from spirit, and ignores time and space. H refuses to accept time as duration; he's opposed to Proust's central thesis. The counterpoint in *Point Counter Point* does not give a sense of time duration. Neither Quarles nor H sees coexistence of the past and present. *Eyeless in Gaza* is even more discontinuous than *Point Counter Point*. H finds the past too painful to recall. Beavis's and Miller's "time" of mysticism is a "timeless present." H's concept of time uncoordinates the human experience.

150. ————. "Concepts of Time in the Novels of Virginia Woolf and Aldous Huxley." *Modern Fiction Studies*, 1 (May, 1955), 19-24.

Woolf uses Bergsonian time; H rejects this concept. H deplored Proust's "discontinuity" (see *Proper Studies*); hence, H has to limit himself to "abstract inquiry on an intellectual level." H parodies Proust's "remembrance" thesis in *Those Barren Leaves*. *Time Must Have a Stop* again negates Proust, but it introduces mysticism, which in no way denies his earlier reliance on clock time. Life

of the spirit is led entirely in the present (note Uncle
Eustace); it knows no past or future. Because H's time
concepts are both abstract (clock time and timelessness),
his novels flow into theory, are more truly essays where-
in he expounds his ideas.

151. Ciocoi, Pop Dumitru. "Dilema morală în opera lui Aldous
     Huxley." *Steaua*, 23 (Feb., 1972), 23-24.

152. Clareson, Thomas D. "The Classic: Aldous Huxley's *Brave
     New World*." *Extrapolation*, 2 (May, 1961), 33-40.

     H uses three basic techniques: extrapolation; parody
     and juxtaposition of detail; and sharp contrasts in point
     of view. The novels themselves don't give H's views;
     only in the later introductions to *Brave New World* and
     Brave New World Revisited does H give his opinions. H's
     prophecy came true for Western technology: "self-indulgence
     up to the very limits imposed by hygiene and economics."
     H juxtaposes the familiar in odd ways, e.g., "Ford's in
     his flivver, all's right with the world." Use of parody
     is shown in the contrast between 1931 and the society of
     Brave New World, as well as the contrast between Savage's
     society and that of *Brave New World*. Savage's and Mus-
     tapha Mond's dialogue, chapters 16 and 17, parallels
     "The Grand Inquisitor" in *Brothers Karamazov*. H attacks
     both the utopian society and Savage's values: (1) The
     utopia that provides bread and pleasure for the many.
     (2) The intellectuals who can't lead, but who escape into
     Rousseauism, alleged simplicity, and benevolence of nature.

153. Coates, J.B. "Aldous Huxley," in *Ten Modern Prophets*.
     London: Frederick Muller, 1944. Pp. 39-55.

     Some of the other prophets include Gerald Heard, Julian
     Huxley, C.E.M. Joad, D.H. Lawrence, Karl Marx. The
     message of *Point Counter Point* is expressed by Rampion
     (Lawrence) in his praise of William Blake: "Christianity
     made us barbarians of the soul, and now science is making
     us barbarians of the intellect. Blake was the last
     civilized man." H praised polytheism in *Do What You
     Will*. In *Eyeless in Gaza* H experienced a moral and in-
     tellectual conversion. *Do What You Will* expresses H's
     earlier philosophy, *Ends and Means* his later philosophy:
     "The ideal man is non-attached." *After Many a Summer*
     expresses a brand of pacifism that also has no hope of
     appealing to the masses. H's later mysticism assumes
     that to know God "one must escape from the bondage of
     the ego, the personality, which has dominated one's con-

sciousness hitherto." H is sympathetic with democracy
because it respects individual personality, but he
deplores all large-scale political activity. H's mysticism perceives evidence that God is both transcendent
and immanent. But H is disinterested in the idea of
God as love.

154. Coleman, D.C. "Bernard Shaw and *Brave New World*."
Shaw Review, 10 (Jan., 1967), 6-8.

Although Shaw ridiculed *Brave New World* upon its publication in 1932, his own "Don Juan in Hell" sequence
from *Man and Superman* shows Hell to be much like the world
of H's novel: tiresome, sensual, indifferent to politics
and religion.

155. Collins, Joseph. *Taking the Literary Pulse: Psychological
Studies of Life and Letters.* [n.p.], 1924. Pp. 164-
165.

H's novels are clever and unpleasant; *Antic Hay* is
tiresome for its vulgarity, facetiousness, blaspheming,
etc. The characters aren't human, they aren't interesting.

156. Conner, Frederick W. "'Attention'! Aldous Huxley's
Epistemological Route to Salvation." *Sewanee Review*,
81 (Spring, 1973), 282-308.

"Truth becomes so only when it has been realized by the
speaker as an immediate experience." Quarles, in *Point
Counter Point*, tries to absorb the view of Rampion: "The
problem for me is to transform a detached intellectual
scepticism into a way of harmonious all-round living."
In *The Perennial Philosophy*, the distinction between
knower and known is ideally lost. "The present moment
is the only aperture through which the soul can pass out
of time into eternity."

157. Connolly, Cyril. "Under Which King?" *Living Age*, 341
(Feb., 1932), 533-538.

"Lawrence, advocating the worship of the body, advocates
all the non-productive alternatives to taking up the
pen." "Huxley is the type of intellectual whose attacks
upon all the things worth living for are most insidious
because he conceals himself--perhaps from himself--behind
a respect for them." (This *tour de force* essay berates
the opposite trends represented by H and Lawrence.)

158. Craft, Robert. "Stravinsky and Some Writers." *Harper's*,
237 (Dec., 1968), 101-108.

August 10, 1949, Hollywood (Stravinsky and H were
neighbors): H's intellectual ammunition included on this
occasion the "haeccei ties of the late Persian mystics,"
an apt quotation from the *Biathanatos*, new information
about amino acids and cellular differentiation. Isherwood played a younger double to H in this "Vedanta in
the Wild West."

159.   ———. "With Aldous Huxley." *Encounter*, 25 (Nov.,
          1965), 10-16.

Gives reminiscences of visits with the Huxleys and
the Stravinskys, who were friends and neighbors near
Los Angeles. H's remarkable encyclopedic knowledge was
revealed in ceaseless conversation. H is more engaging
to listen to than to read. Nothing in his talk suggests
the Tolstoi-like sermonizing of his later books.
Stravinsky used H as a source for encyclopedic knowledge;
H revered Stravinsky as a creative genius.

160.   Croce, Benedetto. "Osservazioni a una pagina di Aldous
          Huxley. 'L'infelice condizione della storia.'" *Quaderni
          della Critica*, 6 (Nov., 1946), 85-87.

161.   Cunliffe, John William. "Aldous Huxley," in his *English
          Literature in the Twentieth Century*. New York: Mac-
          millan, 1933. Pp. 239-245.

H and Brooke introduced a note of cynicism to Georgian
poetry. Cynicism and cold intellectualism also appear
in H's early novels, *Crome Yellow* through *Point Counter
Point*. Not until *Brave New World* were H's readers
generally assured that he was a satirist, rather than a
free-liver condoning immorality. H's aim was "to arrive
technically at a perfect fusion of the novel and the
essay." But H is a better essayist than a novelist—he
didn't separate the essay portions from the novel proper
the way Fielding did. His best compromise is his travel
books. H suffered from a constant state of revulsion:
"The dread of sentiment and the habit of disillusionment
are too strong for him."

162.   Daiches, David. *The Novel and the Modern World*. Chicago:
          University of Chicago Press, 1939. Pp. 188-210.

Daiches complains that the chapters in *Eyeless in Gaza*
are out of proper sequence. Daiches's 1967 revision of
this book omits H altogether. Daiches believes that the
cynicism of H's fiction grows out of his frustrated

romanticism; furthermore, the fiction is dominated by the essay.

163. ———. "Novels of Aldous Huxley." *New Republic*, 100 (Nov. 1, 1939), 362-365.

H is bitter in the early novels because he wants to believe in progress, science, romanticism, but the facts around him won't let him do so. As a disillusioned romantic, he becomes a fierce satirist. Then he moves to satisfied mysticism. The characters are caricatures representing dried-up sources of values--e.g., love, art, social reform, epicureanism, cynicism. *Those Barren Leaves* introduces the option of withdrawn mysticism, a concept further developed in *Eyeless in Gaza*. H's "experiments" in technique aren't organically essential to the novels--primarily he's an essayist, a writer of character sketches, tracts, or fables.

164. Dalglish, Doris N. "Aldous Huxley's Poetry." *London Mercury*, 38 (Sept., 1938), 437-444.

H wrote poetry, as well as the pacifist pamphlets and *Ends and Means*, but this "inconsistency" is like that of Milton and Shelley, poets who also became involved in public affairs. H is both Puritan and visionary. His technique may be French, but the spirit is in the English tradition. "There is not one modern poet who can express pain as significantly." In the 1925 collection of poems, some pieces are Georgian. "Thought has frozen many of the poems...." "The Cicadas" is a rare poem "in which intellect forgets to be ambitious and tranquillity is achieved." Despite his fame as a master of prose, there is a part of H that is a poet; it may even account for some of the unsatisfactory parts of the novels. "He might easily continue what is great in the elegiac Arnold tradition of English verse...."

165. Dardis, Tom. *Some Time in the Sun: The Hollywood Years of Fitzgerald, Faulkner, Nathanael West, Aldous Huxley, and James Agee*. New York: Scribner's, 1976.

The general theme is the economics of authorship versus those of motion pictures. The basic facts are covered. Not a particularly analytical or interpretive book, it is useful primarily for film buffs. H is treated somewhat better than are others in this account.

166. Day-Lewis, Cecil. "Mr. Aldous Huxley." *London Mercury*, 34 (July, 1936), 269.

Review of *Eyeless in Gaza*. Day-Lewis confesses surprise at seeing the facetious H preaching a doctrine of
love. In this novel, Beavis gives up his self-serving
world success, becomes a pacifist and a sort of mystic.
All characters in the novel are flat—they're the same at
the end as they were at the beginning.

167. Delatte, F. "La société contemporaine vue par l'auteur
     de 'Contrepoint.'" *Le Thyrse* (Bruxelles), May-June,
     1931, pp. 219-228.

H finds company with experimental novelists like Woolf,
Joyce, Proust, Gide (*Point Counter Point* is patterned
after *The Counterfeiters*). *Point Counter Point* is a
compendium-type work, with vertical perspective rather
than a horizontal view of the traditional novel-as-history.
H does use the novel-as-history technique to present
two sympathetic characters, Walter Bidlake and his sister Elinor. But for the rest, all time is superimposed
as one time. Using cinematic techniques, or the "musicalization of fiction," H drops transitions, exposition, or
preparation for changes of time and place. H imitates
Gide's device in *The Counterfeiters* of a novelist writing
his novel, and Proust's association of ideas, as in the
account of the madeleine. H's characters represent hyper-
sensitive intellect, or sensuality, or imagination, or
desire for power. H was well aware of the dilemma of the
novel of ideas; its personae exclude the majority of the
human race, who are nonthinkers. Religious mysticism has
corrupted Burlap; scientific mysticism has ruined Quarles
and the Tantamounts; artistic imagination has ruined
Spandrell. Rampion alone, modeled after H's friend Lawrence, expresses H's cherished ideas at the time of
writing *Point Counter Point*. Rampion is not only a
Swift-like satirist, but also a moralist, with a constructive solution to the decadence of his time. Rampion's is the interior drama of H himself.

168. Demondion, Pierre. "Aldous Huxley: L'ange et la bête."
     Cahiers de Paris, 8 (Feb., 1940), 269-271.

169. De Parville, A. "Romans d'Angleterre et de Pologne."
     Études, 205 (Dec. 20, 1930), 714-723.

Quarles, the novelist of *Point Counter Point*, states
the purpose of his novel: its view of multiplicity. H's
experiments are not new: they have been done already by
Proust and Gide. Quarles also expresses the novel's
purpose as encyclopedic, but he wants to make it so with-

out pedantry, and to avoid the interminable delay of writing a novel-as-history. Some of H's episodes, interesting in themselves, are not sufficiently attached to the main fabric of the novel, or the subtle invention of attachment is not sufficiently apparent at first sight. There is a lack of central action or conflict; the only exception is the assassination of Webley. The novel has no all-embracing thesis. Rampion comes closest to expressing one: that man must learn to treat body and soul as equal parties. He assumes that otherwise one becomes a barbarian of the intellect, or else of the body. But Rampion's method is heavyhanded when he wishes to destroy false concepts, just as he is when he tries to illuminate. His theory of equilibrium, if not basically false, is superficial and imprecise. The "equilibrium" isn't defined in terms of restraint, or of latitudes. The question is posed by Rampion, but he doesn't resolve it. He remains only on the surface of his problem.

170. De Vries, Alex. "De muziek in het oeuvre van Proust en Huxley." *Nieuw Vlaams Tijdschrift* (Antwerp), May, 1952, pp. 975-994. (See also 106, 115, 158, 255, 293, 300, 538, 565.)

171. Diego, Celia de. "Unidad y sentido en la obra de Aldous Huxley." *Ficcion*, 45/47 (Sept., 1963-Feb., 1964), 152-156.

172. Dingle, Reginald J. "Life-Worshippers: Study of Neohumanism." *Month*, 134 (Dec., 1929), 496-504.

H denies "Historical Truth"; a fierce hatred of Catholicism runs through his work, as well as through that of Richard Aldington, Robert Graves, and other "moderns." Dingle attacks H's views on Pascal. H gives no impression of intellectual discipline; his creed of worshipping vitalism is a cult with no authority. The "attempt to explain views by viscera" is foolish; if Carlyle was gloomy because of bad health, why then was Stevenson cheerful? "It is obvious that the Life Worshipper can only carry out his programme at the expense of the maimed lives and ruined characters of his fellow humans."

173. Doi, Kochi. "Chikaku no Tobira: Tengoku to Jigoku." *Figo Seinen* (The Rising Generation) (Tokyo), 114 (1968), 214-215.

This essay discusses *The Doors of Perception* and *Heaven and Hell*.

174. Dommergues, André. "Aldous Huxley epistolier." *Études
      Anglaises* (Vanves, France), 26 (1973), 420–434.

      H must have written about 10,000 letters, but
      some have been lost or destroyed. The survivors fall
      into three general categories: (1) the formal letter-
      dissertation, often addressed to H's eminent associates;
      (2) the letter as brief message; (3) halfway between,
      the all-purpose letter for family or friends, spontaneous
      and omitting ceremony. Category 3 is like conversation.
      The letters display no sense of deep emotion, even about
      people he cared for deeply, like Lawrence, or either his
      first or second wife. Judging by his intimate letters,
      H is a mediocre correspondent. H classified himself as
      a cerebretonic, following Sheldon's psychophysiological
      system. This is borne out in the letters--his insatiable
      curiosity, his astonishing range of interests, his pro-
      digious erudition.

175. ———. "Aldous Huxley: Une oeuvre de jeunesse: *Crome
      Yellow*." *Études Anglaises* (Vanves, France), 21 (1968),
      1–18.

      Other H novels have titles that are literary allusions;
      Crome Yellow presents more of a problem with its title.
      "Crome" is of course Garsington, 10 kilometers from Ox-
      ford, where Sir Philip and Lady Ottoline Morrell housed
      a number of conscientious objectors during World War I,
      and where many famous people visited for some 12 years,
      all engaged in spirited, frank conversations. T.S.
      Eliot has identified the real people for whom H's charac-
      ters in *Crome Yellow* stand. Yellow, and gold, are the
      dominant colors of the great house in the novel; at the
      time he wrote this book, H was recovering his eyesight,
      and colors delighted him. Contrasting with the bright
      sunny colors are the darkness and shadow, in keeping with
      the pessimism and postwar gloom. H recalls in the contem-
      plated suicide of Denis the real suicide of his own
      brother. The mode of the novel is borrowed from Peacock.
      Denis is much as H was when he wrote the book, a parody
      of himself as a young man. Scogan (i.e., Bertrand
      Russell) is an elderly philosopher from whom Denis learns
      wisdom, and with whom Denis debates. Sir Hercules, the
      dwarf and poet-philosopher, tries to create his own small,
      ideal world. H borrows from the account of Sir John
      Harington's invention of the water closet. Paintings by
      George Stubbs and Caravaggio are described in the novel,
      but are attributed to imaginary painters. (The relevant
      paintings are reproduced along with this article.)

176. ———. "Deux lettres inédites d'Aldous Huxley." *Études Anglaises* (Vanves, France), 26 (1973), 435-439.

H praises French as the best language for expressing indecency. The French "can combine grossness with grace in a way no other nation can." The two letters are in French. Letter 1 is to Jean Bruno (1950), Bibliothèque Nationale; it expresses interest in the work of Alexis Preyre. The letter also relates that Aldous and his brother Julian are interested in establishing an organization to study transcendental experiences. Letter 2 is also to Bruno (1958). H had just visited Brazil and Peru, where he'd been honored; then he had gone to France, England, Italy. Again H expresses interest in the scientific study of mysticism: the use of the electroencephalogram.

177. Dottin, Paul. "Aldous Huxley, romancier du monde ou l'on s'ennuie." *Revue de France*, 11 (Sept. 1, 1931), 176-183.

After a summary review of *Those Barren Leaves* and *Point Counter Point*, Dottin remarks that "After the Fireworks" and "Brief Candles" show further progression in H's achievement. The common element in all these works, Dottin says, is characters who are bored with themselves.

178. Dyson, A.E. "Aldous Huxley and the Two Nothings." *Critical Quarterly*, 3 (Winter, 1961), 293-309. Reprinted in his *The Crazy Fabric: Essays in Irony*. London: Macmillan, 1965.

H offers the reader a choice between two nothings: Mrs. Viveash's boredom in *Antic Hay*, or the nothing of Mr. Propter's God in *After Many a Summer*. The degradation and disgust of H are not masochistic, but result from his ruthless, uncompromising honesty. Dyson discusses *Antic Hay*, *After Many a Summer*, *Point Counter Point*, *Brave New World*, and *Eyeless in Gaza*. Rampion in *Point Counter Point* doesn't come through as a character, but as if he were a series of lectures on Lawrence. Rampion is insulated against irony, however; and his message can't answer the deplorable sufferings of the others. *Brave New World* reverses T.H. Huxley's theory that science can be the generous friend of man. *Eyeless in Gaza* experiments with time, to produce psychological suspense. But H loses more than he gains by the distortions. *After Many a Summer* is a flawed novel because of the extended exposition by Mr. Propter on God "as a

nothingness capable of free power." This is H's most
extreme statement, thus far, on the dichotomy between
flesh and spirit. H's resolution of the dilemma is ar-
tistically inadequate.

179. Eaton, Gai. "Monk at Large: Aldous Huxley," in his *The
      Richest Vein: Eastern Tradition and Modern Thought*.
      London: Faber & Faber, 1949. Pp. 166-182.

      H regards Puritanism as a heresy, but considers asceti-
      cism a legitimate discipline. H's *The Perennial Philos-
      ophy* created a great fad in England and the U.S. for
      Oriental doctrines, but it gave a false impression of
      them. The "sheer effectiveness of half-truths makes
      Point Counter Point such a fascinating, yet such an
      unsatisfactory novel." "Again and again that type of
      person who might destroy H's thesis by pointing a way
      between naked sensuality and complete denial of the body
      is caricatured." Beginning with *Eyeless in Gaza*, H takes
      a cautious step beyond satire: salvation through "non-
      attachment" and withdrawal. Eaton also rejects *After
      Many a Summer*, *Grey Eminence*, *Time Must Have a Stop*.
      Time has an Epilogue, in which H describes the "good
      life"--an admission that the novel itself has failed.
      H's philosophy is Western--concern for morality, obsession
      with guilt and sin, exaggeration of the differences be-
      tween spirit and matter, a desire to impose a single rule
      on all men. H is the victim of Protestant Christianity.
      His *Perennial Philosophy* is an example of syncretism, not
      synthesis. H "has filched from various doctrines, with-
      out any regard for their context, those elements which
      seem to support his own attitude of life." Despite his
      "mysticism" H is still a modernist, a rationalist, and a
      scientist.

180. Ebon, Martin. "The Psychic World of Aldous Huxley."
      Psychic, 2, no. 4 (Jan.-Feb., 1971), 26-30.

      This is largely a summary, with extended quotations,
      of H's views, with little analysis. Its only point is
      that H's "interest in mysticism, Eastern mythology, and
      in the biochemical elements of the human personality
      absorbed much of his time and interest."

181. Edgar, Pelham. "Aldous Huxley," in his *The Art of the
      Novel from 1700 to the Present Time*. New York: Mac-
      millan, 1933. Pp. 278-293.

      Meckier ("Mysticism or Misty Schism?" [370]) includes
      this book among others that are subject to his strictures

on "histories" of the novel. "The last half of the
book proves to be little more than a sheaf of loosely
joined essays.... Treatment of individual authors is
often sound, but not enough aware of underlying forces
to bring much order to a field which hasn't yet got itself composed and labeled neatly under glass."

182. Ehrenpreis, Irvin. "Orwell, Huxley, Pope." *Revue des
Langues Vivantes* (Brussels), 23 (1957), 215-230.

The three authors imply a civilization they admire,
and its collapse is described. H (*Brave New World*) foresees a harmonious, but sterile, society; this paradise
is an artifice--but it is in fact a counter-utopia. In
H's view, animal contentment is less desirable than wisdom, love, the arts, values achieved only through conflict
and pain. H's good life is not opposed to science, but
one's values must come from another source, intuition.
Both Orwell and H agree that the nonrational elements of
human nature are essentially good. Evil comes from intellect and is perpetuated by organized society. Pope's
view is that man's duty is to submit to his environment,
knowing what its miseries are. H and Orwell blame man's
fate on environment--they absolve the instincts and
passions of responsibility. Pope never believed, even
to begin with, that man's intellect could ever devise a
utopia.

183. Eliot, T.S. "Le roman anglais contemporain." *Nouvelle
Revue Française*, 1 (May, 1927), 669-675.

Eliot refers to Lawrence, Woolf, David Garnett, H.
Citing Henry James's book on Hawthorne, Eliot notes an
interest in the soul and conscience of man, which are of
moral interest. Hawthorne's psychology focuses on this
issue (as does that of James). Contemporary novelists
deal with a less profound psychology, and they lack James's
"moral preoccupation." The contemporaries depend greatly
on insights made by psychoanalysts. H is among those
novelists who have to write 30 bad novels before writing
one good one. H has a natural disposition, which has
scarcely been developed, for being serious. He assimilates
what's not essential, and what is chic, or chic religiosity. *Those Barren Leaves* seems to have been composed
under a momentary mystical impulse. But he's also heavily
laden with sentimentality which brings the possible danger
of H's becoming a modern René or Werther. H is a tormen-
ted man.

184. Elliott, Robert C. "L'estetica dell'utopia." *Strumenti Critici* (Torino), 3 (1969), 301-320; also in his *The Shape of Utopia: Studies in a Literary Genre*. Chicago: University of Chicago Press, 1970. Ch. 7.

Elliott is unaware of the Manichean elements in *Brave New World*, both in structure and theme. Also, he fails to sense H's skepticism about the possibility of a self-sustaining utopia, or H's determination to annihilate Pala (*Island*) after it has been set in motion.

185. Enroth, Clyde. "Mysticism in Two of Aldous Huxley's Early Novels." *Twentieth Century Literature*, 6 (Oct., 1960), 123-132.

H's mysticism can't be accounted for as simply a "conversion" to Gerald Heard, beginning with *Eyeless in Gaza*. Mysticism appears even in the early novels, as well as in *Point Counter Point* and *Brave New World*. *Crome Yellow* (1921) seems to express H's contempt for mysticism, but one character, Scogan, takes it seriously. In *Antic Hay* (1923), Gumbril worries about how to reconcile religious intuitions with skeptical intellect. Gumbril also notes the "quiet places of the mind" which can become central to the mystical experience. But he doesn't act on this discovery: he proceeds as nearly everyone else does, by building bandstands or factories over the "quiet places." *Point Counter Point* and *Brave New World* express primarily H's adoption of Lawrence's life-worship, and hence these novels disallow mysticism. Lawrence supposedly emphasized the body, mind, and spirit living in balance. In *Brave New World* the World Controller suppresses the means for "some intensification and refining of consciousness"-- because it contravenes the aim of accepting happiness as the Sovereign Good. Also, the Emotional Engineer refers to the "something which is not"--a second allusion to the mystical experience. Therefore, H showed a consistent movement toward mysticism throughout his career.

186. Eschmann, E.W. "Zu den Schriften Aldous Huxleys." *Merkur*, Jan. 16, 1962, pp. 176-183.

187. Estrich, Helen Watts. "Jesting Pilate Tells the Answer: Aldous Huxley." *Sewanee Review*, 47 (Jan., 1939), 63-81.

Anthony Beavis's ideas in *Eyeless in Gaza* and much in *Ends and Means* cohere; presumably, these represent H's views. The world is unity, though manifest in diverse forms. Good is what makes for unity; evil, that which

makes separateness. Much of *Eyeless in Gaza* depends on
the theories of F.M. Alexander, which H expresses in the
character of Dr. Miller. Beavis takes lessons from Dr.
Miller, who cites Alexander as his authority. Virtue,
including awareness, and meditation are ends in themselves
and means to the mystical experience. But Alexander is
an untrustworthy authority; H's argument is weakened by
accepting his theories. H's use of science is likewise
flawed in support of his philosophy in *Eyeless in Gaza*.
He assumes that biology proves that cooperation improves
the survival qualities among species. H's analogies from
the lower species to "prove" that forbearance and brother
love are the best conduct are at best forced.

188. Evans, B. Ifor. "Aldous Huxley," in his *English Litera-
     ture Between the Wars*. London: Methuen & Co., 1949.
     Pp. 58-67.

     H is the most representative English writer between the
     two World Wars. He expressed shifting attitudes, showed
     an appreciation of the other arts, and was able to bridge
     the arts and sciences. Lawrence was the only contemporary
     with a profound influence on H; they were complementary
     souls--H cerebral, Lawrence passionate. H mingles biology,
     religion, and mysticism in what seems a profane manner--
     as if Swift had studied science and abandoned his Chris-
     tian faith. But occasionally H's mysticism creeps in in
     a more sentimental way, as if his cynical eye had been
     momentarily closed. In *Ends and Means* (1938) H turned to
     the essay to formulate those views he had expressed in
     his earlier novels. The concept of "non-attachment," a
     theme to be expanded on in his later *The Perennial Philos-
     ophy*, is central. But H's later books are much less in-
     fluential than those written between the wars.

189. Fabre-Luce, Alfred. "Huxley, Morand, Gide." *Revue des
     Deux Mondes*, Oct., 1975, pp. 59-70.

190. Fairchild, Hoxie Neale. "Towards Hysteria," in his *Re-
     ligious Trends in English Poetry*. New York: Columbia
     University Press, 1962. Vol. 5, pp. 620-626.

     H's *The Burning Wheel* is technically conservative; the
     poems are versified discussions of problems. The major
     theme is mysticism, a perilous way unless it is pursued
     to the very end, though he himself has never experienced
     the holy darkness. In matters of love, he's torn between
     a rather grubby realism and a rather misty idealism.
     The Defeat of Youth introduces some frivolous nihilism.

The juxtaposition of romance and realism is crude rather
than witty; H may have tried to imitate Donne, but he
achieved something less than Donne. Christianity too is
debunked; Jonah and Simeon Stylites suffer accordingly.
H gives the impression of mostly putting on his frivolity;
it's not really cynicism, but a cultivated naughtiness.

191.   Farmer, David. "The American Edition of Huxley's *Leda*."
        Book Collector, 18, no. 2 (Summer, 1969), 220-221.

"Each of the five copies at the University of Texas
differs in five respects [here listed] from the description in Hanson Duval's 1939 bibliography."

192.   ———. "The Bibliographical Potential of a Twentieth
        Century Literary Agent's Archives: The Pinker Papers."
        Library Chronicle of the University of Texas, 2 (1970),
        27-35.

H sent J.B. Pinker, his literary agent, over 230 letters
between 1920 and 1934. These often list titles of articles that H had written. An example of an unrecorded
newspaper article is for February 11, 1933, "Thinking
with One's Hands," in the *New York American*. For March
11, 1933, the title given is "Human Instincts" (bibliographies list "The Bantus of Dr. Freud" for that date).
Since considerable differences developed between the New
York and London editions of H's works, H complained to
his New York publisher; he wanted to see proof sheets to
eliminate errors. The May 29, 1929, *Vanity Fair* essay
entitled "A Disagreement with Mr. Shaw" reappears in *Do
What You Will* as "Revolutions" (Eschelbach and Shober do
not note that these are the same). "One and Many" appeared in *Harper's* for Sept., 1929, called "One God or
Many?"--but it is 210 lines shorter than the version
printed in *Do What You Will* (Eschelbach and Shober do
not cite the difference).

193.   ———. "A Note on the Text of Huxley's *Crome Yellow*."
        Papers of the Bibliographical Society of America, 63
        (1969), 131-133.

"The Doran edition (New York, 1922) made 30 changes in
the Chatto & Windus text (London, 1921) in order to bring
about consistency in the use of British spellings; at
the same time the Doran edition introduced 31 errors in
wording, spelling, or punctuation (most of which are perpetuated in the 1955 Bantam edition)."

194. Fay, Eliot. *Lorenzo in Search of the Sun*. New York: Bookman, 1953. Passim.

H "splendidly edited" the letters of D.H. Lawrence and wrote a "penetrating introduction" for them. Lawrence and H first met in 1915; Lawrence was master, H the enthusiastic disciple. They often met on their travels, at intervals, until Lawrence's death. Lawrence wrote some mocking, short verses about H's portrayal of Lawrence as Rampion in *Point Counter Point*. Maria Huxley, Aldous's first wife, was with Lawrence at the time of Lawrence's death.

195. Firchow, Peter. "The Brave New World of Huxley Studies." *Journal of Modern Literature*, 1 (1969), 278-283.

Reviews Bowering, *Aldous Huxley* (see 4); Clark, *The Huxleys* (see 10); Laura Huxley, *This Timeless Moment* (see 24); Watts, *Aldous Huxley* (see 47).
H became reincarnated into too many different forms during his lifetime for the critics to fossilize him. Clark's book is the most comprehensive biography (will be superseded by Bedford's). Clark observes of H, "the most provocative and incandescent of T.H. Huxley's grandchildren." Clark is a better biographer than critic. Laura Huxley preserves several unavailable documents about H. Bowering and Watts limit themselves to literary study, give little biography. Bowering's book is more intellectual than literary; this treatment sometimes becomes routine, dull. Still, since H is a highly intellectual writer, Bowering's approach has some merit. Watts's chapter on "The Mind of Aldous Huxley" is the best in his book. Watts also covers H's use of repeated character types, but he tends to overdo structural criteria in evaluating H's novels. Firchow himself concludes that H was a novelist of ideas and a satirist; H is not to be confused with such novelists of sensibility as James. Firchow praises Watts for doing the only extended account to date of *Grey Eminence* and *The Devils of Loudun*.

196. ————. "Mental Music: Huxley's *Point Counter Point* and Mann's *Magic Mountain* as Novels of Ideas." *Studies in the Novel*, 9 (Winter, 1977), 518-536.

H's reputation still looms larger outside of, rather than within, Anglo-Saxondom, and the writers he seems most to resemble are French, Russian, and German. Mann's *Magic Mountain* is a massively learned and searching fictional synthesis, which H achieves almost as well in

Point Counter Point. Like *Magic Mountain*, it presents
the major philosophical and scientific concerns of the
age, it uses a musical analogy for structure, and it
offers conversational duels between "liberals" and "con-
servatives." H liked Mann's work, but not so much as
that of Kafka, and his knowledge of things German
(except German music) was limited. Mann, however, felt
H to be his peer and saw him as expressing similar
principles. Both authors had encyclopedic minds, both
were heavy on philosophy, and had great fondness for
science, sociology, psychology; both knew French literature very well, as well as English literature--Mann being
particularly fond of the humorous 18th- and 19th-century
English novelists. Both distrusted the dark underworld
of Nietzsche and Dostoevsky, yet as vitalists they opposed systems that explained the world by rational or
"mechanistic" means. Both were noncongenital novelists,
frankly using their medium to express ideas on politics,
society, religion. Both showed literary precocity, and
both were attracted to vacationing or living in the same
sorts of places. H's anti-intellectual Rampion is a
more subtle and credible creation than Mann's intellectual
nonintellectual, Castorp. Both authors admit that their
characters are mouthpieces, but deny that this makes the
characters lifeless.

197.   ————. "The Satire of Huxley's *Brave New World*." *Modern
        Fiction Studies*, 12 (Winter, 1966), 260-278.

Any kind of significant internal life is banished in
Brave New World, a book written to demolish the myths of
progress and nationalism. Both myths are stupid because
they stress externals only. Scogan in *Crome Yellow*, H's
first novel, anticipated *Brave New World* when he theorized
about a "Rational State." *Jesting Pilate*, written after
H's first visit to the U.S. while on world tour, describes
Los Angeles as "Joy City," a kind of prototype for *Brave
New World*; American culture in general is satirized in
Brave New World. Despite the happiness-regimentation in
Brave New World, vestiges of individuality survive among
some of the characters. John, the Savage, is the most
exceptional among these. (See also 13, 33, 85, 225, 363,
365, 369, 402, 516, 548, 560, 611, 614.)

198.   ————. "Science and Conscience in Huxley's *Brave New
        World*." *Contemporary Literature*, 16 (1975), 301-316.

Science permeates much of H's fiction, but *Brave New
World* is his most powerful account of the effects of

science; its antipathy has become proverbial. *Brave New World* is an inspired pastiche, not strictly borrowed from any one source. H's prophecy that man is genetically modifiable and psychologically conditionable is still a valid one. Some of H's science prophecy comes from H.G. Wells. *Brave New World* makes many additions to Scogan's "Rational State" (*Crome Yellow*). H was a friend of Bertrand Russell, J.B.S. Haldane; he could easily have adapted their ideas in the planning of *Brave New World*; also, H's brother Julian was an expert on genetics. Haldane developed the idea of the test-tube babies; and his wife Charlotte wrote an anti-utopian novel, *Man's World* (1926), that in several ways anticipates *Brave New World*. H also despised behaviorist psychologists. The names Foster, Bernard, Helmholtz, and Watson in the novel show H's disparagement of the known defenders of mechanistic physiology and psychology. But Freud is also satirized, as in the rationale-giver for the Hatchery and Conditioning Center. The novel shows the world as it is in danger of becoming, unless individuals insist on being disparate, dissident, and unhappy.

199. —————. "Wells and Lawrence in Huxley's *Brave New World*." *Journal of Modern Literature*, 5 (1976), 260-278.

Brave New World is an attack on Wells's type of utopia; Wells took offense. H questioned the bad conclusions, not the good intentions, of Wells's future worlds. H doubted that Wells's socialistic equality could ever be accomplished. Science, education, and democracy do not, in H's view, bring on the millennium. H began writing *Brave New World* as a parody of Wells's *Men Like Gods*, but it ended up as much more than that. H borrowed many technological aspects of *Brave New World* from Wells, but Wells was not his only source. H was apprised of Wells's admiration for Alfred Mond, a powerful industrialist and political leader of England. The alternative to the Fordian future in *Brave New World* is the savage past, that of the Pueblo Indians H had learned about from Lawrence's writing. The picture of them in the novel is also satirical, and H uses them in various ways to debunk Lawrence's ideas about primitivism.

200. Freeman, John. "Aldous Huxley." *London Mercury*, 15 (Feb., 1927), 391-400.

H remains thoroughly English, for all his meandering in foreign countries. He did well to retreat from poetry because his poems become at times oversentimental and at times oversophisticated and witty. "Leda" is the only poem that makes one regret that H turned to prose. But the novels too are objectionable; they display H's "heedless use of his considerable gifts." *Crome Yellow* and *Those Barren Leaves* are filled with "the stalest of figures repeating the stalest of chatter." *Two or Three Graces* and *Uncle Spencer* are more valid as fiction. H is much better as an essayist. He's a perceptive critic of Edward Thomas and Joseph Conrad. He knows Italy well, pretends to like it better than England out of perversity. The moralist in H always emerges, despite the intellectual fireworks. H believes that our sense of values is intuitive, purely personal; but there are limits to toleration, and one cannot deny the fundamental values.

201.   Frierson, William C. "Postwar Novel, 1919-1929: Sophisticates and Others," in his *The English Novel in Transition, 1885-1940*. Norman: University of Oklahoma Press, 1942. Pp. 244-245, 258-265.

H won popularity early and quickly because he wrote first-rate satire about first-rate people. His novels use a multiple point of view; many of his characters are scientific intellectuals. The interest of the novels is independent of the events in them; precise information becomes an esthetic ideal in itself. "Man is freed from illusions only to find that he needs an illusion to live for." H is "the thwarted romantic with a critical sense that demands the castigation of hope and effort." H's early admirers disappeared when he became a pacifist. *After Many a Summer* was an attempt to regain his audience, who admired the cynical realist in him. After *Brave New World*, H's philosophy became mysticism. "Separateness, and hence anarchy and evil, was the lot of mortals under an empiric-materialistic dispensation."

202.   Fuller, John. [Untitled]. *Saturday Review* (New York), 42 (June 13, 1959), 7-8.

Fuller notes that H received the 1959 Award of Merit for the Novel; H had just returned from Brazil full of admiration for its history and for its series of bloodless revolutions.

203.   Fuller, Roy. "Gilding by the Ruolz Process." *Listener*, 85, no. 2190 (March 18, 1971), 343.

Review of *The Collected Poetry of Aldous Huxley*, ed.

Donald Watt.

H's poems are not important for their own literary interest, but they relate significantly to his early fictional period (up to *Point Counter Point*). Still, H's technical skill with the poems increases; it is best in *Leda* (1920). He remained interested in poetry throughout his life; his early essays on the subject are perceptive.

204. Garman, Douglas. "Those Barren Leaves," in *Towards Standards of Criticism*, ed. F.R. Leavis. London: Wishart, 1933. Pp. 43-47.

In *Antic Hay*, H is for the most part amused at his conjuring of characters, but there are a few signs of his getting bored with them. In *Those Barren Leaves*, the boredom intensifies; H's self-consciousness "seems to have vitiated his outlook, and to have impaired the spontaneity of his inspiration." When H expresses an uncynical view, he does so through a potentially laughable character --to escape the personal responsibility for expressing it. In *Those Barren Leaves*, Calamy demonstrates a new point of view--H is no longer shamefaced about him. H is now writing from a richer and better assimilated experience of life.

205. Gathorne-Hardy, Robert, ed. *Ottoline at Garsington: Memoirs of Lady Ottoline Morrell, 1915-1918*. London: Faber & Faber, 1974. Contains many photographs, including ones of Huxley.

Lady Ottoline does not herself appear as a character in *Crome Yellow*, but most of her household and regular visitors do; she was offended by what she regarded as the unfeeling caricature of them all. H was a frequent visitor, and for a time a resident, at Garsington, where he did "farm work" along with other conscientious objectors during World War I. H met Lawrence and Frieda there, along with Maria Nys, who became his first wife. Lady Ottoline saw H "as if he is looking down on the human race as odd specimens of the animal kingdom." The people H met at Garsington included Bertrand Russell, Katherine Mansfield, Lytton Strachey, Desmond McCarthy, Virginia Woolf, Clive Bell, J.M. Murry, T.S. Eliot. According to Lady Ottoline, H "has been able to satirize and to ridicule by his cynicism, but not to shed light on a new path." Of Maria Nys, she said, "she was so completely foreign that she had no understanding of English ways or traditions, and in this she has never changed." (Maria was a Belgian refugee.) Lady Ottoline held that *Crome Yellow*

mocked and distorted Garsington; many pages mocked the
sermons of the Garsington rector; Asquith and Russell
were also ridiculed. H's defense was: "characters are
nothing but marionettes with voices, designed to express
ideas and the parody of ideas." H denied he was really
writing about Lady Ottoline's friends. She had been
previously offended by Lawrence's *Women in Love*, which
depicted her and Garsington. Of H she also said, he
"is now singularly lacking in the imagination of the
heart." She heard him admire very few people, except
Albert Schweitzer, whose ideas influenced him greatly.
For a time, he was much influenced by Lawrence; and,
since Lawrence's death, by Gerald Heard. (This important
book gives a great deal of first-hand information about
the circumstances from which H derived the ideas, setting,
and characters for *Crome Yellow*.)

206. Gayo Nuno, Antonio. "El lider fascista en la novela
inglesa de nuestro tiempo." *Cuadernos Hispanoamericanos* (Madrid), 72 (1967), 632-640.

This article discusses *Kangaroo* and *Point Counter
Point*.

207. Gellner, Ernest. "Prepare to Meet Thy Doom. A Sermon
on the Ambivalence of Progress, Reason, Liberty,
Equality and Fraternity." *Listener*, 61 (March 19,
1959), 510-514.

H's *Ape and Essence* describes the horror of a society
in which both power and benevolence are lacking. Orwell's *1984* describes the horror of a world in which power
joins with malevolence. H's *Brave New World* shows the
horror of a world in which power and benevolence coexist.
Brave New World is the most interesting of the three
novels because of the philosophically "ideal" situation:
it is not really ideal, however, because the sense of
freedom, and the enjoyment of unpredictable personal
experiences, are disallowed. *Brave New World* is an effective exposé of Utilitarianism, forcibly applied by
modern technology.

208. Gérard, Albert. "Aldous Huxley, ou celui qui croit
devenir sage." *Revue Générale Belge* (Brussels), Sept.,
1955, pp. 1839-1851.

With H, the classic idea of satire has been lost; it no
longer presumes a positive concept of man and his destiny.
H sees man as only the author of his own vanity. H poses
as the supreme, detached judge of intrinsic human folly.

Without a constructive base, H's satire is only a sterile, universal derision, suspended in an intellectual void. Despite H's gaiety, beneath is an anxiety relating not to the presence, but to the need for, a constructive ideal. By writing a novel of ideas (see Quarles's definition in *Point Counter Point*) H leaves out what is most human: emotions and dreams which do not pertain to the rational. Each of H's characters is thus reduced to a fraction of humanity. The characters in *Point Counter Point* don't evolve or change: they're trapped in the author's concepts. H's two basic assumptions have to do with the futility of the world and the need to abandon oneself to hedonism. The characters in *Point Counter Point* are not allowed to find meaning in themselves. In *Eyeless in Gaza* H abandoned the neo-paganism of his theory of balanced excesses (derived from Lawrence) and turned to mysticism, which he has preached ever since. He pieced together *The Perennial Philosophy* from a variety of religious mystics. But his egotism in expressing this philosophy can only be compared with that of the New England Calvinists of the 18th century. The forms of H's novels are weak; for example, *Eyeless in Gaza* compares poorly with the execution of form in Faulkner's *The Sound and the Fury*. H's greatest quality is his ease of style; but he loses much of that in the late works, in which only the idea interests him. He lost the ability to create such self-parodying characters as Quarles in *Point Counter Point*.

209. Gerard, Jo. "Aldous Huxley et notre generation." *Revue Générale Belge*, 41 (March, 1949), 738-744.

Gide remarked that H, though a very intelligent writer, encountered problems along the way, but scarcely suffered from the experience. H never left the happy, cynical spirit of the universities. He lacked the sympathy which comes from suffering that would allow him human company and lead him to arrive at the truth of religious doctrines or morals. All his characters are masks for his own preoccupations and theories. His mysticism of the California era is a *Reader's Digest* compendium of a variety of religious mystics.

210. Gide, André. *The Journals of André Gide*, trans. Justin O'Brien. New York: Knopf, 1949. Vol. 3, pp. 154-155.

Gide discusses his problems in trying to read *Point Counter Point*. Picking up the novel for the third or fourth time, he had found in the first 70 pages "not a

single line somewhat firmly drawn, a single personal
thought, emotion, or sensation, the slightest enticement
for the heart or mind to invite me to go on" (March 18,
1931). Two days later Gide recorded, "I definitely drop
Huxley's book, in which I cannot get interested."

211.   Gilbert, Arthur N. "Pills and the Perfectibility of Man."
       Virginia Quarterly Review, 45 (Spring, 1969), 315-328.

       Compares H's and Koestler's interest in the use of
mind-altering drugs. H's objective was to achieve self-
transcendence, but not the kind that destroys the social
order. Koestler disparaged H's desire for a "Pop-Nirvana."
(See also 427, 477, 493, 515, 594, 599, 600.)

212.   Gill, Stephen M. "*Antic Hay*: A Portraiture of Psycho-
       logical Dislocation." *Calcutta Review*, 1, no. 4 (April-
       June, 1970), 513-518.

       Antic Hay depicts the social and psychological disloca-
tion of England after World War I rather than the economic
and political disorders of the time. The novel was called
obscene when it appeared, because it depicted sex openly.
The characters are based on models from life, each with
his own obsession, and each without any sense of real
destination or coherence to life. The overall picture
is one of nothingness.

213.   Gillet, Louis. "Aldous Huxley et le Père Joseph." *Revue
       des Deux Mondes*, 77 (Sept. 1, 1943), 86-107.

       Strachey is H's model in *Grey Eminence*. But the novel-
ist is overcome by reality: the union of the mystic and
the diplomat of a great state in one man. *Grey Eminence*
gives the events that represent the mysticism in Father
Joseph's life, but the threat of the Hapsburg Empire un-
settles Joseph's sanctity. H argues that all mystical
experiences share common elements. He tries to account
for the paradoxical role of Father Joseph by saying that
the affairs of the Church also become those of the Empire.
(See also 38, 185, 214, 222, 229, 296, 310, 370, 477,
507, 597, 601, 612, 613, 626, 632.)

214.   Glicksberg, Charles I. "Aldous Huxley: Art and Mysti-
       cism." *Prairie Schooner*, 27 (Winter, 1953), 344-353.

       "When Huxley came to the parting of the ways, the artist
was swallowed up by the prophet and the saint." "With
Huxley ... everything comes first as an idea; only later,
if at all, is it transmuted into feeling." Characters in

the earlier novels intellectualize, abstract, all of life; hence they prepare the way for a timeless Nirvana. Glicksberg examines *Crome Yellow*, *Antic Hay*, *Those Barren Leaves*, *Point Counter Point*, *Brave New World*, *Eyeless in Gaza*, *After Many a Summer*, *Time Must Have a Stop*, *Ape and Essence*. In *Point Counter Point* Quarles is symptomatic: a writer who tries to feel with his intellect, but lacks vital faith to live by. Unlike Lawrence, H was too intellectual to become a primitivist. He's a great ironist, but not a relentless cynic. *After Many a Summer* shows H giving up as an artist, receding into the preacher and prophet. *Time Must Have a Stop* preaches the virtue of mystical discipline. H is now a modern-day Tolstoy, who's decided to live the life of the saint in order to understand what sainthood is all about. *Ape and Essence* is a satirical Judgment Day about carnality and nationalism. "Huxley is exploiting the resources of fiction as a means of disseminating mystical propaganda."

215. ———. "Huxley, the Experimental Novelist." *South Atlantic Quarterly*, 52 (Jan., 1953), 98-110.

H's eclecticism and inclusiveness of vision, and the diversity and counterpointing of existence, led him to bold experiments in fiction. Glicksberg describes *Crome Yellow*, *Antic Hay*, *Those Barren Leaves*, *Point Counter Point*, *Eyeless in Gaza*, *Brave New World*, *Time Must Have a Stop*, *Ape and Essence*. *Antic Hay* is more complex than *Crome Yellow*, but each philosophy expressed has its intrinsic interest. *Those Barren Leaves*, Part 2, uses the autobiography of Chelifer, who is especially like H in his stubborn, irreverent skepticism. In *Point Counter Point* sociological objectivity is given fictional embodiment. Quarles, the central character and novelist, wants to remove the film of familiarity that clothes everything and makes the world become incredible and miraculous. The "musicalization of fiction" is the application of the theory of relativity to fiction. H's philosophical outlook and creative method in *Point Counter Point* force him "into the arms of a paralyzing skepticism." *Brave New World* is witty, ingenious, but without human warmth. *Eyeless in Gaza* is spoiled by its didactic strain, but its framework is experimental. H distorts chronology to show that genetic, environmental, and historical forces shape human destiny. Beavis is still another projection of H's search for "self." *Time Must Have a Stop* almost drops the pretense of being fiction. H doesn't dramatize the freeing of Sebastian; when time

stops, so does the action of the novel, which then turns
into a tract. *Ape and Essence* is even more of a polemic;
H's career as a fiction writer has since ended.

216.   ————. "The Intellectual Pilgrimage of Aldous Huxley."
        Dalhousie Review, 19 (July, 1939), 165-178.

H's poems and novels are those of a highly trained
critical intelligence. He's both a journalist and a man
of letters who shows unflinching skepticism. "What
finally determines the nature of truth is psychological
affirmation." He seeks to be sincerely and completely
himself: intuitive and intellectual, instinctive and
rational. Life is its own end, filled with inconsistency
and incongruity. Science can enrich the writing of
poetry. Democracy is derived from a mythical concept of
human nature: it embodies wish-fulfillment about human
"equality." Contra Marx, the proletariat is being in-
corporated into the bourgeoisie. But economic equality
won't solve social problems. H opts for a government by
the intellectual elite. *Ends and Means* holds that
economic motives are no more important than metaphysical
beliefs in the determination of social action. Pacifism
and decentralization are needed for current reforms. H
abandoned the philosophy of complete meaninglessness with
which he began his writing career; he is now associated
with the Peace Pledge Union. H's range has shifted from
"celebrated skepticism to full-blown social faith."

217.   ————. "The Literary Struggle for Selfhood." *Per-
        sonalist*, 42 (1961), 52-65.

Glicksberg discusses H, Proust, Sartre, Gide, and
Bowles. Personality is self-fulfillment, but the modern
novelists deal with characters that have so many conflicts that personality disintegrates. H's characters
are introspective, analytic, and self-dissociative to
the point of mania. Personality cannot exist under such
self-conscious circumstances.

218.   Godfrey, D.R. "The Essence of Aldous Huxley." *English
        Studies*, 32 (June, 1951), 97-106.

"The artistic failure ... is itself the outcome of an
inadequate philosophy." The earlier novels, through
Point Counter Point, show H's failure to face reality.
H's fascination with Lawrence was due to H's attempt to
encounter reality. In *Eyeless in Gaza*, for the first
and last time in H, the characters approximate reality.

The conversion of Beavis from irresponsible to responsible living is a part of H's own conversion--specifically, in H's personal participation in the pacifist movement. H's next book, *Ends and Means*, shows him once more in an intellectualized retreat from reality. *After Many a Summer* shows H once more in total isolation. "Goodness must be sought for only where it is. Goodness is God; the universe is evil." Mysticism was only another shape for H's earlier lapse into cynicism; but now the universal misanthropy totally separates H from the world.

219. Goetsch, Paul. Review of Lothar Fietz, *Menschenbild und Romanstruktur in Aldous Huxleys Ideenromane* (see 12). *English Studies* (Amsterdam), 54 (1969), 300-302.

Fietz's study concentrates on *Eyeless in Gaza*, *After Many a Summer*, *Time Must Have a Stop*, and *Island*. It is concerned with H as a thinker. This book is comparable in quality with Holmes's study of H (19)--both interrelate H's fiction and nonfiction. Both books show H's movement from multiplicity of the early novels to the visionary books of the final period. Holmes's book is more comprehensive, but Fietz focuses on H's development as a thinker and writer. In the 1920's, H believed in a diversity of selves. In the 1930's, he strove for transcending time and personality. H is "a writer who owes much to 19th century materialism, remains true to his scientific temperament even when he turns to psychological mysticism." Fietz makes the novels of ideas appear to be more radically such than they really are. His approach tends toward overabstraction.

220. Gordan, John D. "Novels in Manuscript: An Exhibition from the Berg Collection." *Bulletin of The New York Public Library*, 69 (May-June, 1965), 317-329, 396-413.

An account of the typescript in the Berg Collection, New York Public Library, of *Those Barren Leaves* follows a brief biographical sketch of H. This is the typescript from which the American edition was set. H made very few corrections on it. It is one of a few survivors, since most of H's manuscripts, typescripts, and other papers were destroyed by fire in 1961 when his house in California burned.

221. Gorman, Herbert S. Review of *Limbo*. *New Republic*, 24 (Oct. 13, 1920), 172-174.

Gorman sees the influence of T.S. Eliot and Laforgue in H's early poems. Characteristic are H's "insolence of

youth" and "fastidiousness of cynicism." There is also
a kinship with Beerbohm, one of mood, as in such sketches
as "Cynthia" and "The Bookshop." But H is not consistently a humorist--he's serious on occasion. *Limbo*
shows "a fine maturity in a writer so young."

222.   Graham, Dom Aelred, O.S.B. "Aldous Huxley and Christian
       Mysticism." *Tablet*, 179 (March 28, 1942), 156-157.

       In his biography of Father Joseph in *Grey Eminence*, H
       neglects three basic points: (1) His view of Christianity
       is intellectual and philosophical; it recognizes the
       primacy of love, but it turns out to be intellectual
       love.   (2) H views mysticism from the perspective of
       Hindu thought.   (3) H doesn't see the full relationship
       between the church's dogma and moral teaching, and the
       spiritual life of the church's mystics. Finally, H's
       mysticism is syncretist; he makes it more of an intellec-
       tual exercise than a grace-given enlightenment.

223.   Gray, James. "Obituary for the Human Race," in his
       On Second Thought. Minneapolis: University of Minne-
       sota Press, 1946. Pp. 165-174.

       Gray attacks H for his "snobbish hauteur" and his
       "intellectual fatality" in the later works. H's mysticism
       ignores the rest of humanity. He engages in escapism; he
       makes up for the emptiness of his own skepticism by
       casting off traditional values; therefore, there is some-
       thing skewed in H's mind. He set himself up "in such an
       equivalent of the saint's wilderness sanctuary as
       California has to afford."

224.   Green, Martin. "More Than a Clever Man." *Commentary*,
       8 (Dec., 1959), 551-552.

       H's extraordinary cleverness gives the reader the
       feeling that "This is all *mentally* known, purely *mental*;
       there should be so much more to life than this." This
       imbalance comes about because H has not accepted his
       limitations. He has chosen the philosophies most fatally
       unadapted to his temperament. His essay on Lawrence is
       the best in *Collected Essays*; here he gives a moving
       human response.

225.   Greenblatt, Stephen Jay. *Three Modern Satirists: Waugh,
       Orwell, and Huxley*. New Haven: Yale University Press,
       1965. Pp. 77-101.

       H's novels are "made-up affairs" with paper-thin charac-
       ters. H is not greatly concerned with the great social

and political issues. His characters talk, do nothing;
this is symptomatic of the times about which H writes.
Although there is a balance of conflicting ideological
views, H's position is unclear. His "ameboid" mind is
the reason why his novels fail. *Crome Yellow* rejects
the whole notion of progress. *Antic Hay* depicts its
characters in a rapid search for diversion, debauchery;
but they are bored, much like some of the characters in
"The Waste Land." *Brave New World* presents the dangers
of scientific materialism, faith in progress, hedonism;
these dangers are present now, not just for the future.
In this novel, H for once writes without pedantry, un-
certainty, lapses in style; he has boldness, assurance.
After *Brave New World*, H adopts a philosophy of non-
attachment and mysticism with Buddhist origins. H's
dilemma is "a conflict between a skeptical, sophisticated
mind and essentially Victorian morals. It was as if the
spirits of his two famous ancestors, T.H. Huxley and
Matthew Arnold, were locked in a mortal embrace in Huxley's soul."

226. Gross, Beverly. "In a World of Analysis." *Nation*, 210
      (June 8, 1970), 693-695.

      Reviews the *Letters* of H, edited by Grover Smith.
      H's letters are often miniature essays on select topics.
      He effaces himself in his correspondence--he held that
      the self exists only in relation to outside circumstances.
      He is much more like his grandfather T.H. Huxley than he
      is like his great-uncle Matthew Arnold. *Point Counter
      Point*, his best novel, grew, like the others, out of a
      thesis, rather than a character or situation. H always
      referred to the novels as he planned them in terms of
      the germinal idea. He saw imagination only as a technical
      means to fill out an idea to fictional dimensions. H
      thought of his novels as "fables," doubted them as novels.
      Concern and emphasis in the letters centers on *The Art of
      Seeing*, *Grey Eminence*, *The Devils of Loudun*, and *The Doors
      of Perception*. *Brave New World* and its sequel get little
      attention. H spent the last years of his life in the
      U.S. because he saw it as the laboratory for the future.
      His psychedelic drug experiments were conducted in a
      purely scientific manner, in search of psychic phenomena
      and "gratuitous graces."

227. Grube, G.M.A. "Aldous Huxley." *Canadian Forum*, 10 (Aug.
      2, 1930), 401-402.

      As H's novels succeed one another, he is less inclined
      to suffer fools gladly. He becomes more emphatically a

moralist; comes to express violent hatred of human weaknesses. *Point Counter Point* is his masterpiece to date.

228.   Grushow, Ira. *"Brave New World* and *The Tempest."* *College
       English*, 24 (Oct., 1962), 42-44.

       Chapter 5 of *Brave New World* begins with a parody of
       Gray's "Elegy." The novel contains many allusions to
       Shakespeare; the Savage speaks largely in such quotations,
       since Shakespeare is his principal source of education.
       Most of these allusions are ornamental, not functional.
       But the parallel to *The Tempest* works more closely. John
       Savage and Miranda are parallel innocents whose "educa-
       tion" in a brave new world arouses apprehension. Bernard
       Marx is like Caliban. John, in another sense, reminds
       one of Ferdinand; but John's Miranda is Lenina, a parody
       of Miranda's freshness and innocence. Mustapha Mond is
       like Prospero, but again, distortedly: Mond is an oppor-
       tunist, whereas Prospero is an idealist. Gonzalo (*Tem-
       pest*, II,i) describes an ideal commonwealth, whose objec-
       tives in some ways are achieved in A. F. 632. Caliban's
       plot is subverted by wine; the rebellion by Bernard,
       Helmholtz, and John is overcome by Soma. Thus H writes
       shifting visions of *The Tempest* in *Brave New World*.
       (See also 281, 374, 586, 588, 640.)

229.   Gumbinger, C. "Aldous Huxley vs. Christocentric Mysti-
       cism." *Homiletic and Pastoral Review*, 42 (Aug., 1942),
       1011-1023.

       Gumbinger takes issue with H's ideas on mysticism in
       Grey Eminence. He accepts H's main thesis that the world
       can be saved only by theocentric saints, but he says H
       errs in denying the Divinity of Christ throughout *Grey
       Eminence*. H favors the Dionysian tradition of mysticism.
       Benet erred from this in meditating on the Passion, as
       did Père Joseph, who thus thought himself a mystic, but
       also allowed himself to become Richelieu's tool. But H
       is wrong in thinking that Catholic Mysticism is only
       Dionysian, and that the latter is Christ-less. *Grey
       Eminence* should be kept under lock and key; it's a dan-
       gerously non-Christian book.

230.   Gump, Margaret. "From Ape to Man and from Man to Ape."
       Kentucky Foreign Language Quarterly, 4 (1957), 177-185.

       In *Brave New World*, semi-moronic simian types are bred
       specifically to do menial tasks; in *After Many a Summer*,
       a man in search of longevity regresses to apehood. Gump

reviews other works on ape themes--Hauff's "The Ape as
Man," Hoffman's "News About a Cultured Young Man,"
Kafka's "A Report to an Academy," O'Neill's "The Hairy
Ape." H's apes in *Ape and Essence* have forced scientists
to do their whims. The lovers who escape to northern
California to start life again go to uncertainty--H is
much more knowledgeable about what Hell is like than
about what a new Eden might be. Despite its "happy ending," *Ape and Essence* is the most bitter of all the
works cited in Gump's essay.

231. Hacker, Andrew. "Dostoevsky's Disciples: Man and Sheep
     in Political Theory." *Journal of Politics*, 17 (Nov.,
     1955), 590-613.

     Dostoevsky's Inquisitor shows as deep an understanding
     of human needs as do H's Controllers in *Brave New World*.
     Indoctrination of castes is used in *Brave New World* to
     make them accept their status; Soma is the chief means
     whereby they are drugged into acceptance. The 10 World
     Controllers function in a manner similar to that of the
     Grand Inquisitor. The difference is that the Inquisitor
     says "hundreds of millions" come to him and plead to be
     relieved of the "terrible gift" of freedom of choice.
     Brave New World shows the failure of liberalism to keep
     its own control of freedom.

232. Haferkamp, Bertel. "Aldous Huxley--Ein moderner englischer
     Essayist im Unterricht." *Neusprachliche Mitteilungen
     aus Wissenschaft und Praxis*, 25 (1972), 159-169.

233. Hahn, Emily. "Huxley Finds God." *Living Age*, 358 (Aug.,
     1940), 593-598.

     In *Eyeless in Gaza*, H turns specifically to search for
     God, and many readers were disappointed with the changed
     approach. It is more Buddhist than Christian, but re-
     lates to certain Christian saints too. Concerning *After
     Many a Summer*, "It is as if he had examined his many per-
     sonalities and then discarded some of them, throwing them
     out with affectionate contempt to sprawl on the pages of
     his novels." H proves, scientifically, that God is not
     mocked.

234. Hall, James. *The Tragic Comedians: Seven Modern British
     Novelists*. Bloomington: Indiana University Press,
     1963. Pp. 31-44.

     Hall successfully discusses why roles and role-playing
     are so outstanding in *Antic Hay*. In fact, H's early

novels were significant models for other fiction writers.
Antic Hay is the expression of H's personal myth.

235. Hamilton, Robert. "The Challenge of Aldous Huxley: 'The
      Perennial Philosophy.'" *Horizon*, 17 (June, 1948), 441-
      456.

      H's theocentrism challenged the modern world--but it
      also expanded the future potential of his art. *The
      Perennial Philosophy* expresses a Manichean tendency,
      which derives from H's earlier pessimism. *The Perennial
      Philosophy* works out the philosophical implications of
      Time Must Have a Stop. *Eyeless in Gaza* and *After Many
      a Summer* are inclined toward a neo-oriental view of God
      as impersonal. In *The Perennial Philosophy* H cites only
      mystics for evidence; doesn't include any philosophers.
      There are many obscure points in *The Perennial Philosophy*
      --H is not clear whether immortality assures a personal
      or impersonal union with God. H exhibits a lack of
      logical architecture in his thinking. Oriental vagueness
      is revealed in the quotations from the Indian and Chinese
      saints. Perhaps, beneath H's sophistication and irony,
      he found fundamental humility.

236. Handley-Jones, W.S. "The Modern Hamlet." *London Quar-
      terly and Holborn Review*, July, 1950, pp. 240-247.

      H's problem may be stated thus: "when you understand
      everything, all possible views become equally plausible,
      until in the end there is no difference between knowledge
      and nescience." Distrusting the intellect, H has the
      characters in his novels indulge in studied vice--e.g.,
      Gumbril in *Antic Hay*. Lawrence's "dark wisdom of the
      flesh" offered another temporary solution to H's intel-
      lect problem, which H tried to express as a "mysticism of
      sexuality." In *Point Counter Point*, both Burlap and
      Elinor, Quarles's wife, warn Quarles of the "danger of
      letting the heart dry up."

237. Hansson, Knut. "Livssyn och förkunnelse." *Samtid och
      Framtid*, 21 (1964), 215-221.

238. Hara, Ichiro. "On Aldous Huxley's 'Time Must Have a
      Stop.'" *Rising Generation* (Tokyo), 93 (1947), No. 11.

239. Hart, E.P. "Huxley's 'Eyeless in Gaza.'" *Adelphi*, 13
      (1936), 100-107.

      Eyeless in Gaza is of philosophical interest because
      the hero makes a "jump" from one level of consciousness

to another, and the "jump" appears to have occurred when the novel was being written. On one level, the plot deals with characters like those in *Point Counter Point*, except that they're now older. But Beavis becomes convinced that the vital life force of Lawrence is not now adequate as a philosophy; and one can see H abandoning the ideas he expressed in *Do What You Will*. Beavis's need is met by the philosophy of Dr. Miller, a combination of Gerald Heard and E.M. Alexander. Beavis abandons the cynical view of self as a series of disconnected states. It must be reconditioned to the values H formerly derided as the three dowagers--goodness, truth, and beauty.

240. Hart, Hubert. "Aldous Huxley." *The Catholic World*, 175 (June, 1952), 204-208.

Hart admires H for his erudition, his despising of worldly values, his winning satire; but H has certain confused notions in his mode of inquiry on ultimate questions. H rejects the idea that God is a Person--a concept he holds responsible for religious wars, inquisitions, etc. In H's view, man's salvation lies in his own exercise of his "super-rational will"--but H rejects the idea of salvation by grace. In Hart's view, H is guilty of the old heresy of Pelagius.

241. Hartz, Hedwige. "Les influences françaises dans l'oeuvre d'Aldous Huxley." *Bulletin de la Faculté des Lettres de Strasbourg*, 17 (1938-1939), 214-217.

242. Hauge, Ingvar. "Aldous Huxley." *Samtiden*, 73 (Jan., 1964), 46-53.

The growth of H's philosophy reflects the general changes of our century: (1) materialism, (2) alternation between skepticism and puritanism, (3) assumption that certain absolute values could be reasoned from sensory information, (4) mysticism--a set of philosophical values whereby the characters can be measured.

243. Hauserman, Hans W. "Aldous Huxley as a Literary Critic." *PMLA*, 48 (Sept., 1933), 908-918.

In H's view, the primary basis for literary criticism is scientific integrity, to observe all forms of life. H showed no basic changes in his mode of evaluation during a 10-year period (1923-1933). In H's view, Balzac is a preeminent writer. Both H and Balzac praise aristocracy. But Balzac showed no understanding or appreciation

of mysticism, a subject that greatly interested H.
Nevertheless, H felt called on to perform the same mission
as a novelist as Balzac did. H prefers the Renaissance
writers for their ethical qualities, for their broad, un-
prejudiced view of the world. H praises Donne, deplores
Spenser: poetry must have a wider scope than Spenser
allows it. Gide is too exquisite; Proust is a "scientific voluptuary of the emotions." Rolland insists too
much on the purity, idealism, of his beliefs. D'Annunzio
protests too much, is overly rhetorical. Conrad and
Mansfield don't know what's going on in the minds of their
characters--they leave too much to the reader's imagination. Chapter 4 of *Those Barren Leaves* indicts Wordsworth's nature philosophy. Shelley fills H with terror
and disgust; he's bloodless and boneless. 19th-century
Romanticism closed its eyes to reality, industrialism.
At least modern literature doesn't limit itself to stereo-
types. Although H denies it, he's basically a classical
critic. He believes that the creative impulse is col-
lateral with the working of the intellect.

244. Haynes, Renée. "Aldous Huxley, 1894-1963." *New Black-
        friars*, 46 (Nov., 1964), 97-102.

Haynes summarizes biographical facts about H with occasional insight. "The soul of Uncle Eustace, the sensual
egotist, tallies with the belief of St. Catherine of
Genoa that the love of God which is overwhelming joy to
the blessed is a glaring light or burning heat to those
who have chosen to remain enclosed and absorbed in themselves." *Ends and Means* is concerned with exterior, and
The Perennial Philosophy with interior, life. Examples
are given of H's widely varied interests: traditional
Chinese medicine, William James, problems of educating
Puerto Rican children in American schools, ESP, the
navigational sense of migratory birds, allegorical in-
terpretations of the Bible, whether Jung's psychology is
truly empirical. Haynes concludes, "I never knew a man
of letters so close to being a saint."

245. ————. "Aldous Huxley: Herinneringen." *Streven*, 17
        (1964), 525-531.

246. Heard, Gerald. "The Poignant Prophet." *The Kenyon
        Review*, 27 (Winter, 1965), 49-79.

H's irony and satire, directed against pretense and
hypocrisy, presume the real qualities of truth, beauty,
and dignity. H moved from satire (*Brave New World*) to

prophecy (*Island*). Heard describes H's appearance,
mannerisms, conversation, from their personal friendship,
which began in 1930. Despite his poor eyesight, H was
an eminent art critic. Maugham said of H, "he isn't interested in people because his real interest is in ideas."
But H wrote novels because it paid better than writing
essays. Wells was angry at H's *Brave New World*--said it
was treason to science. H wrote *Ends and Means* while
visiting Lawrence in New Mexico, but H could never in
any complete sense be called a philosopher. Heard analyzes *After Many a Summer* and *Grey Eminence* (he thinks
Grey Eminence will be H's most enduring book). After
writing *The Devils of Loudun*, H wrote *The Perennial
Philosophy*, the key idea of which is that immoral means
do not make possible any moral ends. Heard and H served
as subjects for medically supervised mescalin experiments,
for 10 years beginning in 1953. For H, mescalin gave
total attention, awareness of beauty, to a degree he
never achieved otherwise. Maria, H's first wife, died
in 1955. H finished *Island* in 1961, the year in which
fire destroyed his house; the manuscript of *Island* was
the only thing he was able to save. Afflicted with
cancer of the tongue, H refused traditional medical
treatment, and survived two years. "Shakespeare and
Religion" was his last essay.

247. Hébert, R. Louis. "Huxley's *Brave New World*, Chapter
      V." *Explicator*, 29 (1971), Item 71.

      The opening of Chapter 5 is a skillful parody of the
      first four quatrains of Gray's "Elegy." Each detail in
      Gray is converted into a burlesque counterpart of the
      mechanistic age. (The relevant passages from both texts
      are quoted for comparison.) (See also 379, 500.)

248. Hemingway, Ernest. *Death in the Afternoon*. New York:
      Scribner's, 1932. Pp. 190-192.

      H in *Music at Night* (p. 201) criticizes Hemingway in
      Farewell to Arms for quickly passing over an allusion to
      Mantegna; Hemingway replies in *Death in the Afternoon* by
      saying this sort of learning doesn't lend itself to
      building character.

249. Henderson, Philip. *The Novel Today*. London: John Lane,
      1936.

      Concerning emotional maturity, Henderson discusses H's
      prolonged adolescence, and says this is the real reason for
      the highly civilized skeptical outlook of H's first novels.

250.   Herzog, Arthur. "Una visita a Aldous Huxley." *Brecha*,
        4 (May, 1960), 22-23.

251.   Hicks, Granville. "Huxley Revisited." *Saturday Review*
        (New York), Nov. 15, 1958, p. 12.

        H is preaching again in *Brave New World Revisited*;
        Brave New World was the transition between the flippant
        H and the serious H. *Brave New World* was "wrong" for
        1932, when the world was in the midst of the Great
        Depression. By 1958, however, the more important features
        of *Brave New World* were more apparent: comic inventive-
        ness, ingeniously built plot, valid prophecy. H properly
        censured in *Brave New World* I and II the "nonstop dis-
        traction provided by newspapers and magazines, by radio,
        television, and the cinema." Also, H showed a keen
        awareness of the newest means of mind control and ex-
        pressed concern over its threats.

252.   Hodson, James Lansdale. "Julian and Aldous Huxley," in
        his *No Phantoms Here*. London: Faber & Faber, 1932.
        Pp. 256-261.

        "In some degree each is doing what the other would
        have preferred." Julian's earliest interests were lan-
        guage and literature; Aldous's were in science, but bad
        eyesight prevented his studying medicine as he had
        planned to do. Hodson repeats the various popular
        anecdotes about the appearance, mannerisms, and in-
        terests of Julian and Aldous.

253.   Hoffman, Charles G. "The Change in Huxley's Approach to
        the Novel of Ideas." *Personalist*, 42 (Winter, 1961),
        85-90.

        H abandoned the technique of counterpoint in his later
        novels and became personally committed to presenting
        his concepts. The later novels became tracts in which
        allegory did away with common credence. All of H's
        novels are of ideas (i.e., are used for theme and dia-
        logue; also, ideas are basic to structure, character
        portrayal, dramatic incidents, and satire). The novels
        written after *Brave New World* are less artistically suc-
        cessful because H changed his approach. *Point Counter
        Point* maintains an artistic balance between allegorical
        intent and character portrayal through dramatic incidents.
        In *The Genius and the Goddess*, however, plausible charac-
        ter development is sacrificed everywhere to stress
        allegory. The earlier novels use the "counterpoint"

method to present differing points of view. But beginning with *Brave New World*, H forgets or forgoes counter-
point--he uses simpler approaches such as "either-or"--a
choice, for example, between John Savage and Mustapha Mond
in *Brave New World*. In *Eyeless in Gaza*, H has a personal
commitment to Anthony Beavis; H is no longer the detached
author. All the novels that follow are similar dramatic
essays--the author's mouthpiece talks down to the other
characters. H also uses satire less effectively in the
later novels; it is no longer a controlled attack on
such victims as scientists. The later novels place too
much emphasis on one philosophy over others.

254. Hoffman, Frederick J. "Aldous Huxley and the Novel of
     Ideas." *College English*, 8 (1946), 129-147; reprinted
     in *Forms of Modern Fiction*, ed. William Van O'Connor.
     Minneapolis: University of Minnesota Press, 1948.
     Pp. 189-200; also reprinted in *Aldous Huxley: A Collec-
     tion of Critical Essays*, ed. Robert E. Kuehn (see 30),
     pp. 8-17.

     Quarles's notes in *Point Counter Point* on the "novel
     of ideas" define a novel which uses ideas instead of
     characterization and other standard aspects of traditional
     narrative. H uses ideas in the sense that they possess
     dramatic qualities: "Multiplicity of eyes and multiplicity
     of aspects seen." Quarles has comments to make on the
     several views toward morality. The essays in *Do What You
     Will* expand on this concept. A single, specific philos-
     ophy is fearful and unable to allow for the flux that
     exists in the modern age. H's *Crome Yellow* through *Point
     Counter Point* are all "novels of ideas." Thereafter, H
     becomes more the essayist than the novelist. Ideas have
     the ability to "appropriate the fortunes and careers
     which ordinarily belong to persons." The later novels
     fail to maintain a proper esthetic distance from the
     philosophy expressed.

255. Hogarth, Basil. "Aldous Huxley as Music Critic." *Musical
     Times*, 76 (Dec., 1935), 1079-1082.

     For a man of letters, H has an outstanding knowledge
     of music, showing it early on as music critic for *West-
     minster Gazette*, 1922-23. He showed his dislike for
     "sensuous" and "pedantic" music. Devoted to Beethoven,
     he expressed his disgust with such moderns as Scriabin
     and Stravinsky. "Beethoven was transcendental in the
     direction of heroism, of the soul, of infinity." "Stra-
     vinsky's 'Ragtime' is transcendental in the direction of

soullessness and mechanics" (i.e., "inverted transcendentalism"). H finds Rimsky-Korsakov and Richard
Strauss limited, uninteresting. Of all the romantics,
H preferred Debussy and Delius. At his best, Delius
shows a "certain limited, Wordsworthian emotion."
"Brahms seems strangely grandiloquent, romantic and
sentimental ... a lesser artist than Beethoven because
he is a less resourceful and fertile creator." But
Brahms is superb in his "Variations on a theme by Haydn."
(See the Robert Craft essays [158, 159] to see how H
changed his view of Stravinsky.)

256. Holmes, Charles M. "Aldous Huxley's Struggle with Art."
      Western Humanities Review, 15 (Spring, 1961), 149-156.

H is a potential artist who has never developed, or
really accepted, his gifts. From the beginning, he
presented a series of satires on artists and critics.
"Vulgarity in Literature" also shows that H didn't take
the art of writing seriously. Beavis in *Eyeless in Gaza*
also expresses strong reservations about the truthfulness
of literature. Propter in *After Many a Summer* says that
the values supported by literature are the cause of much
human suffering, and are therefore evil. H's antiheroes
portray a succession of quarrels that he had with himself.
Many are retiring, and scholarly, like H. Many have
awkward feelings about sex and are would-be ascetics.
Many distrust the intellect. H's ineffective novels
show his inability or unwillingness to transform his
inner conflicts into art.

257. ———. "The Early Poetry of Aldous Huxley." *Texas
      Studies in Literature and Language*, 8 (Fall, 1966),
      391-406; reprinted in *Aldous Huxley: A Collection of
      Critical Essays*, ed. Robert E. Kuehn (see 30), pp.
      64-80.

Writing the early poetry taught H the "formidable and
lovely freedom of the novel" that he really needed to
express his inner struggles. H's shifting style shows
he has inner problems that are mixed up with the ways
of dealing with them in art. The poems show an inconsistency of style; some are designed to shock, whereas
others express conventional sentiment. Some poems present
an unresolved dialectic, which was to become the basic
structure for the house party discussions in such novels
as *Crome Yellow*. Many poems exhibit a strongly ironic
method which exhibits human beings as if they were zoo
creatures (an idea borrowed from Rimbaud). Other ironic

approaches were suggested by Laforgue. H's ironic mask in the poems was a temporary solution, but before *Leda* (1920) he had already begun writing the short stories for *Limbo*; these were to provide an alternative means of expressing H's complex attitudes.

258. Holz, L. *Methoden der Meinungsbeeinflussung bei Orwell und Huxley*. Hamburg: n.p., 1963.

259. Hoops, Reinald. "Die Weltanschauung Aldous Huxleys." *Englische Studien*, 72 (1937), 73-92.

260. ———. *Der Einfluss der Psychoanalyse auf die englische Literatur*. Heidelberg, 1934. Pp. 185-194.

261. Houston, P.H. "The Salvation of Aldous Huxley." *American Review*, 4 (Dec., 1934), 209-232.

Although H rejects orthodox religious faiths, he's a humanist and inclines toward mysticism. After World War I, H played Thersites to his contemporaries. He sided with Lawrence's return to pagan vitalism, but he never gave up the sovereign value of reason. *Crome Yellow* and *Antic Hay* are full of meaningless depravity. At the end of *Those Barren Leaves*, Calamy escapes to a life of self-mastery. The Harlequin-Hamlet view of Laforgue is completed in the character of Quarles in *Point Counter Point*. *Do What You Will* and *Music at Night* show H's hatred of Puritanism, St. Francis, Pascal, Baudelaire, Wordsworth, and Swift. H admires those who serve the cause of vitalism: Burns, Blake, Shakespeare, Mozart, Rubens, the early Tolstoy. Vital equilibrium comes through the balancing of opposing hostilities. In a later stage, H believed that an inner harmony of the soul was for the individual to discover in the midst of modern chaos, if he had the will to do so. H has more affinity with Swift than with Voltaire. There is a future possibility for H: "he may trust more implicitly that hidden mystic sense of unity between himself and the world of absolute values which will finally leave him detached from the repercussions of his own wrath and give him the peace he so evidently yearns for."

262. Howe, Irving. "The Fiction of Anti-Utopia." *New Republic*, 146 (April 23, 1962), 13-16.

Anti-utopian fiction is the resort of leftist visionaries who fear that their imaginary society will turn out to have weaknesses. In the machine age, they fear that tech-

nology will lose touch with values partly because people
don't bother to defend values in such an environment.
This is most true of H's *Brave New World*, which in other
respects is inferior to Orwell's *1984* and Zamiatin's *We*.
This genre differs from regular novels because the
characters are generalized and suspense is missing.

263.   Huxley, Julian. "My Brother Aldous." *Humanist*, 25
          (Jan., 1965), 25.

       AH has been falsely accused of being a mystic, a cynic,
anti-scientific, anti-religious, etc. He was in fact a
humanist, positive and constructive in his views, and
one who aimed for "the better realization of human possibilities." *Brave New World* was not simply an attack
on science, but rather a satire on the belief that
science and technology alone could solve all human problems. *Island* should be read as a novel about a "good
utopia." *The Perennial Philosophy* is a careful study of
the phenomenon of mysticism, which can have great value
and significance, just as love can. *The Doors of Perception* studies the intensification of perception, the
enlargement of human consciousness, through the controlled
use of certain drugs. AH was greatly interested in all
forms of modern science. He was also much concerned about
problems in education, conservation of resources, and
overpopulation. He saw religion "as a natural phenomenon
and an inevitable organ of man in society." (Sir Julian
tends to play down the role of mysticism in his brother's
life; he forgets, for example, the important role that it
plays in *Island*.)

264.   "The Huxley Brothers." *Life*, 22 (March 24, 1947), 53-
          54 ff.

       This article includes an unusual collection of photo-
graphs of Aldous, Julian, and their family. Julian was
elected director general of UNESCO in Dec., 1946; he
proposed to attack illiteracy, to reconcile the philosophies of communism and capitalism, and to promote the
study of psychoanalysis. Julian is described as a
materialist and an atheist; Aldous, as the mystic, believes that all religions are one and that God is everywhere.

265.   "Huxleyan Heaven and Earth." *Time*, 44 (Aug. 28, 1944), 90.

       Reviews *Time Must Have a Stop*, a novel full of rascally,
odd characters, and containing lengthy passages on art,
politics, and society. Two-thirds of the book deals

with the same time period as *Point Counter Point* and
Antic Hay; the remainder deals with H's most recent
religious views. "One of the indispensable conditions
of peace" is the establishing of a single religion by
East and West. H is now at work on *The Perennial
Philosophy*--"an anthology of the highest common factors
in world religion and metaphysical systems" (H's statement).

266. "Huxley's Conversion." *Ave Maria*, n.s. 62 (Oct. 20,
      1945), 242.

267. Hyde, Lawrence. "Aldous Huxley: Life Worshipper." *The
      New Adelphi*, Dec., 1929-Feb., 1930, pp. 90-102.

      H's essay on Pascal shows H to be a "Life-Worshipper,"
      a belief which holds that all logic is the result of
      chemical and biological processes in the human body.
      Also, all modes of thinking and acting are equally valid:
      an ultra-Pyrrhonistic point of view. Serious psychic
      damage is done by refusing to admit to all manner of
      impulses, good or bad, existing in the soul and crying
      for satisfaction. The "self" is a composite; therefore,
      an unimpeded development of as many aspects of it as
      possible is needed. The ideal is Greek--one of full and
      harmonious development of the self. But H has ended by
      making "life-worship" synonymous with complete irrespon-
      sibility. He holds that the law can be epicurean on
      Monday, mystic on Tuesday. But this philosophy is false
      to the facts of life.

268. Iancovici, Gheorghe. "Eseistitca lui Aldous Huxley."
      Steaua, 25 (1974), 68-69.

      This article discusses H as an essayist.

269. Inge, William Ralph. "On Huxley's *Perennial Philosophy*."
      Philosophy, 22 (April, 1947), 66-70.

      H reveals himself as a mystical philosopher, deriving
      his ideas from the philosophy of India. The higher
      religions appeared concurrently, and shared some common
      elements: India, China, Persia, Greece, Israel. But
      their modern descendants are mutually exclusive. H finds
      his resolution of these differences in a mystical com-
      munion with God. Disinterestedness, non-attachment, are
      its manifestations. H showed great interest in psychical
      research; he believed telepathy and clairvoyance to be
      proven facts. Inge believes that H was credulous on
      these matters.

270.   "Intellect and Intuition." *TLS*, Dec. 18, 1969, pp. 1437-
        1438.

        A review of H's *Letters*, and of the books by Bowering
        and Laura Huxley. One year before his death H remarked,
        "I remain an agnostic who aspires to be a gnostic--but
        a gnostic only on the mystical level, a gnostic without
        symbols, cosmologies or a pantheon." This article gives
        a competent review of H's career. It notes that as H
        grew older, he praised the very things which he had
        earlier derided. It was H's weakness as a thinker that
        ideas came bubbling up too easily. He is at his best
        in *Grey Eminence* and *The Devils of Loudun*--"given the
        discipline of historical fact, his intellect could en-
        lighten the strange, dark contradictions of human nature
        that at the same time fascinated, delighted and repelled
        him."

271.   "Intelligent Talk: All Grist to Mr. Huxley's Mill."
        TLS, Dec. 30, 1960, pp. 837-838.

        A review of H's *Collected Essays*. The elements under-
        lying H's essays are: (1) Confidence: in his provocative
        subject, in his ability to seek out writers and informa-
        tion from other ages; (2) Facility: his being able to
        write about everything, his almost indifferent skillful-
        ness; (3) Frivolity: his ability to make other writers
        sound the worse in the context of his own elegant,
        light-handed prose. In general, the essays are "over-
        allusive, under-engaged."

272.   Isherwood, Christopher. "Aldous Huxley in California."
        Atlantic Monthly, 214 (Sept., 1964), 44-47.

        H remained sharply observant up to the time of his
        death, always looking for truths in life, even in such
        commonly disparaged sources as the Vedanta, which H
        openly admitted was an important inspiration for his
        later books. He felt that he could discover more truth
        and beauty through mysticism than he could through
        literature, which indulged in futile exercises of tech-
        nique; H was upset over the attempt to replace religion
        with art.

273.   Janssen Perio, E.M. "Huxley's Ideologieën: Fragment
        uit een gelyknamig essay." *Gids*, 120 (May, 1957),
        335-337.

274.   Jehin, A. "The Burning Wheel," in *Aldous Huxley and T.S.
        Eliot*. Buenos Aires: Talleres gráficos Contreras, 1943.
        Pp. 15-24.

H's poem "The Burning Wheel" contains the essential
philosophy of his later novels, which is the mystic
ideal of perfection--absolute detachment from personal
and worldly cares. The wheel image symbolizes the attempt of the mind to cast off all that interrupts its
quiet. Still, the world's appeal for action appears to
be the only way to dispel death. Most of H's novels
have a character who considers the problem of finding
freedom from his own personality and from his social and
intellectual environment: Scogan in *Crome Yellow*;
Gumbril in *Antic Hay*; Spandrell in *Point Counter Point*;
Beavis in *Eyeless in Gaza*; Mr. Propter in *After Many a
Summer*.

275. Joad, C.E.M. "Aldous Huxley: The Man and His Work."
      The Outline (*Supplement to John O'London's Weekly*),
      25 (July, 1936), 597-604.

276. ————. "Aldous Huxley and the Nature of the Universe,"
      in his *The Recovery of Belief*. London: Faber & Faber,
      1952. Pp. 167-169.

H's later works stress the idea that individuality is
transitory, not permanent. Mystical consciousness shows
that God is infinite and non-personal; the individual
soul eventually merges with God. H's views are best expressed in the essay "Beliefs" (Chapter 14 of *Ends and
Means*): (1) Desire is the source of illusion, hence the
need for an attitude of "non-attachment." (2) Nonattachment being achieved, we have a direct experience with
the spiritual unity underlying all diverse, independent
consciousness. (3) Thus we can transcend the limitations
of personality. (4) The mystic can draw moral and physical
powers from the underlying spiritual reality. (5) The
underlying reality lacks ethical qualities. (6) We can
never totally transcend our individuality. (7) Virtue is
the essential preliminary to mystical experience. However, Joad cannot accept these principles because of
logical, ethical, and personal reasons.

277. ————. "Constructive Pacifism." *New Statesman and
      Nation*, 12 (Aug. 8, 1936), 185-186.

H's new novel preaches doctrine, pleads a cause, but
H writes entertainingly; he can never be dull. His
argument is that peace can't be pursued by politics and
diplomacy; the League of Nations creates delusions.
Peace will come only if individual men love one another.
Loving others is possible through self-control, which
begins with body discipline, proper sitting, etc. Mental

discipline, such as Indian "yogi" and Japanese "zen," is also useful. The ideal approach is for small groups to form communities, which in turn love each other. Mass conversion is needed to achieve constructive pacifism. But the objection is that law backed by force is needed for any national commitment. H's is not the most immediately effective method for creating a peace movement--but he has to be admired for serving a worthy cause.

278.   ———. "Huxley and the Dowagers," in his *Return to Philosophy*. London: Faber & Faber, 1935.

Joad restates what are traditional beliefs, values-- "reason, if properly employed, can give us truth; beauty is a real value which exists, and we can train our minds and form our tastes to discern it; some things are *really* right in a sense in which others are *really* wrong." Joad attacks modern pragmatism, subjectivism; he seeks to identify the fallacies in the philosophy of such men as H and D.H. Lawrence.

279.   ———. "Philosophy and Aldous Huxley." *Realist*, 1 (July, 1929), 99-114.

Joad responds to H's article on Pascal in the first issue of *Realist*, in which H implies that philosophy is "moonshine." H disavowed metaphysics--the process of using logical reasoning to determine the nature of the universe. H says that the universe is to be known through scientific observation, and he censures philosophers like Pascal who deal in "vicious abstractions which have no existence outside the classifying intellect." Joad notes that H uses traditional philosophical methods to arrive at his own conclusions. But science, too, draws philosophical conclusions from observed evidence, uses these conclusions to generalize about other situations. H argues against philosophical rationalism (Descartes) and philosophical mysticism (Pascal), but he doesn't always distinguish between them. He fails to see that some truths--e.g., mathematical ones--are not based on sense perception. Intuitive mystical insight justifies the validity of such abstractions as Goodness, Beauty, Truth; they are based on universal human needs. Scientists themselves admit that perceiving "reality" depends on mental constructs.

280.   Jones, Joseph. "Utopias as Dirge." *American Quarterly*, 2 (Fall, 1950), 214-226.

Jones compares Orwell's *1984*, H's *Brave New World*, and Twain's *A Connecticut Yankee in King Arthur's Court*. Of the three, *Brave New World* seems to be the most mechanical; *1984* has the greatest satiric dignity; and *A Connecticut Yankee* is the most humorous. In the novels by H and Orwell, the hero has the cards stacked against him, whereas Twain's hero seems to have an equal chance. *Brave New World* expresses the fear that the scientist gives in to the political boss. *Ends and Means* prescribes Eastern modes of thought to replace Western will-worship, which is the real cause of war. But H's rhetoric is too cool to convince readers of the need for action. Self-conscious intellectualization is the Hamlet-flaw of H. *Grey Eminence*, *The Perennial Philosophy*, *Time Must Have a Stop*, all express the mysticism that H developed after his retreat to California. *Ape and Essence* shows the bitterness of an idealist gone sour. H always lived with a subconscious fear of his own intellect.

281. Jones, William M. "The Iago of *Brave New World*." *Western Humanities Review*, 15 (Summer, 1961), 275-278.

John Savage is the prime mover of action in Part 2 of *Brave New World*. Although the World Controller doesn't want anything to do with Shakespeare, the incidents that follow his confrontation with Savage parallel the events of *Othello*. H's Othello, who is a "Negro" and an outsider, loves a blonde girl, has his mind poisoned against her by society, not by a single Iago. Both H's and Shakespeare's Othello are just, honest men who are duped.

282. Kabiljo-Šutić, Simha. "Filozofija vitalizma D. Lorensa i O. Makslija: Uticaji i paralele." *Knjizevna Kritika*, 4 (1976), 29-54.

283. Kamp, Fritz. "Aldous Huxley, et tilbageblik." *Gads danske Magasin*, 40 (Jan.-Aug., 1946), 384-396.

284. Kanters, Robert. "Aldous Huxley, jugé par Blaise Pascal." *Cahiers du Sud*, 210 (Nov., 1938), 797-807.

285. Karl, Frederick R. "The Play Within the Novel in *Antic Hay*." *Renascence*, 13 (Winter, 1961), 59-68.

Although H tries in all of his novels to make order out of disorder, he succeeds only in *Antic Hay*, by the use of a play within the novel. The Monster in the play, like the characters in the novel, is only half living; at the end it commits suicide. The Monster in the drama

expresses all the faults, and an attempt to overcome
them forcibly, as shown by the characters themselves in
the novel.

286. ————, and M. Magalaner. "Aldous Huxley," in *Reader's
      Guide to Great Twentieth-Century Novels*. New York:
      Noonday, 1959. Pp. 254-284.

The authors describe H's weaknesses as a novelist, but
praise him as a representative of the 20th century. They
rank him with a group including Conrad, Forster, Woolf,
Lawrence, and Joyce. H is a novelist of ideas whose
ideas are not well expressed in the characters and incidents of the fiction, but these ideas are the important
ones of his age.

287. Kennedy, Richard S. "Aldous Huxley: The Final Wisdom."
      Southwest Review, 50 (Winter, 1965), 37-47.

Kennedy surveys the various "periods" of H's career,
from the early sophisticated novel of manners to the later
accounts of vision-producing drugs. From the late 1950's
on, H was in a period of synthesis, with the *Collected
Short Stories* (1957), the *Collected Essays* (1959), and
his final work, in 1963, *Literature and Science*, which
dealt with the Snow-Leavis controversy. *Island* (1962)
was H's best effort at synthesis; its purpose was to put
together the best elements of East and West: as if
Gandhi and Thomas Henry Huxley were to share their best
thoughts. Pala, the "Island," uses Western scientific
discoveries, but it doesn't let technological advances
dominate the culture. The educational system of Pala
combines Hinduism and Sheldon's theories on body and
personality types. But H ends the novel and his utopia
by having a foreign dictator invade the Island in order
to exploit its oil resources. H realized that utopia is
only utopia.

288. Kessler, Martin. "Power and the Perfect State: A Study
      in Disillusionment as Reflected in Orwell's *Nineteen
      Eighty-Four* and Huxley's *Brave New World*." *Political
      Science Quarterly*, 72 (Dec., 1957), 565-577.

Brave New World and *1984* show that modern technology
makes possible the exercise of absolute power by government. Dystopia works in both books; its justification
is pragmatic, to assure the preservation of the present
power structure. Happiness in *Brave New World* is created
for the masses to perpetuate the state, not vice versa.

Corollary to "happiness" are mind conditioning and a directed consumption economy, as well as controlled production of human beings. The state gratifies conditioned desires, and it does not allow any other kinds of desires to develop.

289. Ketser, G. "Aldous Huxley: A Retrospect." *Revue des Langues Vivantes* (Brussels), 30 (1964), 179–184.

H's constant theme is a doomed world--from *Crome Yellow* (1921) to *Island* (1962). H was always worried about antagonism between passion and reason: body vs. mind, instinct vs. intellect, unconscious vs. conscious. His approach was always that of the detached rationalist. Until *Point Counter Point*, none of his characters leads a satisfactory life. Rampion in *Point Counter Point* expresses a "religion of blood" (from Lawrence) which H was later to abandon for the mysticism suggested in *Eyeless in Gaza*. But H always sees his characters from the outside; he doesn't really participate in Rampion's point of view, or in the point of view of his characters who are mystics. Buddhism appealed to H because it allowed for his empiricism and his detachment from the world of unreason.

290. Kettle, Arnold. *An Introduction to the English Novel*, Vol. 2. London: Hutchinson, 1953. Pp. 167–173.

Point Counter Point is not a true cross section of English society, but a picture of two intersecting groups: Mayfair socialites, and a literary clique including characters representing Lawrence (Rampion) and H (Quarles). Lawrence himself found Rampion a bore because Rampion spends all of his time in a Soho restaurant. Most of the other characters only talk, or have sex, or sometimes listen to music or write. H never creates a living organism--he is too intent on dissecting it. The best of the book is motivated by malice or masochism, but H's cynicism is basically shallow. "There is neither compassion nor indignation behind *Point Counter Point*, the performance is nearer to a perverse, cerebral masturbation." Kettle quotes Lawrence's response to *Point Counter Point*: "It's a *perverse* courage which makes the man accept the slow suicide of inertia and sterility: the perverseness of a perverse child."

291. Keyishian, Harry. "The Martyrology of Nymphomania: Nancy Cunard in *The Green Hat* and *Point Counter Point*." *Proceedings of the Sixth National Convention of the Popular*

Culture Association, Chicago, Illinois, April 22-24, 1976.

Both H and Michael Arlen fell in love with Nancy Cunard and both depicted her in their fiction. She was the symbol of shockingly free youth of the 1920's. Jessica Mitford said, "Going too far was her way of life." Maria Huxley ended Aldous's infatuation and pursuit of Nancy by packing him off to Italy and putting him to work there at his writing.

292. King, Almeda. "Christianity Without Tears: Man Without Humanity." *English Journal*, 57 (July, 1968), 820-824.

"Unhappiness" is that vestige of humanity remaining in John Savage, an outsider to the "new world" of *Brave New World*, but conditioned out of the dystopians' lives. Ford's principle of universal happiness exists to per-petuate efficient mass production. The finitude of the Fordian goals prevents man from finding any deeper meaning in life. The infinite is a threat to Fordian stability; science has made life bearable without God. "Soma" = "Christianity without tears." Religion, pure science, and art are discountenanced in the brave new world. Ford substitutes for God, sex for love, "the feelies and the scent organ" for art—all to curb the urge for the in-finite. Despite the filth and disease of John Savage's reservation, he has insights provided by suffering that the conditioned citizens of the brave new world know nothing about. Savage is a "redeemer" who is "crucified" but whose sacrifice isn't understood by those conditioned to a Christianity without tears.

293. King, Carlyle A. "Aldous Huxley and Music." *Queen's Quarterly*, 70 (Autumn, 1963), 336-351.

A great deal of H's fiction and nonfiction relates to music. In *Point Counter Point* H juxtaposes an ironic account of acoustics with an artistic description of playing Bach's Suite in E minor. Music often furnishes metaphors and symbols for H. It furnishes the climactic device for *Point Counter Point*: Spandrell plans for the murder of Webley, and then his own murder by the same assassins, to be accompanied by the playing of a portion of Beethoven's A minor Quartet. In *Eyeless in Gaza*, music is the only thing that makes life tolerable to Mark Staithes. H despised jazz and other forms of popular music. *Brave New World* parodies music; in the novel, it is used only as a pain reliever. *Ape and Essence* also

parodies Hollywood-type music. The climax of *Island*
uses Bach's Fourth Brandenburg Concerto in order to put
heaven and earth together as one. "Through the therapy
of the music Farnaby faces evil as an essential part of
Being and accepts compassion as part of enlightenment."
(Compare this essay with Baldanza's; see 69.)

294. ————. "Aldous Huxley's Way to God." *Queen's Quarterly*,
61 (Spring, 1954), 80-100.

Even in H's early fiction, there are hints of the mysticism he later made his important subject: a sensitive,
awkward character with a propensity for quietude decides
instead to become noisy and intellectual. In *Those Barren
Leaves*, Chelifer is superficial and smart. Calamy is the
maturing intellectual who wants "something new." Cardan,
the satanist, makes the wittiest, most cynical remarks.
Eleven years and fifteen books later, H returns to
Calamy's interests. But H's essays point in the direction
of mysticism before the fiction does. *Point Counter
Point* (1928) through *Beyond the Mexique Bay* (1934) show
the impact of Lawrence, though the last book shows H dis-
engaging himself from Lawrence's life view. After *Brave
New World* H qualifies or rejects the neo-paganism he had
adapted from Lawrence. The change is begun in *Grey
Eminence* (1941) with H showing the conversion of François
Leclerc. *Eyeless in Gaza* shows the important influence
on it of Gerald Heard's mysticism and Dick Sheppard's
pacifism. *Ends and Means* (1937) presents H's creed as
that of a rational idealist: "Men's final end is the
knowledge of the immanent and transcendent Ground of all
being." *The Devils of Loudun* shows how men can escape
from the horror of selfhood: Grandier does, Surin does
not. (This is an important, comprehensive essay because
of its overview of H's writing in relation to a single,
important theme.)

295. Kirkwood, M.M. "The Thought of Aldous Huxley." *University of Toronto Quarterly*, 6 (Jan., 1937), 189-198.

An important feature of H's writing style is the enter-
taining verbal scintillation. H's purpose is to teach
skepticism; his first esthetic purpose is to express
love of life. In *Eyeless in Gaza*, Staithes criticizes
the untruthfulness of literature; this is H's defense of
his own all-inclusiveness in his fiction. Morality means
balancing the claims of the society and of the individual.
H overrules the benevolence of God, the machinations of
fate, and puts us to the perpetual task of constantly
rebuilding the values by which we live.

296. Knox, Ronald A. "Cardinal Bérulle and Mr. Huxley."
      Tablet, 179 (May 2, 1942), 221-222.

      H misreads Cardinal Bérulle in his portrayal of him
      in *Grey Eminence*. H assumes that Bérulle as a mystic
      chooses as the object of love not the Godhead, but a
      person and personal qualities; this view led, according
      to H, to a reaction against mysticism in the second half
      of the 17th century in France. But what Bérulle meant
      was, "We have to identify ourselves mentally with
      Christ.... in that framework we can try to contemplate."
      H read only the first five volumes of Bremond's (still
      incomplete) eleven volumes, in which Bérulle is one of
      the heroes.

297. Knuth, Werner. "Freiheit oder Planung--von Huxley zu
      Russell." *Denkendes Volk* (Berlin), 3 (April, 1949),
      179-181.

298. Kohn-Bramstedt, Ernest. "The Intellectual as Ironist:
      Aldous Huxley and Thomas Mann." *Contemporary Review*,
      155 (April, 1939), 470-479.

      A comparison of the fiction of Mann and H shows that
      Mann's characters are more substantial, but that H has
      the shrewder brain, better scientific training, and
      philosophic elegance. Both deal with the same basic
      conflict, body and spirit. H accepts compromise in true
      English manner. H's irony is realistic; Mann's is meta-
      physical. H is the puritan with the sensibility and
      contradictions of an intellectual. H longs for two sets
      of eyes so that he would be able to read Voltaire and
      Thomas à Kempis simultaneously. Irony is the dominant
      mode of both authors because neither one submits to a
      single philosophy or clique.

299. Kolek, Leszek. "English Novel of Ideas: An Attempt at a
      Preliminary Definition and Description of the Genre."
      Zagadnienia Rodzajów Literackich, 17 (1974), 21-38.

      Frederick J. Hoffman's essay (254) is the best analysis
      of the "novel of ideas," but Hoffman doesn't explain its
      historical development. H's first four novels are recog-
      nized as belonging to the genre; the library at Crome is
      a fine setting for "ideas." In fact, *Crome Yellow* sets
      the pattern for the next three works, since all lack the
      conventional framework of a carefully formed plot. As
      H's novels progress, the characters increasingly become
      mouthpieces for ideas. Balzac defined "novel of ideas";

George Eliot and E.M. Forster contributed such works;
but H is more like Peacock than he is like Eliot or
Forster in that he is interested in the play of ideas
more than in defending specific ideas. His later novels
continue this trend. (Kolek's essay promises more than
it delivers; it is mostly a summary of what many critics
have already said.)

300. ————. "Music in Literature--Presentation of Huxley's
      Experiment in 'Musicalization of Fiction.'" *Zagadnienia
      Rodzajów Literackich*, 14 (1972), 111-122.

Though H often represents music in his essays and fiction, he also recognizes that literature can't fully
express what music is about. H rejected the French
symbolists, who "subordinated sense to sound." He admires the "wholeness" of music, but he aims for a "multiplicity" in his novels. H's "musicalization" of fiction
is a matter of structure, not of sound: he imitates
variation, modulation, counterpoint--all typical modes
of polyphonic music. But his analogies with musical terminology don't produce anything really new; the characters he juxtaposes remain flat conceptions. He also
tries to depict simultaneous actions--but this effect
works well (as in *Brave New World*) only when the scenes
are short and the shifts are frequent. All of these
devices had been used earlier by other authors. After
Point Counter Point, H made no overt allusions to parallels of music and literature.

301. Koljević, Svetozar. "Pucine i obale Hakslijeve misli."
      Izraz (Sarajevo), 5 (1961), 55-72.

302. ————. "Smisao strukture Hakslijevog roma ideja."
      Delo (Belgrade), 4 (1958), 953-970.

303. Kooistra, J. "Aldous Huxley." *English Studies* (Amster-
      dam), 13 (Oct., 1931), 161-175.

H's writing style is a model of clarity, but his witti-
ness sometimes causes confusion about his real intention.
Do What You Will presents H's theory of balanced excesses. A life-worshipping person must oppose the
Pascalian worship of death. Not a man of one principle
(like Pascal), H is a man of many principles. He remarked, "I can't help wallowing in the excitement of
mysticism and the tragic sense ...," even though he has
defended science. H is definitely not a revolutionary,
although he has been accused of being one. "The Claxtons"

attacks sham spirituality; Burlap in *Point Counter Point* is subject to the same vitriolic attack. H did not trust the writing of drama because the most important thoughts of a character go unspoken. Yet he did try for success in the theater. Kooistra sees the themes of H expressed in the poems and carried throughout the other writings.

304. Koskimies, Rafael. "Aldous Huxley." *Valvoja-Aika* (Helsinki), 1932, pp. 549-565.

305. Krause, G. "Die Kulturkrise in der Utopia Aldous Huxleys," in his and Ludwig Borinski's *Die Utopia in der modernen englischen Literatur*. Frankfurt a/Main: Diesterweg, 1958.

306. Kristof Nagy, Istvan. "Huxley harom utopiaja." *Nagyvilag*, 8 (Nov., 1963), 1701-1704.

307. Kronenberger, Louis. "The Voices and Visions of Aldous Huxley." *Atlantic Monthly*, 226 (July, 1970), 100-101.

"Frequently Huxley's keen sense of human failing salts his letters without staining them; though outspoken and sharp, he is seldom petty or mean." He ridicules the Sitwells as publishers of the early magazine *Wheels*; he doesn't care for Strachey, nor for the novels of Woolf. H did an enormous amount of writing of books, reviews, letters, and he did a good deal of traveling, but the prolific writing decreases after *Eyeless in Gaza*; the tone of his writing also changes. H is a man of increased interests: Vedanta, visionary experiences from LSD and mescalin. He is seeking some overall understanding of the world. Shortly before his death, however, he said he remained an agnostic. His wide range of interests gave him not one, but several, publics.

308. Krutch, Joseph Wood. "Love--or the Life and Death of a Value." *Atlantic Monthly*, 142 (Aug., 1928), 199-210.

H sees love "as a sort of obscene joke." He "mocks sentiment with physiology"; but the joke turns bitter on the tongue.

309. Kuehn, Robert E. Introduction to his edited *Aldous Huxley: A Collection of Critical Essays* (see 30), pp. 1-7.

"The proper way of viewing Huxley is as a *moraliste*, a writer who has more in common with Montaigne and Pascal than with, say, Hardy or Conrad."

310. Kureshi, Maki. "Empirical Mysticism--An Essay in Ex-
      planation of Huxley's Theology." *Venture*, 2 (March,
      1961), 33-43.

      H's wide, eclectic knowledge "makes it difficult for
      him to accept exclusively any particular religion."
      The Perennial Philosophy rises above H's usual way of
      dealing with polarities; he searches for a God's-eye
      approach to solving the human problem, an answer which
      H tries to demonstrate empirically--not merely by philos-
      ophy, but by using parapsychology (telepathy, prevision,
      clairvoyance). He tries to find causal relationships
      between physical matter and the mind. Thus *The Perennial
      Philosophy* is a defense rather than a philosophical
      solution.

311. Lacassagne, Claude. "L'au-delà de l'utopie." *Recherches
      Anglaises et Américaines*, 6 (1973), 22-31.

      These utopias that are earthly paradises eliminate any
      chance of immortality (those of More, Morris, H). They
      are for the present and imply an eternity, and persons
      living in them are not distinguished as individuals.
      Anti-utopias (Swift's Houyhnhnms, Wells's *Island of Dr.
      Moreau*) have a sense of the mysterious and an immortality
      after death. Utopias make no place for the arts, which
      exist surreptitiously in anti-utopias. Utopias oppose
      the indulgence of sense impressions and the institution
      of parenthood. Actually, the utopia concept is a death
      wish because utopias are far from daily life and are in-
      accessible.

312. Lalou, René. "Les fins et les moyens d'Aldous Huxley."
      Études Anglaises (Vanves, France), 2 (Oct., 1938),
      353-371.

      For the last 15 years, H has been an English author of
      outstanding interest to French readers. The English
      have called H "too French," because of his intellect.
      Having had enough of Dostoevsky and H.G. Wells, French
      readers turned with delight to *Point Counter Point*. H
      was indebted to Gide's *The Counterfeiters*, but also to
      the vividness of Dickens. Lalou discusses the problems
      of translating H's titles into French: French readers do
      not recognize the allusions to Shakespeare or to Milton
      from literally rendered translations. Lalou also dis-
      cusses the unusual chronology of *Eyeless in Gaza*. In
      Ends and Means, H notes that the accomplished intellectual
      is far from being satisfied. H retraces in these pages
      his spiritual evolution; he is a rational idealist. Who

would have thought that the author of *Point Counter Point* would become a mystic, borrowing ideas from Buddhism and Christianity?

313.   ————. "Le sentiment de l'unité humaine chez Virginia Woolf et Huxley." *Europe* (Oct. 15, 1937), 266-272.

Lalou compares Woolf's *The Waves* and H's *Eyeless in Gaza*. Both novelists are concerned with the importance of time. H's novel uses complex time--the first seven chapters have dates, but they are not placed in chronological order; the same is true of the last four chapters. Collectively, the dates, rearranged, go from 1902 to 1931. The effect of the ending gives the reader the excitement of witnessing five actions conducted simultaneously, all pursued to their dramatic endings. Beavis, the hero of the novel, says there's no order in time. But H superimposes time, as in a work of art, on the novel, to group the episodes for psychological or dramatic value. Beavis reproaches Proust's attempt to recapture the past, when he should have sought to be free in life. Beavis parodies Wordsworth's wish to join all his days each to each in natural piety; he wants his days separated from each other by an impiety contrary to nature. Beavis is like Bernard in *The Waves*, with his multi-personality.

314.   Lancaster, Clay. "A Critique of the Taj Mahal." *Journal of the Society of Architectural Historians*, 15 (Dec., 1956), 7-11.

H first attacked the Taj Mahal as an example of vulgar architecture in *Jesting Pilate*, in which he compares it to the Pavilion at Brighton. H's objections to the Taj Mahal are its inordinate cost, the slenderness of the four flanking minarets, the monument's "deficiency of fancy, a poverty of imagination." H's English taste causes him to prefer St. Paul's as designed by Wren. Lancaster discusses the "bad taste" of St. Paul's and the superb design of the Taj Mahal.

315.   Lang, P. "Blick in sonderbare Zukunft: Aldous Huxley 'Welt wohin?'" *Neue Zurcher Zeitung*, Nov., 1933, p. 57.

316.   Lanoire, Maurice. "Aldous Huxley." *Revue de Paris*, 1 (Sept. 1, 1934), 145-162.

Lanoire emphasizes H's family background because heredity is significant. To show, to explain, to comment,

are the passions of H's novels, which always revolve
around him. Lanoire describes *Crome Yellow*, *Antic Hay*,
Those Barren Leaves; in the last, Calamy is in the tradition of Matthew Arnold; Chelifer, another man of letters,
is like H himself. Cardan expresses even more strongly
H's ironic antagonism. *Point Counter Point* shows H
giving himself most fully to recounting his intellectual
experiences. Lanoire praises H's familiarity with Anglo-
French culture and says that it would have pleased
Matthew Arnold.

317. La Rochelle, Drieu. "A propos d'un roman anglais."
   Nouvelle Revue Française, 19 (Nov., 1930), 721-731.

   H's *Point Counter Point* is a superb account of what
happens when morality and society deteriorate. It's a
bad novel, but a great book. There are several parallel
actions which don't touch each other, except momentarily
in the form of conversation. There is no progression of
incident. With a passion for knowledge, H attests to an
epoch which does not accord with other passions, and the
effect of the lack of those passions. The book is a
revelation of the misery of our arts and lives. La
Rochelle describes the five families who dominate *Point
Counter Point*; in each is an intellectual, and each is
hostile to the others. Rampion is anti-intellectual,
but from a reasoned viewpoint. Philosophy makes the intellectuals antagonists. For this reason, H takes the
advantage of writing fictionalized essays rather than
pure essays.

318. Laurent, Camille. "Thèmes et structures de 'Crome Yellow.'" *Annales de la Faculté des Lettres et Sciences
   Humaines de Nice*, 18 (1972), 47-54.

319. Lawrence, D.H. *The Letters of D.H. Lawrence*, ed. Aldous
   Huxley. New York: Viking, 1932. Pp. 765-766, 791.

   Lawrence comments on H's *Proper Studies*: "that funny
dry-mindedness and underneath social morality." Lawrence
said of *Point Counter Point*, "I have read *Point Counter
Point* with a heart sinking through my boot-soles and a
rising admiration.... your Rampion is the most boring
character in the book--a gas-bag. Your attempt at intellectual sympathy!--It's all rather disgusting...."
Of H's works in general, Lawrence said, "No, I don't like
his books: even if I admire a sort of desperate courage
of repulsion and repudiation in them.... I feel only half
a man writes the books--a sort of precocious adolescence."

320.   Lawrence, Frieda. *Not I, But the Wind*. New York:
        Viking, 1934.

        Frieda Lawrence makes very few direct comments about
        H, but her book contains some interesting photographs
        of Lawrence and H.

321.   Leeper, Geoffrey. "The Happy Utopias of Aldous Huxley
        and H.G. Wells." *Meanjin*, 24 (1965), 120-124.

        The "happy utopias" of Wells are no longer much admired
        or even noticed today. H, however, has "come full circle"
        from *Brave New World*, which "answered" Wells's *Men Like
        Gods*; "at the end of his life [he] gives us a happy
        utopia after all" (*Island*). Both H and Wells possessed
        "exceptional scientific knowledge," but Wells, "almost
        alone among writers of his generation, belonged to both
        of the Two Cultures."

322.   Lefèvre, Frédéric. "Une heure avec Aldous Huxley."
        Nouvelles Littéraires, 9 (Nov. 1, 1930), 1-2.

323.   LeGates, Charlotte. "Huxley and Breughel." *Western
        Humanities Review*, 29 (1975), 365-371.

        H's essay "Breughel" in *Along the Road* (1925) shows
        how Breughel juxtaposes the light and comic with the gro-
        tesque and despairing. H notes Breughel's use of large
        numbers of figures which are individually dissociated
        but which collectively create a pattern that closely
        imitates life. *Point Counter Point* uses the same strategy.
        H also admired Breughel's multiple vision of life. "The
        world is a horrible place; but in spite of this, or
        precisely because of this, men and women eat, drink and
        dance." *Antic Hay* compares with Breughel's orgiastic
        gaiety--the horror of World War I hangs over the antics
        of the novel. Breughel's "The Magpie on the Gallows,"
        "The Misanthrope," and "Blind Men" also juxtapose com-
        edy and horror. H was impressed by the multiple view-
        points of Breughel's "Ascent to Calvary"; H, too, uses
        multiple viewpoints in his novels. H praises Breughel's
        paintings as "anthropological handbooks," just as H's
        fiction shows curiosity about variant customs of various
        societies. Breughel didn't pursue classical beauty, nor
        was he interested in man as he ought to be. The same can
        be said of H's early novels. Throughout his life, he
        held that life should dominate art, not vice versa.

324.   Le Roy, Gaylord C. "A.F. 632 to 1984." *College English*,
        12 (Dec., 1950), 135-138.

H's *Brave New World* is better written, shows more fertile invention, than Orwell's *1984*, but *1984* was written almost 20 years after *Brave New World* and is a timelier book. *1984* cites war as permanent and necessary, whereas *Brave New World* ignores war as an issue. The slogans used in *Brave New World*, though restricting, are at least rational; those used in *1984*, which involve double think, show the modern attack on reason. The potential individualist is much worse off in *1984*. In *Brave New World*, sex is openly fulfilled; in *1984*, it is highly limited. In *Brave New World* the technology works very well; in *1984*, it often breaks down. Both novels present their ways of life as inevitable. Hence, neither serves a completely satiric function--to make the reader recoil from and resist the horrors portrayed.

325. Lewis, Wyndham. "The Taxi-cab Driver Test for Fiction," in his *Men Without Art*. London: Cassell, 1934. Pp. 295-304.

What passes as fiction these days is only intermittently literature; critics spend their time puffing novels that live for not more than two weeks. Critics are swamped by mediocrity, and so they are at last worn down and give in to it. The opening page of *Point Counter Point* (reproduced by Lewis before being identified) has nothing in it to suggest a high level to follow: it's vulgar, sentimental, the voice of lady-novelists. Great literature must be consistently great.

326. Linati, Carlo. *Scrittori anglo-americani d'oggi*. Milano: Corticelli, 1932. Pp. 9-20.

327. Livi, Grazia. "Huxley vi dice." *L'Europeo*, 685 (Nov. 30, 1958), 37-40.

328. Lloyd, Roger B. "The Odyssey of an Intellectual." *Modern Churchman*, 26 (Dec., 1936), 488-492.

Much of H's writing is anti-clerical: *Texts and Pretexts*, *Do What You Will*, *Point Counter Point*, *Proper Studies*. But now his attitude seems to have changed; *Eyeless in Gaza* is remarkably different from *Point Counter Point*. Anthony Beavis indeed seems to express H's own spiritual struggles. Many parallels exist between H's life and that of Beavis--most conspicuously, H's involvement in the Peace Crusade. H's great gifts which have been used to express derision of the Christian now seem to be used instead in its defense.

329. Logé, Marc. "Trois romanciers anglais contemporaine."
      Revue Politique et Litéraire, *Revue Bleue*, 65 (Sept.
      3, 1927), 534-539.

      H, Arthur Machen, and T.F. Powis are discussed.

330. Loos, Anita. "Aldous Huxley in California." *Harper's
      Magazine*, 228 (May, 1964), 51-55.

      H asked to meet Loos the year after *Gentlemen Prefer
      Blondes* was published; the four met several times there-
      after (H and his wife Maria, with Loos and her husband).
      Loos was living in California when H moved there; a
      group of close friends evolved: Edwin Hubble (astronomer)
      and wife; Gerald Heard; Christopher Isherwood; Charlie
      Chaplin; Paulette Goddard; Greta Garbo. H was interested
      in, and amused by, the oddity and variety of religious
      cults. There were Sunday lunches at Santa Monica with
      Loos, followed by walks on the beach. Later, the Huxleys
      also moved to Santa Monica to avoid the smog. Loos got
      H a commission to work on the script of *Pride and
      Prejudice* for MGM.

331. Lorus, Paul. "L'Inde vue par Huxley." *Revue des Deux
      Mondes*, 70 (July 1, 1942), 99-107.

332. Lovett, Robert Morss. "Aldous Huxley," in his and Helen
      S. Hughes's *The History of the Novel in England*.
      Boston: Houghton Mifflin, 1932. Pp. 453-455.

      The young H followed Jules Laforgue, whose "'Harlequin-
      Hamlet' pose accepts life as essentially tragic but re-
      fuses to take it seriously." H deliberately shocks the
      reader. The long short story is H's forte rather than
      the full-length novel. *Brief Candles* dramatizes H's
      theme, rather than just talking about it through charac-
      ters, as happens in the novels. H's duality of passion
      and reason was also the great preoccupation of the Meta-
      physical poets.

333. MacCarthy, Desmond. "Aldous Huxley." *Living Age*, 307
      (Oct. 9, 1920), 107-111; appeared first as "New Poets
      I--Mr. Aldous Huxley." *New Statesman*, 15 (Sept. 4,
      1920), 595.

      Potentially, H is an important poet, but emotion and
      intellect haven't yet fused in his work. He is not like
      Donne, however, who was passionate; H's poems are cold.
      In revulsion, H dives rather than soars--but the subcon-
      scious is difficult to express. H has science in his

blood; what this point of view creates is curious, gro-
tesque--though it is clear that H is homesick for the
old mythological world. *Leda* is smoothly written, but
it is in the old tradition. H's experiments with non-
traditional forms are, however, unsuccessful. The ideas
H expresses in his essay on poetry in the *Leda* volume
emerge from Mallarmé's *Divagations*. "These poems are
the turnings and churnings of a queasy stomach."

334. ————. "Notes on Aldous Huxley." *Life and Letters*, 5
     (Sept., 1930), 198-209; reprinted in his *Criticism*.
     London: Putnam, 1932. Pp. 235-246.

H's stories in *Brief Candles* show a faultless style
and a complete expression of theme. But H's identity
as a writer is bound to tire his readers: detached,
exacting, inconclusive, looking down, not up, at human
nature. The characters are not necessarily ignoble, but
H focuses on that in them which is demeaning. In *Point
Counter Point* Tantamount is a scientist, but he is gro-
tesquely viewed. H is the most deeply and widely cultured of modern novelists, a student of "Bovaryism" in
all of its forms. Scientific awareness makes it diffi-
cult for him to unify his impression of life. In H one
sees the danger of being unable to distinguish the
assimilator from the assimilated: there is something
ameboid about Philip Quarles's mind. As a writer, H is
"wide" but not "deep." H's "cool indifferent flux of
intellectual curiosity" makes him a more learned Anatole
France who has not yet achieved suavity.

335. McCormick, John. *Catastrophe and Imagination: An Inter-
     pretation of the Recent English and American Novel.*
     London: Longmans, 1957. Pp. 284-286.

H is a pure satirist, and satire defies foreign appreciation. But he is "an increasingly pretentious
bore." "Time has been unkind to Huxley, though just."
His early work was "bright, *chic*, cynical, anarchic";
the later work "monstrous and horrible." H is "the obsessed satirist who turns to allegory." But H really
indulged in "the typical English minor writer's escape
through madmen and fantasy, rather than true allegory."

336. Macdermott, Doireann. "The Zoologist of Fiction: Aldous
     Huxley." *Filologica Moderna* (Madrid), 37 (1969), 27-45

H often classifies his fictional characters according
to zoological procedure: animal and human behavior are

often seen as interchangeable. Greatly knowledgeable in zoology and biology, H praises Chaucer's interest in animals and their "human" behavior. Lions, wasps, bears, often appear in H's writing. Quarles of *Point Counter Point* wants to write a modern Bestiary. H was especially interested in the submarine world. Stoyte, in *After Many a Summer*, discovers that the Struldbug-like 5th earl of Gonister has become ape-like, and *Ape and Essence* emphasizes our simian ancestry.

337. McMichael, Charles T. "Aldous Huxley's *Island*: The Final Vision." *Studies in the Literary Imagination*, 1 (Oct., 1968), 73-82; also in *Studi Linguistici Italiani*, 1 (1968).

Many ideas from all of H's earlier works are here assembled in *Island*; in addition, the belief is expressed that woman is essential for the soul-uplifting of humanity. The novel is utopian, not dystopian; it emphasizes the need for freedom and for mysticism; thus only can man really know himself and the matter of the reality of the spirit. In the earlier works, H stressed that relations of the sexes were hopeless, but in *Island*, woman leads the spiritual quest. Thus H offers his solution to the sick spirit of modern society.

338. MacShane, Frank. "Forest Lawn." *Prairie Schooner*, 35 (Summer, 1961), 137-148.

H ridicules Forest Lawn Cemetery (California) in *After Many a Summer*, as does Evelyn Waugh in *The Loved One*. After describing Forest Lawn in some detail, MacShane concludes, "In its pretentious bad taste and saccharine religiosity it overawes thousands and revolts or amuses the discriminating." The opening of H's *After Many a Summer* describes briefly "The Beverly Pantheon" (Forest Lawn).

339. Maes-Jelinek, Hena. "Aldous Huxley's 'Collected Essays.'" *Revue des Langues Vivantes* (Brussels), 3 (1961), 253-261.

The essays represent 40 years of H's work, and they show the extraordinarily diverse interests of the author. He mastered knowledge of all sorts, but he used it to the purpose of illustrating his own ideas. The essay is the form that best suits H's type of mind. The essays selected for the collection are intended to show H's diversity. H insists on the sameness of human nature, regardless of differences in culture, history, environment. Man is generally stupid, ignorant, superstitious, inconsistent; he is capable of individual greatness, but this is canceled out by group action, which focuses only bad impulses. Religion and politics show men at their worst. Quantity and quality are irreconcilable in human behavior. The essays appeal, despite their pessimism, because of H's lucid style, his vast knowledge, his convincing logic. When he moralizes, the proposals sound utopian because they expect such vast changes to be made in human nature. The essays are strong on thought, but the feeling is usually directed by satirical motives rather than humane ones; anger, rather than love. H always stands aside, is not directly involved.

340. Maini, Darshan Singh. "Aldous Huxley--A Study in Disintegration." *Indian Review*, 54 (July, 1953), 294-296.

The Hollywood H has lost his hold on reality, is "neck-deep in his mystical dreams and fantasies." He has ceased to be a novelist because he presumes to be a prophet. The mysticism implied in the earlier novels becomes specific and definite with *After Many a Summer*. Most of H's fiction deplores the body and its impulses.

341. Mainsard, Joseph. "Aldous Huxley, moraliste." *Études, Revue Catholique d'Intérêt Général*, 214 (Feb., 1933), 279-301.

Kant and Nietzsche are the prophets to whom H declares himself disciple, but without much veneration. H felt that history was without value. He detested the Jews, whom he saw as the spiritual ancestors of Americans. Jews, he believed, were a sterile people who created neither a philosophy nor a politics, and very little literature. How much richer is polytheism! Catholicism is a bastard form of it. H often spoofed progressive evolution, which he often reversed, seeing the modern age as productive of monsters rather than higher types of humanity. One had best live life with all passion, ardor, joy, all the excesses of spirit and body; it is necessary to accumulate these to live without remorse and scruple. H felt that being a serious Christian was committing partial suicide. He accounted for St. Francis as Nietzsche did: vain and greedy for power, he sought it by an excessive display of asceticism and humility. *Brave New World* is a synthesis of all these moral views. H proposes a desperate optimism: the indispensable unity of life can be achieved by spontaneous equilibrium: each

excess finds another, and by mutual constraint they produce harmony. Just as H considered Baudelaire a returned
Christian, so H can be considered a returned Puritan.
For fear of asceticism, H proposes a mortification more
radical than that of the *Thebaid*: he deprived man of
reason and will.

342.   Mais, Stuart P.B. "The Poems of Aldous Huxley," in his
       Why We Should Read. London: Richards, 1921. Pp. 88-96.

       Because of his perversity of intellect, H is "the
       neurasthenic Rabelais of 1920." Sensuous beauty is to
       be found in the poem "Leda," but in other poems, H laughs
       at the transitoriness of human passion. Sometimes the
       verse isn't even poetry, but it can be funny on occasion.
       John Ridley in "Soles Occidere ..." is "feebly skeptical,
       inefficient, profoundly unhappy." Compared with Jove in
       "Leda," Ridley is anemic. H "makes us feel that we ought
       to be more fastidious, that we ought to think more, that
       we ought to accept less."

343.   Makino, Seiichi. "An Aspect of Aldous Huxley's Style,"
       in Braj B. Kachru and Herbert F.W. Stahlke, eds.
       Current Trends in Stylistics (Papers in Linguistics
       Monographs Series, 2). Edmonton, Alberta; and Cham-
       paign, Ill.: Linguistic Research, Incorporated, 1972.
       Pp. 243-250.

344.   Manolescu, Dan. "Dilema morala la Aldous Huxley."
       Orizont, 18 (July, 1975), 8.

345.   Manolescu, Nicolae. "Grefele lui Aldous Huxley." *Con-
       vorbiri Literare*, Feb., 1975, p. 2.

346.   Maraini, Yoi. "A Talk with Aldous Huxley." *Bermondsey
       Book* (London), 3 (June, 1926), 76-80.

       An interview with H at his villa in Montici, on the
       hillside outskirts of Florence, scene of "Young Archi-
       medes." H looks the part of a scholar, dreamer, poet.
       He says his books express that part of his mind which is
       the product of an excessively intellectual upbringing.
       Intellectuals tend to decry their vital instincts and
       find themselves removed from the mainstream of life.
       Dadaism in literature is the result of the absurd theory
       that form takes precedence over content. H's own aim is a
       perfect fusion of the novel and the essay. A great
       talker, avid listener, and prolific writer, he most ad-
       mires Dostoevsky among writers.

347.   Margolin, Jean-Claude. "Erasme et Aldous Huxley."
       Moreana, 15-16 (1967), 58-62.

       A characteristically "Huxleyan" dialogue occurs in
       Crome Yellow between the naive young poet Denis and the
       wise and aged Scogan. Scogan presents the idea of the
       rational state, in which men are classified into three
       species: those of intelligence, faith, and the multitude.
       H is writing a parody of Plato's Republic. Erasmus,
       says Scogan, typifies the man of reason; Luther, the
       man of faith. Erasmus placed higher in the ranking than
       Luther. Nevertheless, Luther's passion aroused men to
       bloody action, whereas Erasmus's more reasonable appeal
       was ignored. Scogan says that to get men to behave
       reasonably, one must persuade them in a maniacal manner.
       H is of course using ideas from Erasmus's *In Praise of
       Folly*. H saw in this example a sane and reasonable use
       of the forces of insanity. As he remarks, "The madman
       appeals to what is fundamental, the passion and the in-
       stincts. The philosopher, to what is superficial and
       supererogatory--reason." The man without passion is
       not human; he is equally deprived of intelligence.
       Erasmus himself said, "stupidum et ab omni prorsus humano
       sensu alienum."

348.   Markovic, Vida E. "Aldous Huxley." *Filoski Pregled*
       (Belgrade), 3-4 (1964), 103-118.

       Because it accepts more of life than any other H work,
       Point Counter Point is the only H novel that deserves
       to become a classic. The other novels stress man's tech-
       nological genius too much, ignore the complicated matters
       of human relationship. H's intellectual candor gives
       him a place in English letters. He can't remain loyal
       to past values, but he's too idealistic to confront the
       future--but his dealings with this problem have helped
       others to face it.

349.   Marovitz, Sanford E. "Aldous Huxley and the Visual Arts."
       Papers on Language and Literature, 9 (Spring, 1973),
       172-188.

       The Palanese guide in *Island* conveys ideas that are
       similar to H's own views as expressed in various essays
       written during the 10 years preceding the writing of the
       novel. These ideas differ markedly from those of H's
       early years: the new emphasis is on the arts, religions,
       mystical roles, as well as the traditional intellectual
       functions H had always attributed to the novel. H began

his career as a novelist with the idea of satirizing art,
but by 1930 he was more concerned with harmonizing the
disparate elements of life, and by 1945, in *The Perennial
Philosophy*, he openly accepted a religious dimension to
art. He had no tolerance for non-representational art,
and he always retained his attitude that art must be
rated first of all according to a moral concept.

350.   ———. "Aldous Huxley's Intellectual Zoo." *Philological
       Quarterly*, 48 (Oct., 1969), 495-507; reprinted in *Aldous
       Huxley: A Collection of Critical Essays*, ed. Robert E.
       Kuehn (see 30), pp. 33-45.

       H described man as "amphibian," "triphibian," "animal
       and intellect," and apelike yet capable of self-transcen-
       dence." Animal imagery is used to give physical identity
       to the people in H's novels who represent ideas as well.
       Quarles decides that the leading figure in the novel he
       is writing must be a zoologist who is writing a novel in
       his spare time. In *Crome Yellow*, Scogan looks like an
       extinct lizard (Bertrand Russell was the model for
       Scogan). Shearwater, in *Antic Hay*, is named for a
       skimming type of gull. In *Those Barren Leaves*, Miss
       Elver is described as bird-like: a cumbersome bird is
       used to suggest a moronic woman. In *Time Must Have a
       Stop*, Uncle Eustace is said to be like an elephant.
       Apes are the most common animal image, which comes to
       a climax in *Ape and Essence*.

351.   Matson, Floyd W. "Aldous and Heaven Too: Religion among
       the Intellectuals." *Antioch Review*, 14 (Sept., 1954),
       293-309.

       H's conversion is an important model for modern times:
       to show how intellectuals can adopt a religion. H is
       not an originator, but rather is significant because he
       defines the classic means of his accomplishments. He
       set the example of searching for and achieving values,
       even though his specific values may not be acceptable
       to all.

352.   Matsushima, Takeshi. "Aldous Huxley no Buntai ni Tsuite,"
       in *Gengo to Buntai: Higashida Chiaki Kyoju Kanreki
       Kinen Ronbunshu*. Osaka: Osaka Kyoiku Tosho, 1975.
       Pp. 185-194.

       This essay deals with H's style.

353.   Matter, William W. "The Utopian Tradition and Aldous
       Huxley." *Science-Fiction Studies*, 2 (1975), 146-151.

Brave New World, *Ape and Essence*, and *Island* show H's awareness of and dislike for many aspects of utopian literature. Until the 20th century, utopian literature had largely been positive in tone. H prefaced *Brave New World* with a comment by Nicholas Berdiaeff: in the new century men may seek to avoid utopias because they prefer a less perfect, but more free, society. H disallowed the view that science could bring a perfect world. *Island*, nevertheless, is close to being a traditional utopia. The outsider, Will Farnaby, is skeptical, but he's won over by the unshakeable logic of the people of Pala. *Ape and Essence* shows the worst characteristics of East and West (it's anti-utopia), even though H himself hoped for the best of East and West to merge. In *Island* science serves man, though *Ape and Essence* and *Brave New World* show the opposite. In *Island*, H finally permits heroic struggle and sorrow to enter his island paradise.

354. Maugham, W. Somerset. *Introduction to Modern English and American Literature*. Philadelphia: Blakiston, 1944. Pp. 335-336.

Maugham ranks H's essays with Hazlitt's. Qualities needed for a good essayist are character, encyclopedic knowledge, humor, ease of manner, ability to combine entertainment and instruction. H didn't succeed as a novelist because of "deficiency of sympathy with human beings." He sees people as an anatomist does. Still, he has high readability, narrative skill, and originality.

355. Maurois, André. "Aldous Huxley." *La Revue Hebdomadaire*, 44 (May 4, 1935), 60-82.

Like his great-uncle Matthew Arnold, H had a great knowledge of France and French culture. *Point Counter Point* is not a chronological novel; it is a compendium novel. H represents, better than any other writer, the attitude toward life which belongs to his generation, both in England and in France. He was an encyclopedist; indeed, *Encyclopedia Britannica* was among his favorite reading. H believed that a novelist should be an amateur zoologist—depicting people as if he were studying animals or insects. When he traveled, he was deeply interested in the variety of customs he observed. H is highly intellectual, but aware of the risks of being overintellectual. There is courage in H's hard freedom of intellect, courage that is almost a voluptuous masochism. Intelligence, boredom, desire, a cruel sensuality, all of these traits of Baudelaire inhere in it.

356. ————. "Aldous Huxley's Progress." *Living Age*, 339
        (Sept., 1930), 52-55.

     With *Point Counter Point* H joined the company of the
     great novelists. It is not a "novel-river," but rather
     a novel of additions; it is not a thesis novel, but one
     of intellectual counterpoint. Quarles is like H the
     novelist; Rampion expresses the ideas that H sympathizes
     with. Rampion's ideas are similar to those of H in his
     essay on Pascal, which opposes the doctrine of *memento
     mori*; Rampion attacks St. Francis and Shelley. One must
     be neither a mystic nor a voluptuary. H is the only
     living novelist with a solid scientific culture, but
     sometimes his learning submerges the novels. His charac-
     ters possess the force of the characters of Dickens.

357. ————. *Magiciens et logiciens*. Paris, 1935; trans. by
        Hamish Miles as *Prophets and Poets*. New York: Harper,
        1935. Pp. 287-312.

     This series of studies of English authors describes
     those who have played an important part after the "begin-
     ning of the century in the spiritual moulding of one or
     two generations of human beings." The writers include
     Kipling, H.G. Wells, G.B. Shaw, G.K. Chesterton, Conrad,
     Strachey, D.H. Lawrence, H, K. Mansfield. Written for a
     French, popular audience, the book betrays the weakness
     of a series of lectures; it leads to no overall conclu-
     sions.

358. ————. "Maurois despre Huxley." *Tribuna*, 2 (May 18,
        1967), 8.

359. ————. Preface to *Point Counter Point*, trans. Jules
        Castier. Paris: Plon, 1930.

360. ————. "Private Universes," in his *A Private Universe*.
        New York: Appleton, 1932. Pp. 104-109.

     Maurois says that H's views on Pascal are "those in-
     dividual views of the world, impenetrable each to others,
     which men take as truths and yet are merely projections
     of their own states." Pascal's sick body was naturally
     Christian; it couldn't be pagan.

361. May, Keith. "Accepting the Universe: The 'Rampion-
        Hypothesis' in *Point Counter Point* and *Island*." *Studies
        in the Novel*, 9 (Winter, 1977), 418-427.

     Lawrence appealed to H in that H found in him a "con-
     fident, intuitive rejection of Platonic idealism."

"Lawrence apprehended God as the *being* of each individual plant or creature, existence rather than essence, yet quite beyond analysis or explanation." Throughout his career, H despised all the attitudes expressed in *Point Counter Point* other than Rampion's own. In this favorite character, H was inveighing against living by one ruling principle. Rampion is content with Shelley's dome of many-colored glass, has no wish for the white radiance of eternity. Spandrell, his opposite, seeks this eternity in Beethoven's A minor Quartet. But Spandrell is a death-worshipper, the final stage of the self narrowed to any single principle. When these two characters debate about music (before Spandrell's death scene), Rampion is almost won over by his opponent, but not quite. The conflict expresses an unresolved problem with H himself. *Island* is the synthesis that H could not make when he wrote *Point Counter Point*; in this last novel, H "came down to earth again, but an earth shot through with celestial gleams." Hence H's final point is that there is no Manichaeism, no Platonic idealism, no unknowable God—only a "non-stop, perpetual creation." H found further understanding of Rampion in Abraham H. Maslow's *Motivation and Personality* (1954), a book which claimed to "have discovered empirically the phenomenon of the 'self-actualizing' individual." This person's chief merit is his ability to reconcile psychological dichotomies.

362. Maynard, Theodore. "Aldous Huxley, Moralist." *Catholic World*, 144 (Oct., 1936), 12-22.

H was at first thought to be a wit, dilettante, satirist, without a moral viewpoint; but as his moral viewpoint has emerged, his former admirers have become critical of him. Alexander Henderson thinks H is moving toward Communism. Gerald Vann thinks H will move toward Catholicism. H has this in common with Dickens: "the characters are observed rather than understood ... and each writer is at his best when he is funny." But none of H's characters comes to life in the way Dickens's characters do. Maynard admires H's stories "The Claxtons" and "Chawdron." He holds that H's essays are weakened by loquacity, but are often dazzling. *Texts and Pretexts* is his most satisfactory book. Some of the humor in *Brave New World* verges on clowning. H's own brand of humanism includes a sort of polytheism, the purpose of which is to enable man to live with all of his faculties and properly exercise them. "When writing of Christianity he seems to make no distinction between Catholic and Calvinist, Manichee and Puritan."

363. Meckier, Jerome. "Aldous Huxley: Satire and Structure."
      Wisconsin Studies in Contemporary Literature, 7 (1966),
      284-294.

      Meckier shows how Chelifer in *Those Barren Leaves*
      recognizes that being normal is no longer common; there-
      fore, he deliberately adopts strange, odd mannerisms
      already inherent in other people. Hence, Chelifer is
      like an artist in an age that has no values for a guide.
      In this novel and in his others, H welded satire and
      structure together by the use of his method of counter-
      point.

364. ―――. "Cancer in Utopia: Positive and Negative Elements
      in Huxley's *Island*." *Dalhousie Review*, 54 (1974-1975),
      619-633.

      "Unlike most utopians, Huxley tries to confront several
      inescapably negative factors in his perfect society, and
      these ultimately convince him that utopia is not of this
      world." "Plans for Pala's destruction begin almost
      simultaneously with the account of its merits." Will
      Farnaby comes to admire Pala, but he contributes to its
      ruin. The exposition in *Island* is more dramatic than it
      is in earlier utopian novels because it becomes Will's
      therapy. McPhail is like Prospero; Colonel Dipa is like
      Caliban. Will's Aunt Mary died of cancer; so does Dr.
      McPhail's wife. H's mother, and his first wife, died of
      cancer; H himself was suffering from it when he wrote
      Island. The greed inspired by Pala's oil deposits is
      also a metaphorical cancer that destroys the island.
      Will's drug experience brings him both heaven and hell;
      there is no such thing as utopia alone.

365. ―――. "The Case of the Modern Satirical Novel: Huxley,
      Waugh, and Powell." *Studies in the Twentieth Century*,
      14 (1974), 21-42.

      Common elements shared by these authors' satirical works
      include: (1) The works make profound but discomforting
      observations about the nature of reality; (2) The symbol
      embodies observation in the text and it affects the
      novel's structure; (3) The reader becomes the ultimate
      target; (4) The satire always has more to say than nega-
      tion has; (5) Animal imagery discounts all assumptions
      about inevitable human progress; (6) Time is the novel-
      ist's weapon, even if it leads to the Apocalypse.

366. ―――. "Dickens and the Dystopian Novel," in *The Novel
      and Its Changing Form*, ed. R.G. Collins. Winnipeg:
      University of Manitoba Press, 1972. Pp. 51-58.

Meckier discusses the similarities between *Hard Times* and *Brave New World*.

367. ————. "Fifty Years of Counterpoint." *Studies in the Novel*, 9 (Winter, 1977), 367-372.

Philip Quarles in *Point Counter Point* recognizes that once the world's "essential multitudinousness is displayed, the modern world is no more rational than it is romantic, no more Newtonian than it is Christian, Shelleyan, or Freudian." None of the paradigms fits. After fifty years, *Point Counter Point* is still a viable novel. It is the prime example of the novel of ideas, it is a supreme satirical novel, and it achieves H's large ambitions. Its power to demolish respectable metaphysical complacencies remains unrivaled, and it is worthy of the careful study merited by *Bleak House*, *Middlemarch*, or *Ulysses*.

368. ————. "The Hippopotamian Question: A Note on Aldous Huxley's Unfinished Novel." *Modern Fiction Studies*, 16 (Winter, 1970-1971), 505-514.

H never lost interest in the novel, the genre in which he achieved most. One chapter only was completed, before H's death, of a novel he meant to follow *Island*; the chapter was published in *This Timeless Moment* by Laura Achera Huxley. In this chapter Edward Darley, aged 60, recalls his tenth and eleventh birthdays. Perhaps this new novel was to have followed the method of *Eyeless in Gaza*, which gives various perspectives on the life of Anthony Beavis. "Darley would be a sort of summation of all the self-portraits in the previous novels." H was perhaps planning "the Bildungsroman of the 20th century man of intellect." The scope of the new novel was to have been broader than that of any other H novel, covering the years 1890-1962. H wanted to model the new work on polyphony, not on counterpoint. This novel's being written in the first person is unusual for H, but the character of Darley seems to be the outgrowth of many characters whose notebooks form parts of H's earlier novels.

369. ————. "Housebreaking Huxley: Saint Versus Satirist." *Mosaic*, 5 (1972), 165-177.

Meckier reviews H's *Letters*, as well as books on H by Brander (see 5), Holmes (see 19), Bowering (see 4), and Watts (see 47), along with H's *Collected Poetry*. "One cannot substitute the would-be saint of the '60's for the satirist of the '20's because the roles of saint and

satirist were never mutually exclusive for Huxley."
The books reviewed tend to exalt the later H over the
earlier one. Smith's selection of letters is problemat-
ical; there are serious gaps. Brander and Holmes aren't
very familiar with the earlier scholarship on H, and
they depend too much on Smith's edition of the letters.
Brander misunderstands *Crome Yellow*, *Antic Hay*, *Point
Counter Point*, *Those Barren Leaves*. He does better with
the later books, e.g., *The Perennial Philosophy*, because
he likes them. Holmes's book is guilty of the autobiographical fallacy; he also makes H sound like an escapist.
Holmes doesn't really contribute anything new about H,
but he has read him thoroughly; he has covered H's
poetry better than anyone else has. He mistakenly sees
Island as resolving all of H's problems. Bowering is
more balanced in his account, but he too finally gives
in to H's being "better" as a mystic. Bowering doesn't
see that to the contrapuntalist H, dichotomies are coun-
terpoints, not permanent oppositions. Meckier says
Bowering's book is a good introduction to H for those
not familiar with H criticism--but that Atkins' study,
and his own, are better. Watts's study generally ignores
H's earlier works, defends the later ones on literary
grounds. The *Collected Poetry*, edited by Watt, shows
why H turned from verse to fiction, but there are as yet
no adequate studies of H's poetry. Later criticism
should read H as a poet of ideas, predecessor to the
novelist of ideas. The real problem in current H criticism is that critics haven't read each other--works have
come too close together. New work should be done on the
poetry, the essays, the short stories. Much of the
present difficulty results because H has attracted many
readers of specialized interests, and the critics reviewed in this essay are at fault for seeing him more as
a man than as a writer. (This is probably the most important critical article on H and H studies.)

370.   ————. "Mysticism or Misty Schism? Huxley Studies since
          World War Two." *British Studies Monitor*, 5 (Fall,
          1974), 3-35.

          In the 1940's, critics were "summing up" H in essays
          as if he were finished. Many no longer took him serious-
          ly because of his shift to mysticism in 1936. Yet H's
          last six novels contain some of his bitterest satire.
          He preferred to be both artist and philosopher; to judge
          him as only one or the other is unjust. *The Perennial
          Philosophy* doesn't prove that H had a personal experience

as a mystic; it is his best attempt to prove that mystics
of different ages and places share common attributes.
"Contrary to Hoffman, Dyson, Bentley and others, the
later novels of Huxley are consistently contrapuntal,
even *Island*, which is ostensibly the least dramatic."
Those critics who recognize a coherent progression in
H's works include Rolo, C.A. King, Matson, Enroth, Quina,
Watts, Hoffman, and Baldanza. (This is an excellent
survey of H criticism of the 1940's and thereafter; along
with "Housebreaking Huxley" (see 369), it completes the
best account of H studies.)

371.   ————. "Our Ford, Our Freud and the Behaviorist Con-
spiracy in Huxley's *Brave New World*." *Thalia: Studies
in Literary Humor*, 1 (1978), 35-59.

372.   ————. "Philip Quarles's Passage to India: *Jesting
Pilate*, *Point Counter Point*, and Bloomsbury." *Studies
in the Novel*, 9 (Winter, 1977), 445-467.

In *Jesting Pilate*, H shows his disgust at India's in-
attentiveness to the material world. H's trip to India
in 1925-26 made him see English intellectuals who longed
for spiritual life as "barbarians of the intellect." In
Point Counter Point, Rampion is the only non-Procrustean
of the lot. Chapter 6 of *Point Counter Point*, in which
Quarles returns to England from India, is the one in
which he plans to write a novel like the one in which H
portrays him. India has bemused Quarles with its bewilder-
ing diversity, and "disillusionment with India explains
the militant antispiritual theme in *Point Counter Point*."
Religion is the refuge of grotesques; only Rampion's
noble savagery escapes H's invective. The allusions to
India in the novel discredit or depress the characters
who make them. In fact, *Jesting Pilate* and *Point Counter
Point* say the opposite of what Forster says in *A Passage
to India*: for H, there can be no empathy between East
and West. "Where Forster tests Bloomsbury values in
India to discover their universal validity, Huxley sets
a chapter in India to reveal that discontinuity between
men and between mind and matter is worldwide." Numerous
parodies of *A Passage to India* exist in *Point Counter
Point*, just as another Bloomsbury novel, *To the Lighthouse*, is also parodied. H's purpose is to redo in an
opposite spirit the famous scenes of Forster and Woolf,
and hence H allows none of the structural recovery that
appears in *Passage* and *Lighthouse*. For H, the idealism
of Bloomsbury has no meaning for modern life; Bloomsbury

fails because it tries to reinstate a worn-out humanism
victimized by war and reality. With one exception, H's
characters stay trapped in mutually exclusive provinces.
The exception is the meeting and merging of Mark and
Mary Rampion; they "connect," as Bloomsbury wished to do,
but H relished their doing so by Lawrence's methods rather
than by those of Bloomsbury. Lawrence's method is wholeness before connection, inner balance before association.
"The repugnance H feels for India entices him toward
Lawrence, but his parodies of Forster's Indian novel and
Bloomsbury values comprise all humanist solutions to the
human condition."

373. ————. "Quarles among the Monkeys: Huxley's Zoological
      Novels." *The Modern Language Review*, 68 (April, 1973),
      268-282.

      Both H and Quarles of *Point Counter Point* are actual
      experts in zoology. Quarles is less humane than H; he
      always reduces his friends, in his own concept, to animal
      level. The zoologists Quarles cites also explored human
      body types many years before H learned about Sheldon's
      psycho-physical classifications. Zoologists appear in
      several other H novels; animal imagery often is used in
      Island, *Antic Hay*, *After Many a Summer*, *Ape and Essence*.
      "The world always seemed to trap the enlightened man
      among contemporaries backward enough to appear simian."

374. ————. "Shakespeare and Aldous Huxley." *Shakespeare
      Quarterly*, 22 (Spring, 1971), 129-135.

      This is a more general treatment than that of Robert
      Wilson (586) on this subject; it includes an account of
      H's final essay, "Shakespeare and Religion." The Shake-
      speare plays from which H chose his novel titles must
      have been most meaningful to him. All three utopian
      novels allude to Shakespeare. *Brave New World* counter-
      points its Shakespeare allusions to ones relating to
      works by H.G. Wells. "Both Huxley and Shakespeare are
      awed by the 'pluralistic mystery,' by the multiplicity
      of viewpoints on any given subject."

375. ————. "Sir George Sitwell's Contributions to *Crome
      Yellow*." *Modern Fiction Studies*, 23 (Summer, 1977),
      235-239.

      Osbert Sitwell's anecdote about his father, Sir George,
      collecting peachstones for the war effort was used by H
      in *Crome Yellow*, but H transfers the incident to Mrs.

Budge. The modifications indicate H's gift for satiric
inventiveness: Mrs. Budge's absurdly limited cause typifies "socially useless, morally perverse, spiritually
blind" characters such as appear in H's early novels.
Osbert Sitwell was miffed that H used the anecdote without his permission. However, H disguised the incident
much more elaborately than he did the accounts of many
other characters in *Crome Yellow*, most of whom are based
on real people. Philip Morrell, the real owner and host
of Garsington, where H met many artists, writers, and
intellectuals, is not much like Henry Wimbush of *Crome
Yellow*; Henry is much more like Sir George Sitwell. Sir
George himself often took to bed to avoid houseguests,
and the fictional Wimbush wants "to get rid of all human
contacts." Both men are antiquarians, and prefer objects,
especially buildings, to people. Osbert Sitwell reports
Sir George's eccentricities in his *Great Morning!* Sir
George's castle near Florence is similar to Mrs. Aldwinkle's castle in *Those Barren Leaves*. Wimbush in *Crome
Yellow* is a composite (as many of H's characters are) of
two real people; in this case, of Morrell and Sitwell.

376. Meller, Horst. "Aldous Huxleys affischer Tithones," in
     Lebende Antike: Symposium für Rudolf Sühnel, ed. Horst
     Meller and Hans-Joachim Zimmerman. Berlin: E. Schmidt,
     1968. Pp. 473-488.

377. Merton, Thomas J. "Huxley's Pantheon." *The Catholic
     World*, 152 (Nov., 1940), 206-209.

     H is not a distinguished philosopher, despite his wit,
     erudition, and skill as a writer. Following *After Many
     a Summer*, his mysticism leads him to believe that the
     world is illusory, that matter doesn't exist, and is in
     fact evil. Man can be purified by being detached from
     matter. H's central theme in *After Many a Summer*, the
     vanity of materialism, is buried in too much extraneous
     material. Mr. Propter is "the dullest character in the
     history of the English novel." His soliloquies attack
     anthropomorphic religions. *After Many a Summer* isn't
     out to save the world, just a few well-disposed individ-
     uals. H should stop writing novels and return to what
     he writes best: essays.

378. Miles, O. Thomas. "Three Authors in Search of a Charac-
     ter." *Personalist*, 46 (Winter, 1965), 65-72.

     Miles discusses three authors and one work by each: H's
     Brave New World, Miller's *Death of a Salesman*, and Camus's

Exile and the Kingdom. *Brave New World* exhibits a
society as it was created by man; but man becomes obso-
lete in the rapidly changing society he made. In his
introduction to the later editions of this work and in
the sequel, H said that man lacks the alternative of
sanity in a world almost wholly insane.

379. Millichap, Joseph A. "Huxley's *Brave New World*, Chapter
      V." *Explicator*, 32 (1973), Item 1.

      Grushow (see 228) and Hébert (see 247), who both see
parallels between the opening of Chapter V of *Brave New
World* and Gray's "Elegy," fail to see that H's main purpose is to satirize the sentimental attitudes of the
"Elegy." The area around Stoke Poges in *Brave New World*
has been converted to the uses of a crematorium to process
corpses into fertilizer. Gray's "Elegy" romanticizes the
commonality of the common man; so does *Brave New World*,
except that H satirizes the sentiment that Gray takes
seriously. *Island* also parodies the "Elegy" by referring
to "the mute inglorious Hitlers, the village Napoleons...."

380. Minton, Arthur. "Huxley's 'Leda.'" *Explicator*, 7 (Feb.,
      1949), 31.

      The poem has two major themes: the primacy of the sex
drive, and a satirical view of anthropomorphism.

381. Mirski, Dimitri. *The Intelligentsia of Great Britain*,
      trans. Alec Brown. New York: Covici Friede Publishers,
      1935. Pp. 128-130; 202-203.

      This amusingly biased account deals with such literary
groups as the Bloomsbury circle; biased by a Marxist perspective, it remarks, "Huxley depicts the putrescent
capitalist class with exceptional vim." But H is "unable to use his records and sketches as material for a
work of art, and is completely devoid of historical
understanding." Mirski scolds H for making Illidge, the
communist who turns assassin in *Point Counter Point*, ignorant of Einstein, Eddington, the quantum theory.
Marxists, according to Mirski, are far better educated
than H allows.

382. Miserocchi, Manlio. "Ricordo di Aldous Huxley." *Nuova
      Antologia*, 492 (Sept., 1964), 140-143.

      Living in America, H saw a paradox of the infinite
spirit confronting finite earthly existence. Following
Baudelaire, in whom he took great interest, devotion to

art becomes meaningful because pain is the only way to redeem us from human error. H extends to further dimensions the torments described by Kafka and Freud. He recognizes the errors made by the young in their search for a synthetic heaven. H's broad knowledge is shown by his concern about the population explosion and food shortages. His lay humanism bears comparison with Christian humanism.

383. Misra, G.S.P., and Nora Satin. "The Meaning of Life in Aldous Huxley." *Midwest Quarterly*, 9 (July, 1968), 351-363.

Brave New World shows that even when it is used constructively, technology dehumanizes man. Used destructively, it produces a world of horror such as appears in *Ape and Essence*. Technology equates happiness with external objects. "Scientific modernism is turning the staunchest mathematical physicists into mystics," H writes in *Those Barren Leaves*. H followed Buddhist thought, which holds that sorrow originates in the feeling of individuality. *Eyeless in Gaza* also condemns individuality; unity brings good and peace. Science and technology are not inherently bad; they become so when they are used as ends in themselves rather than as means.

384. Moeller, Charles. "Huxley: ou la religion sans amour," in his *Littérature du XXe siècle et Christianisme*. Tournai: Casterman, 1954. Pp. 178-219.

H was always self-consciously the "enfant terrible" of literature. His works fall into two categories: humanistic (through *Point Counter Point*) and mystical (the works written thereafter). In the latter group of works, H sought for the common denominator of all religions. He rejected the religions of revelation, philosophy in the classical sense, and he adopted an empirical philosophy to serve his own interests.

385. Molina Quiròs, Jorge. *La novela utópica inglesa (Tomás Moro, Swift, Huxley, Orwell)*. Madrid: Prensa Española, 1967.

386. Monch, W. "Der Acte gratuit und das Schicksalsproblem bei André Gide und Aldous Huxley." *Zeitschrift für französischen und englischen Unterricht*, 30 (1931), 429-435.

387. Montgomery, Marion. "Aldous Huxley's Incomparable Man

in *Antic Hay*." *Discourse: A Review of the Liberal Arts*, 3 (Oct., 1960), 227–232.

Everyone in *Antic Hay* is unhappy, and each follows what he thinks is the ideal Complete Man. Lypiatt, Gumbril, Sr., and Coleman are busy, talkative idealists. Mercaptan and Gumbril, Jr. are different, negative, and hence limited idealists. H's irony is to give opportunities to the unmotivated, who of course ignore these chances. H makes many contrasts between the noble incompetents and the competent ignobles.

388.   ————. "Lord Russell and Madame Sesostris." *Georgia Review*, 28 (1974), 269–282.

Eliot's world and that in *Crome Yellow* are comparable. Eliot noted that the characters in *Crome Yellow* were only thinly disguised versions of houseguests at Lady Ottoline Morrell's circle at Garsington. The Wimbushes-Morrells created a haven for World War I conscientious objectors. H invents a Mme. Sesostris in *Crome Yellow* (who is really Scogan, dressed as a fortune teller at a country fair). H said he borrowed the idea from *Jane Eyre*--but Scogan himself is much like Bertrand Russell. Though they were friends for a time, with some interests in common, by the 1930's H and Eliot parted in their philosophical and religious views--H to Eastern thought, Eliot to Anglicanism.

389.   Moody, C. "Zamyatin's *We* and English Antiutopian Fiction." *Unisa English Studies*, 14 (1976), 24–33.

Zamyatin's *We* preceded *Brave New World* by 10 years. An English translation was made in 1924, but H said he never heard of it before he wrote *Brave New World*. Orwell knew the book well before he wrote *1984*. Zamyatin's view blends two antipathetic elements of Russian thought: Marxist dialectics and Dostoevsky's defense of the irrational as the final source of man's independence. Zamyatin's *We* sees nothing good to come of the Bolshevik Revolution, and warns against technological regimentation. Zamyatin, hearing that H said he hadn't read *We* before writing *Brave New World*, remarked, "these ideas are in the air we breathe." Zamyatin knew Wells, and Wells's novels; *We* satirizes books like Wells's *Men Like Gods*. *Men Like Gods* is one of H's antipathies in *Brave New World*, which was first conceived, according to H, as a parody of *Men Like Gods*.

390. Moore, Harry T. *The Intelligent Heart, the Story of D.H. Lawrence*. New York: Farrar, 1954. Passim.

H had never known anyone in his own family who was anything like Lawrence. H believed that Lawrence's beliefs declined for the last third of his novel *The Plumed Serpent*. H and his wife Maria renewed Lawrence's interest in painting. H remained the calm, independent friend that Lawrence needed during times of stress. Lawrence said of *Point Counter Point*, "I refuse to be Rampioned. Aldous's admiration for me is only skin-deep...." The paths of H and Lawrence often intersected in their travels to evade the English climate. H saw Lawrence as "the crusader of ... the reuniting of animal and thinker." Rebecca West remarked, "Even Aldous Huxley, who is so far above the rest of us, feels that he has to look up to Lawrence."

391. Mortimer, Raymond. "Bombination; Review of *Crome Yellow*." *Dial*, 72 (June, 1922), 631-633.

"When the 'amusing' becomes the principal interest, and the only criterion, all capacity and inclination for moral judgment naturally disappears." H was the most extreme example of this approach in England. The subject of *Crome Yellow* is similar to that of Peacock's novels, or of Douglas's *South Wind*. "Brain has become an illness, a parasitic growth." H takes nothing seriously, least of all his own talents.

"Mr. Huxley's Fears." *Commonweal*, 68 (May 30, 1958), 221.

H has strongly expressed his fears about controlling the minds of the masses by the use of drugs, mass media, subliminal advertising, etc. *Brave New World* seems to be borne out as a prophecy of these more recent technological developments.

Muir, Edwin. "Aldous Huxley." *Nation* (New York), 122 (Feb. 10, 1926), 144-145; reprinted in his *Transition: Essays on Contemporary Literature*. New York: Viking, 1926. Pp. 101-113.

H's early rise to fame is unusual; Lawrence and Eliot became known much more slowly. The main interest of H is the pricking of illusions. Beneath his seeming freedom "there persists a certain conventionality, a certain banality." In *Those Barren Leaves*, he misses his chance with Mrs. Aldwinkle; he never reveals her soul, he merely shows her as a nuisance. "His art is not one of compre-

hension; it is one of exposure." H has "the moral rage,
without the morality, of the satirist." The novel gave
H a loose form for his intellectual fantasies.

394. Muller, H.J. "Apostles of the Lost Generation: Huxley,
      Hemingway," Chapter 21 in his *Modern Fiction: A Study
      of Values*. New York: Funk & Wagnalls, 1937. Pp. 383-
      403.

      H and Hemingway are the most important post-World War I
      writers. *The Sun Also Rises* and *Point Counter Point* are
      excellent companion pieces. *Point Counter Point* is a
      synthesis of everything that H had done previously in
      fiction. It owes much to Gide's *The Counterfeiters*; both
      books relate the heterogeneity of modern society. H is
      clearly aware of his limitations as a novelist, but he
      works well within them. *Point Counter Point*, in H's own
      words, is "a made-up affair": he talks about his subject
      rather than dramatizing it. The characters have no real
      life of their own, never take the story into their own
      hands. H's synthesis is incomplete, however, because he
      leaves out the nobler element of human character. "*Brave
      New World* is a cheap professional performance, ingenious
      and amusing at first, but presently as dull as a prolonged
      vaudeville skit whose point one has caught." H was mis-
      understood by Marxist critics as fostering their cause.
      "Despite his flippancy, Huxley misses the Absolute more
      than any other emancipated modern." But the faith "dis-
      covered" in *Eyeless in Gaza* is also a "made-up affair."

395. Muret, Maurice. "Un roman du début de M. Aldous Huxley."
      Journal des Débats, March 8, 1939.

396. Muzina, Matej. "Reverberations of Jung's *Psychological
      Types* in the Novels of Aldous Huxley." *Studia Romanica
      et Anglica Zagrebiensia*, 33-36 (1972-1973), 305-334.

397. ————. "Znanost i likovi Huxleyvih romana ideja."
      Kolo, 11-12 (1967).

398. Nagarejan, S. "Religion in Three Recent Novels of Aldous
      Huxley." *Modern Fiction Studies*, 5 (Spring, 1959),
      153-165.

      Nagarejan approves of H's emphasis on religious themes
      in his later work, but the emphasis is inadequate, and H
      misunderstands his sources. His failure to use Christian
      insight in his fiction limits its potential for success.

399. Nazareth, Peter. "Aldous Huxley and His Critics."
      English Studies in Africa, 7 (March, 1964), 65-81.

      Nazareth cites the importance of Dyson's essay "Aldous
Huxley and the Two Nothings" (see 178) by reopening the
subject of H's importance as a novelist. But he says
that the best way to read H is in the vein of Swift, Ben
Jonson, and Wilde. Like Jonson and Wilde, H specializes
in two-dimensional portraits. Several critics misunder-
stand H, thinking his cynicism degrades humanity. H has
no moral norms within the novels; he simply states them
implicitly by presenting their negatives. Rampion isn't
really the norm of *Point Counter Point*, nor is Quarles.
Brave New World shows the world split into two unnormative
societies: the "happy" technological world, and the "free"
primitive New Mexican reservation. But the solution is
not to recede to primitivism (H didn't totally accept the
ideas of Lawrence). Nazareth defends H as a novelist of
ideas, and he defends *Eyeless in Gaza* against the criticism of Dyson. *Eyeless in Gaza* deals with the theme of
detached freedom. Nazareth agrees with Dyson that the
novels beginning with *Time Must Have a Stop* are inferior.
But then, there is too much cerebral activity in all of
H's novels; his is a subdued vitality when compared to
that of Jonson, Swift, Fielding, and Conrad.

400. Nehls, Edward. *D.H. Lawrence: A Composite Biography*.
      Madison: University of Wisconsin Press, 1958. Vol. 2,
      pp. 96-100.

      Philip Heseltine was the model for a character in
Lawrence's *Women in Love*, and for one in H's *Antic Hay*.
The character in *Antic Hay*, named Coleman, has a blond
fan-shaped beard, bright blue eyes "smiling equivocally
and disquietingly as though his mind were full of some
nameless and fantastic malice." Lawrence depicts Heseltine as Halliday, who is weak, irresolute, ridiculous,
soft, effeminate. H makes Coleman virile, sinister, a
monster of vice; he presents the fictional version of
Heseltine as Heseltine himself was trying to be. Lawrence
created a character such as Heseltine feared to be known
to be. Another character in *Antic Hay*, Gumbril, wears
a false beard in order to ape Coleman's wicked success.

401. Neumann, Henry. "Aldous Huxley and H.G. Wells Seek
      Religion." *Standard*, 23 (April, 1937), 169-174.

      Wells wanted socialism, but with a new morality of
administration. H's *Eyeless in Gaza*, interlarded with

long reflective essays, presents Beavis, a spoiled intellectual, undergoing a conversion to pacifism during
his trip to Central America. It consists of "the freedom to unite one's deepest strength in others for the
sake of a good so worth while that whether or not it is
finally crowned with success, it is well with us that here
is where we are found struggling."

402. New, Melvyn. "Ad Nauseam: A Satiric Device in Huxley,
      Orwell, and Waugh." *Satire Newsletter*, 8 (1970), 24-28.

      The satirist himself may on occasion experience nausea
      from the corruption he describes; examples may be found
      in *Brave New World*, *1984*, and Waugh's *Vile Bodies*. The
      Shakespeare allusions in *Brave New World* represent the
      normative world, as contrasted with the satirized utopia.
      John Savage watches the Delta workers at the factory, and
      comments, "Brave new world that has such people in it";
      then, retching, he dives into a clump of bushes. (New's
      essay then gives similar nausea responses in Orwell and
      Waugh.)

403. "New Satirist of Life's Hypocrisies." *Current Opinion*,
      68 (June, 1920), 830-831.

      This review of *Limbo*, H's first collection of short
      stories, compares H with Jules Laforgue "because of his
      ironic attitude toward sentiment" and with J.K. Huysmans
      "because he writes like a man with a queasy stomach for
      life."

404. Nicholas, Claire. "Aldous Huxley." *Vogue*, 110 (Aug. 1,
      1947), 110; 147.

      A description by H's niece of Llano, H's Wrightwood,
      California, home, located near the Mojave Desert, as
      well as details of his personal living habits: he works
      during the mornings in his study, walks with his wife,
      Maria, and Hindu friend Krishnamurti to the top of the
      mountains in the afternoon, dines vegetarian in the
      evening, listens to Maria read books like *War and Peace*.
      He is pleased with the Hollywood production of *The
      Gioconda Smile*, has successfully recovered his eyesight
      through use of the Bates System. The music of Brahms,
      Beethoven, Bach, provides him great pleasure. He and
      Isherwood are closely involved with the Vedanta Society.
      He warns that science has been misused to strengthen
      government leaders in power, at the expense of the common
      citizens.

405. Nicholson, Norman. "Aldous Huxley and the Mystics."
      Fortnightly, 161 (Feb., 1947), 131-135.

A natural progression of thought may be found in H's
works. The early fiction, despite its surface glitter,
has a cold feeling toward life and a cynical view of man.
A disgust with the physical also emerges. H's way of
explaining art and music on the level of biology, chemistry, and physics tends to debase the arts. In *Ends and
Means* the philosophy of non-attachment relates to H's
pacifism. *The Perennial Philosophy* seeks to discover
the Highest Common Factor, the common element shared by
the religions and philosophies of the world: the result
is a mystical insight. H's "non-attachment" is less of
a sacrifice to him than it was to the great mystics because his disgust with flesh and the material world made
it relatively easy for him to give them up. He has adopted the Manichean heresy, to the extent of doubting the
manifestation of the divine in temporal affairs as in
miracles, sacraments, and incarnation. H's representa-
tion of Western mysticism in *The Perennial Philosophy* is
extremely limited.

406. ———. "Henry de Montherlant, Aldous Huxley and
      Others," in his *Man and Literature*. London: Student
      Christian Movement Press, 1943. Pp. 94-103.

H was Lawrence's most devoted follower, perhaps because
both were basically puritans. H is at his best when he
comments on music, poetry, and philosophy in mock scientific language. Reducing the Natural Man to the level of
biology, chemistry, or physics is a common habit with
H. He often has the air of a high-brow journalist: the
display of erudition for its own sake. Creating character is not H's strong point--he seems to have repeated
the same basic types in successive novels, but with each
repetition the character becomes less pleasant. "It is
not surprising that his youthful preoccupation with the
senses should later turn to disgust and finally to a
wish to escape entirely from the physical world."

407. Nickalls, Rayne. "Some Thoughts on Huxley's Philosophy."
      Friends Quarterly, Jan., 1949, pp. 15-19.

There is a philosophical dilemma in H's having elimina-
ted the concept of "personality" in his mysticism. In
the Christian sense, "personality" relates to certain
divine qualities as they were present in the person of
Christ. In the Gospel of St. John, Christ asserts seven

times, "I am [the door, etc.]." This is true personality. Buddhism, by contrast, assumes an unconscious
merging with the divine, and hence loss of personality.
H's mysticism has strong Buddhist overtones.

408.   Niebuhr, Reinhold. "An End to Illusions." *Nation* (New
       York), 150 (June 29, 1940), 778-779.

       "Aldous Huxley dreams in Hollywood of a method of
       making man harmless by subtracting or abstracting the
       self from selfhood, and stumbles into a pseudo-Buddhist
       mysticism as the way of salvation without understanding
       that this kind of mysticism annuls all history in the
       process of destroying the self." Hitler succeeds because
       of the vapid cultures of the democracies.

409.   Niles, Blair Rice. "Thoughtful Mr. Huxley," in his
       edited *Journeys in Time: From the Halls of Montezuma
       to Patagonia's Plains*. New York: Coward-McCann, 1946.
       Pp. 308-310.

       A brief biography of H, and a summary of his account
       of Mexico and Guatemala in *Beyond the Mexique Bay*, are
       given. Actually, H gives only a sketchy description of
       the local scene; almost immediately, he digresses to
       other cultures, other times; he is constantly making con-
       nections for his digressions. His main concern is whether
       primitive and civilized cultures can ever relate. He re-
       flects on these thoughts with Olympian perspective.

410.   Noonan, Gerald. "Aldous Huxley and the Critical Path in
       Canadian Literature; or, How Imperious Fashion Screws
       Up Local Art--Everywhere." *Journal of Canadian Fiction*,
       2 (1973), 73-76.

       Noonan quotes from *Literature and Science*: "Canadian
       literature is a product of the social forces that shape
       Canada's culture--the forces of class and colonialism."
       Noonan protests against the colonial attitude toward
       Canadian literature.

411.   Nordhjem, Bent. "Aldous Huxley," in *Fremmede digtere i
       det 20 arhundrede*, ed. Sven M. Kristensen. Vol. II.
       Copenhagen: G.E.C. Gad, 1968. Pp. 461-473.

412.   "Notes on Aldous Huxley." *Publishers Weekly*, 175 (June
       1, 1959), 11-12.

       H said that his favorite among his own novels was *Time
       Must Have a Stop*. Lecturing at the University of Califor-
       nia, Santa Barbara, he talked about his plans for his

next novel, an island fantasy, to be the reverse of *Brave New World*.

413. Obayashi, Mikiaki. "Huxley Kyodai to Sofu: Julian, Aldous Kyodai to Sofu Henry Huxley." *Oberon*, 17, ii (1978), 36-45.

    The essay discusses the Huxleys and their grandfather.

414. "Obituary." *New Statesman*, 66 (Dec. 6, 1963), 834.

415. "Obituary." *Newsweek*, 62 (Dec. 9, 1963), 93A.

416. "Obituary." *Public Works*, 184 (Dec. 9, 1963), 27.

417. O'Brien, John. "The Problem of Evil in the Novels of Aldous Huxley." *Listening*, 6 (Fall, 1971), 197-209.

    H began his career as a cynical satirist; he ended in *Island* by saying that an "attack on all fronts" could eliminate evil from the world. In H's first novel, *Crome Yellow*, Scogan describes evil and suffering, but the other characters have their private means of escape; all avoid human involvement. In *Antic Hay*, the advent of science and the decline of religion have brought on the spiritual emptiness of the day: God is dead. Moral judgment is impossible when the laws of psychology and biology apply. In *Those Barren Leaves* everything is provisional and temporary, but out of it comes Calamy's conversion to mysticism, which does not promise a certain solution. *Point Counter Point* confronts the problem of determinism. Quarles's excessive intellectual development weakens his other attributes. To intellectualize is not to resolve. But Quarles is compassionate, whereas Denis in *Crome Yellow* merely saw life as comic. *Eyeless in Gaza* is H's most satisfactory novel thematically and artistically. Here H believes that man can gain self-control. Beavis achieves what no earlier character in H's fiction has done. *After Many a Summer* combines science and mysticism; here is H's first attempt to create the "ideal man"--Mr. Propter. But there is the need for a world application of his principles, through a political solution. *Time Must Have a Stop* returns to religion and mysticism. Rontoni says, "You've got to *be* good to *do* good." *Island* is the social application of individual mysticism as described in the earlier novels: "Nothing short of everything will do." The theme of this novel is the need to avoid all forms of determinism --and yet paradoxically the controls in this society

were a form of determinism, the purpose being to associate
people instinctively with "goodness." H believed that
man was now at the stage in his history when he could
reestablish Eden.

418. O'Brien, Justin. "On Rereading the Modern Classics."
     Nation (New York), 155 (Nov. 28, 1942), 579-580.

       Like Gide's *The Counterfeiters*, H's *Point Counter Point*
     has Philip Quarles holding a box of Quaker Oats with a
     picture of a picture ... of the Quaker holding.... H
     directly imitates Gide, but he doesn't handle the "novel
     within the novel" device as effectively as Gide does.
     Quarles is not at the center of the action. Quarles's
     notebook jottings do not advance the plot of *Point
     Counter Point* (unlike those of Edouard, which do relate
     to the plot in *The Counterfeiters*). Quarles's notebook
     is really an essay-like device to further the ideas of
     Rampion. H's attempt to see all layers and levels of
     life is accomplished mechanically--unlike Gide's approach.
     H's "contrapuntal" device was borrowed from Gide. Edouard
     wants to write novels based on Bach's "Art of the Fugue."
     Several of H's characters are parallels to those of Gide.
     In Gide's novel, there is the hope of youth, but H's
     novel shows no hope. Gide's work depicts a greater
     amount of positive evil, creative evil. H's world is
     shoddily immoral. Gide himself disliked *Point Counter
     Point*; after reading 70 pages he had not found "a single
     line rather firmly drawn, a single personal thought,
     emotion or sensation--not the slightest bait for the
     heart or the mind which might invite me to continue."

419. Ocampo, Victoria. "El recuerdo de Aldous Huxley."
     Cuadernos, 81 (Feb., 1964), 3-6.

420. Oerton, R.T. "End of the Beginning." *Twentieth Century*,
     175 (First Quarter, 1967), 48-50.

       Oerton notes the fulfillment of H's *Brave New World*
     prophecy of the test-tube fertilization of human egg cells,
     and of the possibility of making the fertilized cells
     subdivide into multiples to produce many identical per-
     sons. Also, Oerton notes the actuality of producing
     "super babies" by increasing the oxygen supply to the
     brain of the fetus. Aversion therapy now also exists that
     operates in the way H predicted it would in *Brave New
     World*; sleep teaching also exists. Cryogenics for the
     incurably diseased, spare parts surgery, sperm banks, are
     all futuristic "now" possibilities. But *Brave New World*

didn't sufficiently apprise the reader as to why this
utopia should be rejected; the novel creates only a sense
of disgust, which wears off once the phenomena become
familiar. If the Brave New World actually comes to be,
possibilities for evolutionary change will come to a dead
end.

421. O'Faolain, Sean. "Huxley and Waugh, or, I Do Not Think,
Therefore I Am," in his *The Vanishing Hero: Studies
of the Hero in the Modern Novel*. London: Eyre &
Spottiswoode, 1956, pp. 33-69.

O'Faolain groups H and Waugh together in one chapter,
a comparison which is unfair to both authors.

422. Olney, James. "'*Most* Extraordinary': Sybille Bedford and
Aldous Huxley." *South Atlantic Quarterly*, 74 (Summer,
1975), 376-386.

H's favorite expression--"*most* extraordinary"--relates
to the incommensurable nature of things. Bedford's
Aldous Huxley (see 2) is the culmination of her life work.
She is the ideal artist and H is the ideal subject. Bedford knew H for 35 years, and she had a sense of the high
calling of a writer. She is in and out of the book, sometimes in the first person, sometimes in the third person.
She makes a remarkable use of materials.

423. Orme, Daniel. "L'itineraire spirituel de M. Aldous Huxley." *Le Mois*, Nov., 1936, pp. 174-181.

This is an account of *Eyeless in Gaza*.

424. Orrell, Herbert M. "Huxley as Novelist." *New Republic*,
102 (Jan. 15, 1940), 88-89.

Responds to Daiches's Nov. 1, 1939, article in *New Republic* (1963), in which Daiches assumes that the novelist
must suggest remedies for the problems he presents. Also,
Daiches expressed a dislike for H's mysticism. Orrell
believes that H's real power lies in showing the sterility
of the purely intellectual life. Daiches, responding in
turn, says that he was being critical of H's *solution* to
the problem presented.

425. Orsini, Napoleone. "Aldous Huxley." *Belfagor*, 1 (May,
1946), 348-358.

426. Orwell, George. *The Collected Essays, Journalism and
Letters of George Orwell*, ed. Sonia Orwell and Ian

Angus. New York: Harcourt, 1968. Vol. 2, pp. 30-31;
Vol. 4, pp. 73-75; 479.

Orwell agrees that *Ape and Essence* is an "awful" book;
"the more holy [Huxley] gets, the more his books stink
with sex." H is obsessed with the flagellation of women
in *Ape and Essence*; Orwell suggests that perhaps private
sadism on a small scale would avoid large-scale public
war. In his review of Zamyatin's *We*, Orwell assumes that
Brave New World must be derived from *We*: both rebel
against a painless, mechanized world of the future.
H's book is better written, but Zamyatin's book has a
stronger political point to make. H gives no reason for
the social stratification in *Brave New World*. In Orwell's
review of Jack London's *The Iron Heel* he remarks of *Brave
New World*, "a brilliant caricature of the present (1930),
it casts no light on the future." Orwell also comments,
"A ruling class has got to have a strict morality, a
quasi-religious belief in itself, a mystique."

427.   Osmond, Humphrey. "Peeping Tom and Doubting Thomas."
       Twentieth Century, 154 (June, 1954), 521-526.

       Osmond comments on Alistair Sutherland's review (see
       515) of H's *The Doors of Perception*. Sutherland had
       argued that only H could have had the sort of experience
       he did from mescalin. But, Osmond says, H had a writer's
       genius for memorably describing his experiences.

428.   Otten, Kurt. "Aldous Huxley: Point Counter Point."
       Der moderne englische Roman, 51 (1966), 201-221.

429.   Overton, Grant Martin. "Half-Smiles and Gestures," in
       his *When Winter Comes to Main Street*. New York: Doran,
       1922. Pp. 33-36.

       An expression both serious and smiling appears in the
       person and writing of the young post-World War I writers.
       Overton quotes Michael Sadleir's comments on *Limbo*, *Crome
       Yellow*, and *Mortal Coils*. There are several H's: "the
       artificer of words, the amateur of garbage, pierrot
       lunaire, the cynic in rag-time, the fastidious sensualist.
       I believe only the last ... to be the real Huxley and the
       rest prank, virtuosity, and, most of all, self-conscious-
       ness." In his satire, H manufactures the possible sorts
       of remarks that critics might be making about his writing.

430.   ———. "The Twentieth-Century Gothic of Aldous Huxley,"
       in his *Cargoes for Crusoes*. New York: Appleton, 1924.
       Pp. 97-113.

H learned the art of caricature from Dickens, for whom
he shows an almost indiscriminate fondness. Overton
spends much of his time quoting, and deriding, laudatory
remarks made about H. Not much is gained by Overton's
analogy between H's mind and the intricacies of a Gothic
cathedral.

431. Owen, Guy. "'Prufrock' and Huxley's 'Crome Yellow.'"
      Laurel Review, 10 (Fall, 1970), 30-35.

      Antic Hay owes much to Eliot's *Waste Land*, which was
published one year earlier. Eliot knew H at Oxford in
1914 or 1915, and then at Garsington. Eliot didn't care
for H's verses; perhaps H got back at Eliot by parodying
him in *Crome Yellow*. Eliot apparently borrowed the name
Sosostris from *Crome Yellow*. Denis Stone is composing a
poem which reads like a parody of "Prufrock"--it reads,
"My Soul is a thin white sheet of parchment stretched/
Over a bubbling cauldron"--and then Denis makes revisions
on the lines. Denis himself is like Prufrock, though he
is somewhat like the young H too. Denis reads a lot, his
mind is filled with "rags and tags of other people's
makings," he ineptly pursues a woman he loves. He dreams
of fulfilling his sexual urges, of being a man of action.
Chapter 4 of *Crome Yellow* begins much like "Prufrock"--
Denis decides to wear white flannel trousers, studies
himself in the mirror; Anne puts off his attempts to
declare love.

432. Oye, P. Van. "Een herinnering aan Aldous Huxley." *De
      Vlaamse Gids*, 48 (1964), 68-69.

433. Ozana, Anna. "Der gewandelte Huxley." *Welt und Wort*,
      11 (1956), 344.

434. Ozawa, Takashi. "Sotaishugi kara Kachi no Hakken e:
      Ren-ai Taiiho no Shiso-teki Haikei." *Oberon*, 17, i
      (1978), 49-58.

      Discusses the intellectual background of *Point Counter
Point*, from relativism to the discovery of value.

435. "The Pantaloon in Contemporary English Letters." *Literary
      Digest*, 74 (Aug. 5, 1922), 37.

      Refers to several critics with varying opinions about
H: his "lack of earnestness," his "languid urbanity."
Crome Yellow and *Mortal Coils* are "deeply serious," pur-
poseful, holy, flaming, and passionately true and wise.
H himself, writing in the August, 1922, issue of *Vanity*

Fair about the Sitwells, declared that the "world is
socially and morally wrecked." H believed that the war
and the new psychology had destroyed the institutions and
values that had supported us in the past. What is needed
is a new artistic synthesis, and the only possible one
"is the enormous farcical buffoonery of a Rabelais or an
Aristophanes--a buffoonery which, it is important to note,
is capable of being as beautiful and as grandiose as
tragedy."

436.   Papadache, Frida. "Ultimul roman al lui Aldous Huxley:
       Insula." *România Literară*, 25 (Dec., 1975), 21.

437.   Parmenter, Ross. "Aldous Huxley: Style Was the Man."
       Saturday Review of Literature, 46 (Dec. 21, 1963), 12-13.

       H's mystical commitment left him without a style ap-
propriate to express it. He dropped his easy, flippant,
successful style and turned to earnest exposition. The
new prose was turgid, dull (in *Ends and Means*, 1937; in
The Perennial Philosophy, written eight years later).
After Many a Summer is also a bad stylistic performance.
The novels written after it were somewhat better, but H
never regained his old verve.

438.   _____. "Huxley at Forty-Three." *Saturday Review of
       Literature*, 17 (March 19, 1938), 10-11.

       H is a man troubled by his need to do something to
save the world. He accepts a kind of mysticism, but
not that of the Roman Catholic Church; nor does he understand T.S. Eliot's "solution." Poor at political action,
he is a mild-mannered man who does not pontificate. He
remarked, "I have always aimed at maximum translucency ...
at incisive clarity. I hate obscurity with such passion."
He believed that farce and tragedy are closely related;
they are the same thing seen from different angles. "I
try to get a stereoscopic vision, to show my characters
from two angles simultaneously. Either I try to show
them both as they feel themselves to be and as others
feel them to be; or else I try to give two rather similar
characters who throw light on each other, two characters
who share the same element, but in one it is made grotesque."

439.   Patai, Daphne. "Verissimo e Huxley: Um ensaio de
       analise comparada." *Minas Gerais, Suplemento Liter-
       ario*, Jan. 26, 1974, pp. 6-7; Feb. 2, 1974, pp. 6-7;
       Feb. 9, 1974, pp. 6-7.

440. Patty, James. "Baudelaire and Aldous Huxley." *South Atlantic Bulletin*, 23 (Nov., 1968), 5-8.

Patty develops one aspect of Ruth Temple's long article on H and French literature (521). References to Baudelaire are common in H's works. Patty concentrates on the allusions in *Point Counter Point*, especially in the characterization of Spandrell. *Point Counter Point* contains a host of references to French authors, and H knew a good deal about Baudelaire. Spandrell, like Baudelaire, was most happy as a child with his mother's love, before the mother remarried. "The most Baudelairian part of the novel is a long passage in which H shows Spandrell wallowing in a slough of ennui, sloth, debauchery, depravity." Spandrell himself says, "I really like hating and being bored"--which was H's perception of the character of Baudelaire. Spandrell's destruction of the suggestively phallic foxgloves in the presence of Connie parallels Baudelaire's remark, "A celle qui est trop gai."

441. Pendexter, Hugh, III. "Huxley's *Brave New World*." *Explicator*, 20 (March, 1962), 58.

The emasculated cross, which appears as a "T," symbolizes the triumph of the assembly line--society deprived of feeling, imagination, and self-reliance--it degenerates into an organized pursuit of pleasure. The sign of the T is made, therefore, not over the heart, but over the stomach by the citizens of the Brave New World.

442. Peraile, Esteban, and Lorenzo Peraile. "A vueltas con *Un mundo feliz*." *Cuadernos Hispanoamericanos: Revista Mensual de Cultura Hispanica*, 325 (1977), 160-180.

443. "The Perennial Prophet." *TLS*, Feb. 27, 1959, pp. 105-106.

Most of H's predictions made in *Brave New World* have now come upon us in reality, as H himself noted in *Brave New World Revisited*. But H never quite defines what the "freedom" is that will be our ultimate salvation. *Brave New World Revisited* drops much of the slapstick high spirits of *Brave New World*. H proposes a Higher Utilitarianism, in which the Greatest Happiness would be secondary to the Final End principle. This concept is also present in *The Perennial Philosophy*. Most of H's prescriptions on the achievement of freedom are negative, however.

444.   Perez, Mario Arias. "Quadragesimo aniversario de *Contra-
       ponto*." *Minas Gerais, Suplemento Literario* (Feb. 23,
       1974), 5.

445.   Perruchot, Henri. "Les hommes et leurs oeuvres. L'evo-
       lution spirituelle d'Aldous Huxley." *Synthèses*, 1
       (1949), 66-72.

446.   Petre, M.D. "Bolshevist Ideals and the 'Brave New
       World.'" *Hibbert Journal*, 31 (Oct., 1932), 61-71.

       Bolshevism is a religion with no Beyond--unlike the
       other great religions. *Brave New World* produces universal
       happiness for its citizens. It has a caste system, which
       also applies in Bolshevism, where history, art, and
       science are all made to serve the State. Savage, as a
       "Personality," upsets the planned equanimity of the State,
       or he would if he were to have his way. However, he is
       eliminated.

447.   Poisson, Jean Roger. "Hommage à Aldous Huxley." *Études
       Anglaises* (Vanves, France), 17 (April-June, 1964),
       140-147.

       H's career divides into three parts; the first ends in
       1932, the second in 1946. His best work was done during
       the first period, when he was most doubtful about man's
       future. He became more hopeful as time went on, but the
       quality of his work declined.

448.   Popa, Marian. "Huxley moralistul" (Huxley the Moralist),
       in *Frunze uscate* (*Those Barren Leaves*). Bucharest:
       Univers, 1973. Pp. 5-18.

449.   Pritchett, V.S. "Aldous Huxley." *New Statesman*, 66
       (Dec. 6, 1963), 834.

       H is a daring assimilator rather than an original,
       creative mind. His daring juxtapositions awaken and
       disturb our settled superstitions.

450.   ———. "A Living Symposium." *New Statesman*, Nov. 28,
       1969, pp. 769-770.

       H's achievement is that of a great teacher; he himself
       was aware that he was not congenitally a novelist. He
       was a prodigious letter writer and his books overflow into
       the letters. The later letters tend to emphasize science,
       deal less with H's personal emotions. "The gentle, think-
       ing persuader is strangely violent and melodramatic in

his novels; his comic sense depends a lot on disgust and the grotesque." His curiosity was both infectious and quick. Despite near blindness, he had a passion for reading and travel; he settled near Hollywood because it suited his taste for satirical comedy. His plays and the plots of his stories depend on melodrama; his art is distorted in a theatrical way because he felt compelled to arrange and juxtapose, and to prescribe philosophical viewpoints.

451.   ————. "The Vision from Limbo." *New Statesman*, Sept. 20, 1974, pp. 384, 386.

H's intellect worked in somewhat the same machine-like manner that Shaw's did. The California letters show that he wasn't Americanized during his residence in the U.S. H played two roles: the isolated sage and the friendly wanderer. California is a natural subject for the satirist--the surface-level materialism of America is here ripe for commentary by a moralist. H sought and taught his moral philosophy. His wife Maria monitored his experiences and related them to the world for him. H was keenly interested in oddball performances and performers, but he was never really close to the broad mix of human beings.

452.   Proteus, Hugh Gordon. "Aldous Huxley." *Twentieth Century*, 1 (Aug., 1931), 7-10.

453.   Pryce-Jones, Alan. "Aldous Huxley--A Modern Prophet." *Listener*, 38 (Oct. 16, 1947), 678-679.

H's first lesson in the early fiction was life's meaninglessness. "He is watching intelligent people making fools of themselves--not fools of themselves in a generous or venturesome way, but with a kind of cold triviality." H censures his characters for not adapting to his intellectual plan for humanity. The special neurosis he presents is that of his day--tiresomeness-- an effect that doesn't lend itself to grandeur. He never lets the central idea of his novel expand--he is always off on some new diversion. When he wrote *Ends and Means* H decided that intellectual pursuits were not the primary ones; instead, he sought the transcendental, through self-discipline and contemplation of eternal truth. He is perhaps closest to the 18th-century Deists; he tries to relate transcendence to popular science. His chief merit is "ever-awakened curiosity and vivaciousness of expression."

454.   Puhalo, Dusan. "Romansijer Oldes Haksli." *Savremenik*
       (Belgrade), 3 (March, 1956), 323–340.

455.   Putt, S. Gorley. "The Limitations of Intelligent Talk:
       Huxley's Essays," in his *Scholars of the Heart*. Lon-
       don: Faber & Faber, 1962. Pp. 28–42.

       Putt comments on H's *Collected Essays*, 1960. H shows
       unruffled confidence, facility, frivolity. Some of the
       passing thoughts are perceptive and entertaining. In
       the later essays, he is less frivolous, and even seems
       to be at the point of giving a serious lecture. The
       essays are characterized by "the flittering musings of
       an almost over-volatile mind." Putt expresses concern
       about "the uncritical looseness of so much of [H's]
       writing."

456.   Quennell, Peter. "Aldous Huxley," in *Living Writers:
       Being Critical Studies Broadcast in the BBC Third
       Programme by Denis Johnstone on Sean O'Casey [et al.],*
       ed. Gilbert Phelps. London: Sylvan Press, 1947. Pp.
       128–136.

       Since 1920, H has published twenty-four volumes: seven
       novels, twelve collections of essays, two books of verse,
       one drama, one biography, one philosophical and religious
       treatise. Even as a student at Oxford, H astounded others
       with his finished style. *Crome Yellow*, a very different
       sort of book, was written when the solid realism of Wells
       and Bennett was the current style. In all of H's seven
       novels, the same characters keep turning up. He himself
       was guilty of the weakness he describes in "Vulgarity in
       Literature"--an inborn facility which he didn't subject
       to constant constraint. He is always outside of his
       characters. And in the later novels, he lapses into
       mysticism.

457.   ————. "D.H. Lawrence and Aldous Huxley," in *English
       Novelists: A Survey of the Novel by Twenty Contemporary
       Novelists*, ed. Derek Verschoyle. London: Chatto &
       Windus, 1936. Pp. 267–278.

       H and Lawrence were almost total opposites, but both
       are influential writers. For each, the form of fiction
       was not an issue. H admired Lawrence probably more than
       he did any other living writer. Lawrence feared form
       because it threatened his spontaneity. H feared it be-
       cause it threatened his play of intellect. H pinpointed
       his own weakness as the inability to resist phrases,

situations, that suggest "a whole train of striking or
amusing ideas that fly off at a tangent...." H was in-
quisitive about the senses, but he never quite got through
to them emotionally; but for Lawrence passion was the profound emotional reality. Lawrence's characters are vis-
ceral; H's are built on hard outlines, with amusing or
scandalous details attached. H tends to repeat characters
from novel to novel. His spiritedness and inquisitiveness
helped to lift English fiction out of its contented som-
nolence.

*   ————. "Electrifying the Audience: *Music at Night* and
           Beyond the Mexique Bay," in "A Critical Symposium on
           Aldous Huxley." See 573.

458.   Quina, James. "The Mathematical-Physical Universe: A
        Basis for Multiplicity and the Quest for Unity in *Point
        Counter Point*." *Studies in the Novel*, 9 (Winter, 1977),
        428-444.

        While writing *Point Counter Point*, H was also reading
        E.A. Burtt's *The Metaphysical Foundations of Modern
        Science*, and various characters in his novel refer to
        this book. According to Burtt, "modern man has fallen
        victim to the distorted metaphysical assumptions he
        inherited from the doctrines of Copernicus, Galileo,
        Descartes, and Newton." Further, scientists up to and
        including Newton became entangled with philosophical and
        theological matters. The fallacy is that different
        "modes of being" arouse different modes of truth, but
        each has "just as much right to exist and call itself
        real as every other." H's figurative language in *Point
        Counter Point* contrasts mathematics, physiology, anatomy,
        molecular theory, time, and organic evolution with es-
        thetic and moral experience, religious belief, and human
        values. These alternate modes of being are made even
        more tentative by the portrayal of time from multiple
        perspectives. "Time passes" means that characters have
        separate awarenesses; "time flows" means that the subject-
        object division is partially dissolved into a unitive
        experience. Organic evolution provides H with still
        another variable lens for looking at life and beings.
        Following Burtt, H juxtaposes the mathematical-physical
        with the moral and esthetic. Animal imagery for charac-
        terizing people gives still another means for expressing
        multiplicity. Lucy Tantamount is seen as "a perfumed
        imitation of a savage or an animal," but Spandrell is
        seen as gangrenous, as a gargoyle, and he's fond of

growing mushrooms and fungi. Nearly all characters in
Point Counter Point seek for multiplicity, but fail to
achieve it. Rampion is defined by light or flame
imagery, the other characters, by animal or plant
images. "Like Blake, Rampion portrays man living in
harmony with animals, plants, and nature," and as with
Blake, Rampion's light images express the integrated
man.

459. ————. "The Philosophical Phases of Aldous Huxley."
      College English, 23 (Nov., 1962), 636-641.

A study of H's philosophical development proves that
his characters were always in quest of peace. But until
the last stage of H's novels, the quest was conducted in
self-serving or illogical ways that H deplored. The
problems are defined in the early novels; they are approached more maturely in the later ones.

460. Quinteros, Alberto. "Aldous Huxley y al Promilema de
      la Unidad de Centro America," *Sintesis*, 1 (May, 1954),
      125-129.

461. Ramamurty, K. Bhaskara. "Aldous Huxley and D.H. Law-
      rence." *Triveni*, 42 (Oct.-Dec., 1973), 26-34.

One important distinction between the life views of
Lawrence and H is that Lawrence accepts intuition as
the only way to salvation, whereas H trusts reason.
Similarities between the two writers include the following: both found unhappiness in life; both were interested
in, and influenced by, Indian literature; both are
"novelists of ideas"; both have had a strong influence
on later writers. Lawrence doesn't use H's method of
reason, but he comes to a similar conclusion. H never
really rejected Lawrence, and he borrowed much from
Lawrence for his own novels.

462. Rascoe, Burton. "Contemporary Reminiscences." *Arts and
      Decoration*, 25 (July, 1926), 48.

At New York publishers' parties as the guest of honor,
H gave answers "encyclopedically, teetering back and
forth on his long legs and rattling off statistical and
topographical information like the ineffable husband of
'Two or Three Graces.'" H is a "man incongruously placed
in a social milieu that he finds irresistibly fascinating
and yet abhors."

463. Rather, L.J. "Courage, Mr. Huxley!" *Nation* (New York),
      188 (Feb. 28, 1959), 188-189.

In 1959 H warned of the danger of government use of
mind-control drugs. Police power and propaganda would
be replaced by a "dictatorship without tears." H also
explained how this method worked in *Brave New World Revisited*. However, H's conclusions are based on the
scientific anachronism that humans are conscious automata.
Evidence shows that drugs or other forms of mind control
don't produce uniform results. Human beings in groups
react differently to these influences than they do when
in isolation. Pharmacologic effects are sometimes reversed by interpersonal factors.

464. Ratnam, Kamala. "Chilean Writer Meets Aldous Huxley in
      India." *United Asia*, 16 (July-Aug., 1964), 257-260.

In H's speech in India, 1961, at the Tagore Centenary,
he declared that Tantrism was the philosophy inspiring
the works of Tagore. Tantrism is a branch of Hinduism;
it holds that the basis of the Universe is sex, through
which man is liberated. H's interest in Yoga and mysticism led him to write on the Vedanta philosophy. He
believed in "Mutantes," a superior species of men who
achieve mystical experience through modern scientific
means such as drugs. H remarked that *The Doors of Perception* was "one of my books which I like most."

465. Read, Herbert Edward. "A Culture out of Chaos." *Saturday
      Review*, 43 (Nov. 19, 1960), 44.

Review of *Aldous Huxley on Art and Artists*, ed. Morris
Philipson. H's essays are always characterized by their
variety and digressions. H shows great zest in his inconsistency; he believed that being consistent was only
a verbal concept, not one of life. He expressed this
philosophy of art: "an individual's attempt to reduce the
chaos of appearances to some comprehensible unity."
Tradition enables persons of little talent to produce
good works; they don't have to depend on their inadequate
imaginations. A good tradition is "the ghosts of the
dead artists dictating to bad living artists." Vulgar
art of today is predicated by the large mass of semi-
educated people. The popular arts only serve Fordism,
an incredible industrial monotony. Part 2 of this anthology contains H's appreciations of such great artists
as Chaucer, Ben Jonson, Swift, Baudelaire, Goya, Breughel,

El Greco; H does this sort of thing better than anyone
since Pater. Sometimes the moralist in H displaces the
hedonist, as in his strictures against Baudelaire.

466. Rebora, P. "Aldous Huxley." *I Libra del Giorno*, June,
      1927, pp. 328-330.

467. Richards, D. "Four Utopias." *Slavonic and East European
      Review*, 40 (1962), 220-228.

The utopias described are Dostoevsky's "Grand Inquisitor," Zamyatin's *We*, H's *Brave New World*, and Orwell's
1984. Zamyatin and Dostoevsky attack the fanatical application in practice of rational principles. Unreason
cannot be straightjacketed by reason. Zamyatin and H
deplore the disappearance of art. *Brave New World* and *We*
are both futuristic; both warn of impending dangers; the
industrial regimentation depersonalizes humanity. *Brave
New World* institutionalizes free sex; *1984* restricts it.
1984 is the most frightening of the four utopias. In
Brave New World Revisited, H saw the continuing march of
events depicted in *Brave New World*.

468. Rillo, E. "Aldous Huxley and T.S. Eliot," in *Aldous
      Huxley and T.S. Eliot*. Buenos Aires: Talleres
      gráficos Contreras, 1943. Pp. 5-14.

The short biographies given of H and Eliot show that
both had the best educations available. Both depict
sterility, vanity of modern life; both approach the
mystic ideal, Eliot through faith, H through intellect. In *Those Barren Leaves*, Mrs. Aldwinkle reminds
one of the women in "Prufrock" who talk of Michelangelo.
Cardan himself is like Prufrock. Calamy's meandering
thoughts deal with themes that are also expressed in
"Ash Wednesday." In *Point Counter Point* Lucy Tantamount
is a prose version of the sensual types described in
The Waste Land (part 2) and in "Sweeney Agonistes."
(Most of this essay consists of parallel passages quoted
from H and E.)

469. Roberts, John Hawley. "Huxley and Lawrence." *Virginia
      Quarterly Review*, 13 (Autumn, 1937), 546-557.

Those Barren Leaves expresses the nadir of 19th-century
formulas and values (religion, patriotism, humanitarian-
ism, etc.); Calamy indicates H's first interest in
mysticism. But in 1926, H found a new interest in Lawrence, whom he had met 11 years before. *Point Counter*

Point shows a strong loyalty to Lawrence's ideas. Lawrence preached that man was desiccated by making reason conquer blood. Other than Rampion, the characters in *Point Counter Point* are overintellectualized, or else overemotionalized. *Brave New World* is a utopia from which emotion has been excluded. John Savage is the one character who wants human pain, danger, emotion, and commits suicide when he can't find these in the Brave New World. *Eyeless in Gaza* tries to describe mysticism of the blood, following Lawrence. Anthony Beavis searches for this kind of experience. His ideal combines Platonism and Indian Yoga. Lawrence achieved his goal through the mysticism of the sexual experience. H's experience begins with the body, ends with vision. There is considerable doubt as to whether H's mysticism really solved his intellectual problems.

470. Rogers, Winfield H. "Aldous Huxley's Humanism." *Sewanee Review*, 43 (July-Sept., 1935), 262-272.

There is always a serious philosophical idea behind H's satire. H attacks Wordsworth for erecting a life philosophy on an emotional experience. H's philosophy is based on the oneness and simultaneous diversity of life. A psychological humanist, H saw harmony as a balance between reflection and spontaneity. Man should recognize and fulfill his almost infinite potentiality. "Multiplicity of eyes and multiplicity of aspects seen" and "balanced excess" are two basic precepts of H. The threats to modern society are monotheism and the superhuman ideal; worship of success and efficiency; and the machine.

471. Rolo, Charles J. "Aldous Huxley." *Atlantic Monthly*, 180 (Aug., 1947), 109-115; reprinted as the Introduction to *The World of Aldous Huxley*, ed. Charles J. Rolo. New York: Harper & Row, 1947.

H is the "sceptic, moralist, artist" who looked for moral values in a time when belief based on faith alone was peremptorily rejected. The finest caricaturist of the 20th-century English novel, H attacks false beliefs to provide a thorough account of man's ideas in the present century. The cynic in ragtime of the earlier period coheres with the pacifist, mystic, of the later one. Even in his early essay on Pascal (1927) H leaned toward the moralist and mystic. Counterpoint in fiction is for H "sufficiency of characters and parallel, or contrapuntal plots." Modulation is "several people

falling in love, or dying or praying in different ways—
dissimilars solving the same problems." H's purpose was
to "consider the events of the story in their various
aspects—emotional, scientific, religious, metaphysical,
etc." Rolo reviews the various novels, observing the
evolution of H's philosophy. The discovery of faith in
Eyeless in Gaza makes the satire more bitter. "A review
of H's adventures in negation and belief shows that he
was never satisfied with garbage collecting and smashing
of idols; that early in his career he 'chased the absolute
in remote strange regions' and seemed on the point of
embracing mysticism at the conclusion of *Those Barren
Leaves.*"

472. Rosati, Salvatori. "Aldous Huxley." *Nuova Antologia*,
      370 (Dec. 16, 1933), 643-645.

473. Rose, Steven. "The Fear of Utopia." *Essays in Criticism*
      (Oxford), 24 (1974), 55-70.

      Brave New World shows behaviorist psychology at work.
      Conditioning to happiness produces fear in the reader
      because it threatens the reader's present identity.

474. Ross, Julian L. *Philosophy in Literature*. Syracuse:
      Syracuse University Press, 1949. Pp. 25-31; 97-99.

      Brave New World shows the Platonic-scientific society
      gone wrong because of an exclusive reliance on reason.
      In *Point Counter Point* the characters are not intended
      to be real, but all are excessively articulate and keenly
      self-analytical. H's sense of meaninglessness in life is
      the basis for the hedonism in *Point Counter Point*. Lucy
      Tantamount is a modern Cyrenaic, Philip Quarles, a modern
      Epicurean, but he intellectualizes his experience. H
      turned in his later books from hedonism to mysticism as
      an antidote.

475. Roston, Murray. "The Technique of Counterpoint."
      Studies in the Novel, 9 (Winter, 1977), 378-388.

      In *Point Counter Point* H is not merely satirizing in-
      dividual characters nor condoning them; he is also get-
      ting at the major intellectual issues of his day. The
      novel's title shows that a single or controlling view of
      life is no longer possible: each standpoint is cancelled
      out by another, its opposite. Quarles, the novelist
      whose physical disability prevents him from being physi-
      cally active or socially complete, is "like" H. And so

is Bidlake, the assistant editor who fulminates against
his exploitation by Burlap (a caricature of Middleton
Murry, who was once H's editor). But Walter Bidlake, the
"Shelleyan idea of man ennobled and elevated by love,"
is cancelled out by Philip Quarles with his fascination
for the new biological theories: these characters seem
to be "twin extrapolations of Huxley's inner conflict."
Individual characters also contain their own contradic-
tions; thus Illidge, consciously devoted to the materialism
of communism, is also capable secretly of sending a weekly
allowance to his elderly mother, and hence cancelling
his precept that the body politic transcends the individual.
A final, major conflict is seen in Rampion and Spandrell's
debate about music. Music, Spandrell's symbol of the
soul, meets Rampion's scepticism about absolutes. "The
heart yearns to believe in beauty and in the nobility of
man, while the mind perceives the grotesqueness of his
zoological or physiological state."

476. Routh, Harold Victor. "Aldous Leonard Huxley," in his
      English Literature and Ideas in the Twentieth Century:
      An Inquiry into Present Difficulties and Future Pros-
      pects. London: Methuen & Co., 1948. Pp. 181-185.

Even in H's early poetry, the Oriental mystic and
Western scientist appear on occasion, but not molded into
one view. "He was a humorist, a collector of human
curiosities." H hated the class of people who easily
talked of science, philosophy, but really couldn't think.
"Huxley's skill and literary tact are dedicated to the
evils of educated perversity" in the early novels. In
Brave New World, "The principle of evil must be raised
and redirected, not by totalitarian administration, but
by an enlightened code of self-discipline." "Huxley has
developed an insatiable curiosity in the waywardness
of his fellow-creatures."

477. Sadler, A.W. "The Zaehner-Huxley Debate." *Journal of*
      Religious Thought, 21 (1964-1965), 43-50.

Zaehner, in *Mysticism Sacred and Profane* (601), said
H had confused his drug-induced experience with sacred
mysticism. Also, H confused communion with all of
nature with communion with God. Zaehner also said that
H's experience with mescalin paralleled manic-depressive
psychosis. H himself notes parallels between three types
of individual, the chemical imbalance in whose bodies
all relate to mysticism: the schizophrenic, who is in-
voluntarily subject; the mescalin taker, who is so by

intention; and the mystic, who is so unwittingly. Zaehner's own experiments with mescalin were invalid, Sadler says, because Zaehner resisted the drug's effects, was highly skeptical about its producing any of the responses in him that H said he experienced through mescalin. Sadler also remarks that H did not claim a truly mystical experience from mescalin--rather, he gained insight into the Beatific Vision, Enlightenment. Perhaps H felt that he was lacking in holiness.

478. Saher, Purvezji Jamshedji. *Indische Weisheit und das Abendland; Religionphilosophische Parallellen.* Meisenheim am Glan: Hain, 1965. Pp. 111-140.

479. Sale, Roger. "Huxley and Bennett, Bedford and Drabble." *Hudson Review*, 28 (1975), 285-293.

Review of Bedford's *Aldous Huxley* (see 2) and Margaret Drabble's *Arnold Bennett*. Bedford's biography was written out of personal knowledge and love, but it's too long--and the one-volume American edition is formidable. Bedford was guided by reminiscence; hence, the coverage disproportionately emphasizes the California years; there is only a fitful account of how H arrived at that point. Bedford's tone is too breezy, filled with trivia; she should have told more, or less, about Aldous and Maria's sexual life, and the circumstances of Maria's arranging sexual liaisons for H. Bedford does manage a very complex set of personal ties and circumstances. She reports on H's involvement with innumerable fads: massage, occultism, seances, parapsychology, etc. "He tried so many different things because nothing by itself worked, and the more he worked the more he saw he had to do." Bedford "lets herself be content with chronicling where she should have been a decisive storyteller."

480. Salle, Bertrand de la. "Un romanesque des idées." *Fontaine*, numéro spécial, 37-40 (1944), 171-175.

Point Counter Point is a paradox: the author is outside of, yet consciously within, the book. The Quarles device was borrowed from Gide. It is an oddity to have an Englishman writing a novel of ideas; English education doesn't rank intellectuality high among conversational subjects. The ideas are the products of the characters; they relate mainly to the state of man and society. The points of view are many: emotive, scientific, economic, religious, metaphysical. It's a sign of the times to have characters preoccupied with dis-

cussing ideas. Man has ceased to find emotional and
spiritual satisfaction in the word of God. Social ideas
have assumed that function. Among French writers, ideas
have been held high--Flaubert, Zola, France, Gide, Proust;
it is appropriate that H should make up for this omission
in the English novel. The novel of ideas logically
succeeds the novel of emotions.

481. Salter, K.W., and A.E. Dyson. "Aldous Huxley." *Critical
     Quarterly*, 4 (Summer, 1962), 177-179.

Salter says Dyson misunderstood Mr. Propter's statements about God in *After Many a Summer*. Also, Propter
is referring not to Buddhism, but to the mysticism of
14th-century Europe. But Propter also seeks practical
means of making people independent if they wish to be.
Mr. Propter is the most fully realized of H's idealists.
     Dyson's response: H meant to show similarities among
all types of mysticism.

482. Salvan, J.L. "Le scandale de la multiplicité des con-
     sciences chez Huxley, Sartre, et Simone de Beauvoir."
     Symposium, 5 (Nov., 1951), 198-215.

Salvan compares the existential views of H (*Eyeless
in Gaza*) and Sartre. The persistence of certain Platonic
elements in the esotericism of H and the existentialism
of Sartre: H says at the end of *Eyeless in Gaza*, "Separation, diversity--conditions of our existence. Conditions
upon which we possess life and consciousness.... But
separation is evil. Evil, then is the condition of life,
the condition of being aware, of knowing what is good
and beautiful."

483. Sanin Cano, Baldomero. "Aldous Huxley, o la idolatria
     de la vida." *Repertorio Americano*, 23 (Sept. 26, 1931),
     177-179.

484. Savage, David S. "Aldous Huxley and the Dissociation of
     Personality." *Sewanee Review*, 55 (Autumn, 1947);
     reprinted in *Focus Four: The Novelist as Thinker*, ed.
     B. Rajan. London: Dobson, 1948. Pp. 9-34; also in
     Savage's *The Withered Branch*. New York: Pellegrini
     & Cudahy, 1952; and in *Critiques & Essays in Modern
     Fiction*, ed. J.W. Aldridge. New York: Ronald Press,
     1952.

H's works are thinly disguised autobiographical sequences in the intellectual growth of the man. The

later H (prophet and philosopher of Enlightenment) tries
to disown the earlier H (a youthful entertainer). The
prophet, however, has overshadowed the artist. The
earliest H was the novelist of despair--a "Pyrrhonic
aesthete"--but this also applies to his later works.
Discontinuity is the only continuous factor throughout
H's career. His novels lack dramatic movement because
there's a lack of dynamic movement in the author's mind
--his characters in the novels are caricatures and there
is no dynamic interplay among them. H's later works are
an attack on self-hood, the solution being a withdrawal
from "self," but this detachment is another kind of
futility.

485.   Schall, J.V. "Buber and Huxley: Recent Developments in
       Philosophy." *Month*, 19 (Feb., 1958), 97-102.

       H's and Buber's attitudes toward language differ con-
       siderably. H is highly suspicious of what language can
       do, but this is not necessarily his final, considered
       opinion. H is more concerned about the methods of mind
       control that threaten the conscious self (as in *Brave
       New World Revisited*) than he is about discovering the
       subconscious, visionary self. Western man, like H, is
       "seeking more vigorously to discover self by fleeing
       from it." Buber finds the self, and also the infinite
       and absolute, in intense consciousness generated by
       human verbal communication.

486.   Scheck, Frank Ranier. "Augenschein und Zukunft: Die
       antiutopische Reaktion: Samjatins *Wir*, Huxleys *Schöne
       neue Welt*, Orwells *1984*," in *Science Fiction: Theorie
       und Geschichte*. Munich: Fink, 1972. Pp. 259-275.

487.   Schmerl, Rudolf B. "Aldous Huxley's Social Criticism."
       Chicago Review, 13 (Winter-Spring, 1959), 37-58.

       Brave New World Revisited shows H come full circle
       after a writing career of over 30 years. In the 1920's,
       H criticized democratic processes; in the 1930's he
       defended pacifism as the way to deal with totalitarianism;
       after World War II he called for an international congress
       of scientists to save society from another war; now he's
       returned once more to a bitter picture of the effects
       of materialism on society. Schmerl draws a parallel be-
       tween *Brave New World Revisited* and *Ape and Essence*: both
       reflect, via fantasy, the fears of the time when they
       were written. But H's social criticism is highly de-
       tached, and his wise men--Miller in *Eyeless in Gaza* and

Propter in *After Many a Summer*--are chilling saints.
Education for individual responsibility, and decentralization, are tentative answers, as is civil disobedience,
for overpowering modern governments. But H always sacri-
fices the concrete and the human to what he calls the
"ultimate." He is basically aristocratic, but his social
criticism is filled with inconsistencies.

488. ―――. "The Two Future Worlds of Aldous Huxley." *PMLA*,
      77 (June, 1962), 328-334.

Brave New World and Ape and Essence may be analyzed as
fantasies, in terms of techniques of construction, and
satire on the real world. Fantasy uses the future, not
the past. "Our Ford" sweeps away all history--"History
is bunk." H complicates and blurs the issues by intro-
ducing John, who is a mixture of Zuñi primitive and
Shakespearean tragic hero--he makes the reader recall
Renaissance values. *Ape and Essence* handles the "history
of the future" through the device of a rejected movie
script. World War III is a more significant part of the
past in *Ape and Essence* than in *Brave New World*. "*Brave
New World* represents a strange mixture of desire and revulsion on the part of the author." "The harmony of the
World State is the harmony of Death." *Brave New World*
is not science fiction because it's not based on an ideal
premise; rather, it satirizes the world of 1932: synthetic
emotions of movies, popular music, compulsive pursuit of
"pleasure." *Ape and Essence*, unlike *Brave New World*, has
little humor. The Arch-Vicar of *Ape and Essence* is an
ignorant worshipper of Progress and Nation, on whose
ruins the action takes place. *Ape and Essence* is a much
lesser novel--poorly constructed, with crude symbolism,
and much nagging of the reader by the author. H does
not seem to have gained as a propagandist what he lost as
a novelist.

489. Schwanitz, Dietrich P. "Burgerlicher Relativismus:
      Gesprachskulture und sozialistische Figuren in zwei
      Ideenromanen." *Germanisch-romanische Monatsschrift*,
      Neue Folge, 25 (1975), 463-468.

490. "The Scientific Nightingale." *Spectator*, 211 (Oct. 4,
      1963), 406.

H's *Literature and Science* proposes the middle road
in the Snow-Leavis controversy. After some pleasant
irrelevancies, H gets to the topic of the English
nightingale and its role in English literature. He

notes that the real nightingale sings, not for love, but
to warn rivals to stay out of his territory. It's
"literary cowardice" to ignore this information. H "ignores the process by which imagination has always explained the world to the world." He ignores the undue
pressure of science to influence world affairs, without
"guidance of philosophy" or humane ideas that are the
basis of Western civilization. H only states the obvious
in trying to resolve the Snow-Leavis debate.

491.   Scurani, Alessandro. "Il sincretismo di Aldous Huxley."
        Letture, 25 (1970), 263-282.

492.   Semmler, Clemment. "Aldous Huxley Revisited." *Australian
        Quarterly*, 42 (Dec., 1970), 74-82.

        H noted that every great religious leader was pessimis-
tic about society at large, but most optimistic about
the possibilities of individuals or small groups.
Religious leaders who sought to change the world inevi-
tably got involved in power politics--as in *Grey Eminence*.
Semmler thinks *The Perennial Philosophy* is H's most enduring book, along with *Brave New World*.

493.   Sharma, Arvind. "Mescalin and Hindu Mystical Experience."
        Studies in Religion. A Canadian Journal, 5 (1975), 171-
        176.

        H compares his mescalin experience with the mystical
experiences recorded by Christianity, Hinduism, Buddhism.
Zaehner has already examined the parallel with Christian
mysticism. H was not specific about the particular aspect of Hinduism he had in mind. Similarities between
H's experience and the experience of Brahman include the
following: perception of ultimate beauty--especially in
H's observing the folds of the garment of Botticelli's
Judith; time and space are phased out; the loss of the
"I" consciousness; the total awareness of Mind at Large;
the abolition of such dualities as good and evil, subject
and object, self and other. But some differences also
apply. H could carry on a conversation with others, retained some sense of space and time, and perceived bright
color (none of this was so in the Nirvikalpa Samadhi
state).

494.   Sheppard, Lancelot C. "Aldous Huxley: An Estimate."
        Books on Trial, 11 (Jan.-Feb., 1953), 149, 174.

        The Devils of Loudun achieved nearly the almost univer-
sal praise that greeted *Grey Eminence*. H was held up as

a rare example of humanism in an age of specialized
technocracy, and he is one of the first modern novelists
because he's one of the first with a modern culture.
But despite his scientific knowledge, skillful style,
and wide reading, there is an absence of feeling--and
intense but unobtrusive feeling is the mark of a great
creative work. H is much interested in Catholicism,
but fails with it because of his Manichean viewpoint.
Furthermore, he fails with it because he can't accept
the Incarnation. His sources for *The Devils of Loudun*
are not all trustworthy, and some of the book appears
to be based on surmise, rather than documentation.

495. Shostakov, V. "Sotsial 'maya antiutopiya Oldosa
      Khaksli--mif i real' nost.'" *Novyi Mir* (Moscow), 7
      (1969), 230-247.

496. Simons, John D. "The Grand Inquisitor in Schiller,
      Dostoevsky and Huxley." *New Zealand Slavonic Journal*,
      8 (Summer, 1971), 20-31.

H himself noted the parallel between Dostoevsky's
Grand Inquisitor and his World Controller in *Brave New
World*. He saw the State, not the Church, as withdrawing
freedom, an act which is "an outrage against man's biological nature." Savage rejects the Brave New World
society because he wants the right to be free. Before
writing *Brave New World*, H had read *Crime and Punishment*,
The Brothers Karamazov, *Notes from Underground*, and *The
Idiot*.

497. Slochower, Harry. "Bourgeois Bohemia," in his *No Voice
      Is Wholly Lost: Writers and Thinkers in War and Peace*.
      New York: Creative Age Press, 1945. Pp. 32-40.

The early works of H and Hemingway are bourgeois in
origin, critical of bourgeois standards. H debunked
scientific rationalism and romantic idealism, both
middle-class values. In *Point Counter Point*, the
socially accepted ideals are examined and shown to be
without basis: love comes from hormones; music from
"rosined horsehair" drawn across the "stretched intestines of lambs." But, Slochower asks, of what use is
sensationalism when all taboos cease to exist? H's
point of view is split into "skeptical pluralism," but
no growth ensues from it. Pacifism is expressed by
Gombril in *Antic Hay* and is expanded upon by Miller and
Beavis in *Eyeless in Gaza*. Progress, according to them,
is to come through mystical faith, not scientific inves-
tigation. (Slochower's book is determined to fit literary

figures into categories in order to prove evolution and change in literary and social phenomena.)

498.   Smyser, H.M.   "Huxley's 'Point Counter Point,' Chapter 11."   *Explicator*, 6 (Dec., 1947), 22.

Rampion in *Point Counter Point* doesn't want his books to be sold in "the rubber shops"--i.e., along with pornographic books.   H's parallel is drawn from Robert Graves's *Lars Porsena* (1927), which notes that Aristotle's *Works* (with illustrations) "is sold in every rubber shop in London and Cardiff."   This edition of Aristotle described the physiology of marriage, midwifery, aphrodisiacs, etc.

499.   Snow, C.P.   "Aldous Huxley--Romantic Pessimist."   *New Republic*, 140 (Jan. 12, 1959), 18-19.

Snow dislikes utopias and anti-utopias, but he confesses his indebtedness to the earlier H, who "sharpened our wits and widened our sensibilities."   In Snow's view, utopia is "neither art nor life, but essays at just that kind of abstraction which most distorts the truth."   Snow takes the intellectuals to task for not seeing that "industrialization is the one hope of the poor."   H is "constantly trying to think, or idealize, the individual into a non-social context"; that is, H is a romanticist, with no sense of how human beings really live their lives.

500.   Snow, Malinda.   "The Gray Parody in *Brave New World*."   *Papers on Language and Literature*, 13 (1977), 85-88.

Gray's "Elegy" is parodied in the opening of Chapter 5 of *Brave New World*.   In his close verbal parallels H renders the spirit of the original poem absurd: at the Stoke Poges Golf Club appear the herd-like lower-caste golfers.   Gray's elegant verse is ridiculed by H's deliberately commonplace prose.   Gray's values become twisted or negated in *Brave New World*.   In this novel family life and "useful toil" don't exist; neither does individuality.   Gray's values of privacy and reflection are denied in *Brave New World*.

501.   Snyder, Stephen.   "From Words to Images: Five Novelists in Hollywood."   *Canadian Review of American Studies*, 8 (1977), 206-213.

Review of Dardis, *Some Time in the Sun* (165).   Dardis's thesis that the five novelists he describes in Hollywood generally profited financially and creatively from the experience isn't very well documented.   H, like the others,

felt distressed that words were of subordinate importance
in film. Dardis doesn't really clarify the differences
between literary and cinematic writing, though he assumes
that they exist.

502. Spencer, Theodore. "Aldous Huxley: The Latest Phase."
   Atlantic Monthly, 165 (March, 1940), 407–409.

   Because of its economy, force, and subtlety, *After
   Many a Summer* is H's best novel. *Crome Yellow* has an
   "ironic eye for surface peculiarities of characters."
   The presence of evil is introduced in *Antic Hay*. In
   Those Barren Leaves, H introduces for the first time,
   and tentatively, his sense of moral values. Calamy's
   retirement and contemplation foreshadow Mr. Propter in
   After Many a Summer. H's problems as a satirist are
   greater than Swift's. After all, Swift's contemporaries
   had a commonly accepted sense of values; H's contemporaries did not. But one-fifth of *After Many a Summer* is
   given to expressing Mr. Propter's views--this is too long
   an exposition for the average reader to accept. Also,
   the characters in this novel are too consciously balanced
   as opposites: the effect is "less an organism than an
   argument." Still, H is "one of the most honest and
   fascinating of contemporary minds."

503. Spender, Stephen. "An Open Letter to Aldous Huxley."
   Left Review, 4 (1937), 539–541.

   Spender replies to H's "Case for Constructive Peace."
   He refuses to see any plausibility in H's idea of a World
   Conference for peace, the premise of which was that Hit-
   ler and Mussolini would be peaceable and satisfied if
   given a fairer share of the world's goods.

504. Sponberg, Florence L. "Huxley's Perennial Occupation."
   Mankato State College Studies, 3 (Dec. 1, 1968), 1–18.

   For his final 30 years, H was devoted to self-transcen-
   dence, a means of individual salvation achieved by
   mysticism; but he saw organized religion and drug cults
   as hostile to his approach. H associated mescalin alone
   with his "upward" transcendence. *Eyeless in Gaza*, *Time
   Must Have a Stop*, and *Island* are all concerned with this
   objective. The "gospel" preached in each novel varies
   somewhat, but the hero who discovers it in each case
   transcends himself. H believes that individuals can be
   saved in this manner, but the world at large will be
   victimized by the wicked results of orthodox Western-type
   faiths.

505. Steen, Ellisiv Buch. "Aldous Huxley." *Edda*, 35 (1935),
         55-102.

506. Stevens, George. "Aldous Huxley's Man of Good Will."
         Saturday Review of Literature, 14 (July 11, 1936),
         3-4; 12.

         "*Crome Yellow* and *Antic Hay* had represented an attitude;
         Point Counter Point represented a point of view." *Eye-
         less in Gaza* is no longer skeptical; it is explicit in
         meaning, not, like *Point Counter Point*, implicit.. Beavis
         discovers that human freedom is not detachment, but a
         matter of identifying with other human beings. Juxta-
         posed episodes highlight the special features of Beavis's
         character. "Beavis creates or observes the melodrama of
         others." "Beavis's intellectual life is the subject of
         the novel, and Beavis is not very intelligent." His
         "conversation" isn't very dramatic or alarming. Fiction
         has become an inadequate medium for H to present his
         point of view.

507. Stewart, Douglass H. "Aldous Huxley--Mysticism," in his
         The Ark of God: Studies in Five Modern Novelists.
         London: The Carey Kingsgate Press, 1961. Pp. 44-70.

         "For Aldous Huxley science is not god but idol." "He
         discards scientific utopianism in the name of the soul
         of man." "Every spiritual perception involves this in-
         explicable act of translation out of the physical."
         "Man's destiny lies in man's nature. Man is cause
         rather than effect." H's vision of human nature and the
         human dilemma is Pauline or Augustinian, but when he
         approaches a solution, H removes himself from any form
         of Christianity. The syncretism developed in *Ends and
         Means* and *The Perennial Philosophy* is negative--it with-
         draws from evil. H believes that mysticism can be separa-
         ted from the accidental accretions of historic religion;
         mysticism in its pure form is the way to salvation. He
         held that Christianity is over-obsessed with the cruci-
         fixion. H's religion is "of the philosophers" and con-
         tains no Divine action; it proceeds from man's will.
         H's conversion is expressed in *Eyeless in Gaza*, in which
         Anthony and Helen are washed in the blood of a dog (not
         that of a lamb). But this unclean baptism carries with
         it no awareness of God's eternal love. "H is dreaming of
         escape rather than accepting the redemption of 'the
         whole creation.'"

508. ————. "Aldous Huxley's *Island*." *Queen's Quarterly*,
         70 (Autumn, 1963), 326-335.

Stewart examines Pala as an old-fashioned utopia. H's novel is subject to social, as well as literary, criticism. *Island* is not a parody or a dystopia. H's society in this novel attempts a synthesis of East and West, mysticism and science, individualism and collectivism, the rural and the urban. "Feasible but as yet untried theories are at hand for a new generation of reformers and zealots to play with seriously."

509. ————. "Significant Modern Writers: Aldous Huxley." *Expository Times* (Edinburgh), 71 (Jan., 1960), 100–103.

Brave New World debunks the possibility of progress through science; such "progress" comes at the expense of the loss of the soul. H's novels read in sequence give a sense of deepening human unhappiness. In an extravert age, H approaches all problems as inner: man is torn from within by doubts and frustrations. H's emphasis on mysticism assumes that the initiative for salvation lies with the mystic who seeks out God: but this reverses Biblical dialectic, which holds that only God can rescue us from ourselves. H embraces "the god of the philosophers" rather than "the God of Abraham, of Isaac...."

510. Stössinger, Felix. "Alter und neuer Huxley." *Weltwoche* (Zürich), 17 (1949), 5.

511. Stokes, Sewell. "Aldous Huxley in London." *Listener*, 58 (Dec. 12, 1957), 977–978.

Stokes gives reminiscences of the late 1920's and H's feelings about other writers. Shaw was fond of showing off busts and pictures of himself; H didn't admire Galsworthy; he felt he was of another generation than that described in Waugh's *Vile Bodies*; readers are afraid to approach D.H. Lawrence; Woolf had a lovely sense of words, but never got close to her characters; Dreiser can't write, is unreadable; once H has finished with his novels, he has no interest in rereading them.

512. Stürzl, Erwin. "Aldous Huxley--Zeitgebundenheit und Zeitlosigkeit seines Werkes." *Stimmen der Zeit*, 156 (April, 1955), 49–59.

513. ————. "Aldous Huxleys Gedanken über die Sprache." *Germanisch-romanische Monatsschrift*, Neue Folge, 8 (July, 1958), 286–300.

H often makes etymological and morphological comments, but these show that he is better informed on the artistry

of language than he is in the science of linguistics.
His esoteric, technical terminology shows a many-layered
human experience within his artistic framework.

514. Sullivan, J.W.N. "Interviews with Great Scientists:
      Aldous Huxley." *Observer* (London), Feb. 1, 1931, pp.
      15-16.

Four topics are discussed: Making Things Clear to
Oneself, The One-Sided Genius, Newton as Monster, and
The Age of Silliness. H said he doesn't write for his
readers and doesn't want to think about them. He writes
for writing's sake, to solve literary problems he puts
to himself. His books represent different stages in
his progress toward an outlook, but they are all pro-
visional and all move toward a definitive view not yet
clearly conceived. Progress in one direction hinders
progress in other directions. Newton paid a heavy price
for his discoveries: he was incapable of friendship,
love, fatherhood. The right ideal is Greek: balance and
harmony among all powers. H likes C.D. Broad's theory
of psychic survival; it seems to prove survival after
death. H foresees a time when people will revolt against
their present conditioned passive boredom.

515. Sutherland, Alistair. "Aldous Huxley's Mind at Large."
      Twentieth Century, 155 (May, 1954), 441-449.

In H's *The Doors of Perception*, color and depth senses
are remarkably altered by the use of mescalin. The Mind
at Large is perceptually limited by the brain and central
nervous system under normal conditions; mescalin by-
passes these mechanisms. Through mescalin, H experienced
the "other worlds" of the mystic, the medium, and the
schizophrenic. Art is a poor substitute for the drug-
induced experience. Sutherland doubts that H would have
had a comparable experience had he taken mescalin 40
years earlier in his career.

516. Sutherland, James. *English Satire*. Cambridge, England:
      Cambridge University Press, 1958.

Along with giving brief notes on H, Sutherland remarks
that the satirist is now worried about saving humanity
from extinction, or from the loss of its essential
humanness. He doubts that the Peacock-like novels of H
will survive the end of the century.

517. Swinnerton, Frank. *Figures in Foreground: Literary*

Reminiscences, 1917-1940. New York: Doubleday, 1964. Pp. 185-189.

Swinnerton finds H wandering into "fatal intellectual solitariness." This excursion into mysticism is on an intellectual basis; it is not the naively expressed pure experience of the ancient mystics. Swinnerton knew H from the beginning, with the writing of *Limbo*, *Crome Yellow*, etc. The characters in these earlier novels "were often recognizable caricatures of living people"; the fashionable West End was delighted when they could recognize the victim, but the victim was angered.

518. ————. *The Georgian Scene.* New York: Farrar, 1934. Pp. 439-447.

Despite his career as a novelist, H has remained a poet. Swinnerton gives various biographical anecdotes about H and his appearance. H called his first novel "Peacockian"; like Peacock, H is also a scholar-satirist. *Crome Yellow* dared to laugh at "first-rate people." H has book learning and some practical knowledge of men's actions. Despite its brilliance, Lawrence said that *Point Counter Point* might have been written by a "precocious adolescent." *Brave New World* is the work of a poet, full of thought and feeling, but like all of H's books, it is negative. H tried "by a process of successive loathings to reach some positive philosophy."

519. Sykes, Christopher. "Aldous Huxley and Original Sin." *Listener*, 90 (Nov. 1, 1973), 601-602.

Review of Volume I of Bedford's *Aldous Huxley* (see 2). By 1939, H had done all of his best work. The later books are no longer new or vital; and the longer ones are badly done. H wrote fiction during his earlier years because it sold better than essays and because he needed the money, even though he was better at essays than fiction. His philosophical reasoning is muddled, his view of evil naive, as in *Eyeless in Gaza*.

520. Szladits, Lola L. "New in the Berg Collection: 1962-1964." *Bulletin of The New York Public Library*, 73 (April, 1969), 240.

Early in 1961, H's California home, library, and manuscripts were destroyed by fire. That summer, already experiencing symptoms of a cancer that was to be fatal, H traveled in Europe attending many meetings--that of the Parapsychology Foundation, meetings with experts on

acupuncture and psychedelics. Items in the Berg Collection include a 16-page manuscript, "Notes on a Mental
Journey," concerning the 1961 trip. In 1958, a Broadway
production of *After Many a Summer* was planned; H collab-
orated with Ralph Rose on the typescript (the play was
never produced). In 1962 H wrote a letter to Myrick
Land concerning the feud between D.H. Lawrence and
J. Middleton Murry.

521. Temple, Ruth Z. "Aldous Huxley et la littérature
française." *Revue de la Littérature Comparée*, 19
(Jan.-March, 1939), 65-110.

Crome Yellow quotes a modern young intellectual woman:
"there were very few first-rate things in the world and
... those were mostly French." Rimbaud's poems influenced
the young H. Pantagruel is present in H's comedy; H
admired the conciseness, progression, of French classical
tragedy. La Rochefoucauld's *Maximes* were a favorite of
H. Flaubert is H's "saint of letters." H often refers
admiringly to Balzac and Stendhal. He has a special
interest in Baudelaire (Spandrell in *Point Counter Point*
"is" Baudelaire), but H misunderstood Baudelaire's
reasons for satanism—the "chrétien à rebours." After
Baudelaire, Rimbaud was the greatest French poet. H
also refers often to Mallarmé and Laforgue. Anatole
France is H's first master in the French novel, as may
be seen from *Crome Yellow* and *Antic Hay*. But H develops
a closer resemblance to Gide, as may be seen by comparing
The Counterfeiters and *Point Counter Point*. Remy de
Gourmont provides some of the ideas of Chelifer in *Those
Barren Leaves*. H admired Proust, but with reservations;
he often criticizes him as well. Jules Romains and H
were both interested in science, and both turned to
mysticism. H did excellent translations of Baudelaire,
Gourmont, Mallarmé, Rimbaud, and others. He showed an
admirable appreciation of French literature.

522. Thiébaut, Marcel. "Trois romanciers étrangers: Huxley,
Morgan, Caldwell." *Revue de Paris*, 1 (Dec. 1, 1937),
685-700.

Eyeless in Gaza assembles various episodes by juxta-
posing them; they concern intellectual life, philosophy,
psychology, politics: the technique was used also by
Proust. Association is by idea, not by chronology. The
purpose of this method is to focus on the problem of
personality. Anthony Beavis's search for inner unity is
fully pursued, but isn't convincing to the reader; perhaps
H will succeed better in another novel.

523. Thiry, A. "Zamjatins *Wij* als model voor A. Huxley en
     G. Orwell." *Dietsche Warande en Belfort*, 122 (1977),
     508-521.

524. Thomas, W.K. "'Brave New World' and the Houyhnhnms."
     Revue de l'Université Ottawa, 37 (Oct.-Dec., 1967),
     686-696.

     The Brave New World society, though it sometimes re-
     sembles ours, also shows marked differences: promiscuous
     copulation, lack of family attachments, engenderment in
     bottles, Bokanovsky groups (up to 96 identical members
     in each one, genetically produced). Since Freud deplored
     sexual repression and family tensions, these are elimi-
     nated in *Brave New World*. In the 1920's, Fordism meant
     mass production and the assembly line. H meant to show
     assembly-line production of human beings in *Brave New
     World*. "Freud" and "Ford" are used as catchwords to
     remind the reader of the meaning of H's satire. Swift's
     catchwords "Reason" and "Benevolence" are repeated less
     often in the Houyhnhnm episode in *Gulliver's Travels*;
     Swift is more subtle than H, relies solely on narrative,
     and produces a more complicated work than H does. Swift
     too is questioning the absolute merits of Reason and
     Benevolence; following this method, H questions the
     merits of Freud and Ford.

525. Thompson, Leslie M. "A Lawrence-Huxley Parallel: *Women
     in Love* and *Point Counter Point*." *Notes & Queries*, 15
     (Feb., 1968), 58-59.

     H borrowed a passage from *Women in Love* to use in
     Point Counter Point: the idea that both a murderer and
     a murderee are needed for the crime; both performers are
     temperamentally suited to their parts. But in *Point
     Counter Point* it is Spandrell, not Rampion, who makes
     the observation, and Spandrell is Rampion's antitype.
     H often borrowed material from other literary sources,
     but he adapts them to his particular uses with a cus-
     tomary ironic twist.

526. Thorp, Margaret Farrand. "Is Aldous Huxley Unhappy?"
     Sewanee Review, 38 (July, 1930), 269-277.

     H's "materialism" gets stronger with his later books;
     it is an Elizabethan zest for life. Because he has a
     better eye for detail than for form, H's plays fall a
     little flat. *Antic Hay* is the most sincerely unhappy of
     all of H's books. His later short stories--as in *Little
     Mexican*, *Young Archimedes*, *Two or Three Graces*--are

more sympathetic than the earlier ones. *Proper Studies* sounds as if it were written by Bertrand Russell, not H; here H is more concerned with what he's saying than with how he is saying it.

527. Tindall, William York. *Forces in Modern British Litera-
       ture, 1885-1946.* New York: Knopf, 1947. Pp. 185-223.

In his chapter "The Hunt for a Father," Tindall sees Rampion (*Point Counter Point*) as H's portrait of Law-rence; H remained Lawrence's disciple until Lawrence's death. A second portrait of Lawrence appears in *Brave New World*: the New Mexican savage who dies martyr to the values of H.G. Wells. But H showed his disenchant-ment with Lawrence in *Beyond the Mexique Bay*. Gerald Heard replaced Lawrence as H's idol--"man's disunity can be cured by religion." H told of his conversion to Heard in *Eyeless in Gaza*. Still later, H became involved with the Vedanta Society.

528. ———. "Transcendentalism in Contemporary Literature,"
       in *Asian Legacy and American Life*, ed. Arthur E.
       Christy. New York: John Day, 1945. Pp. 175-192.

Tindall agrees with Gray's censure of H's later works (see 223) as escapism. Tindall sees H as an idealist whose sensitivity has been upset, but who had enormous talent for depicting what was offensive, grotesque, and strange. Still, his later career made only a limited use of this talent.

529. ———. "The Trouble with Aldous Huxley." *The American
       Scholar*, 11 (Oct., 1942), 452-464.

The specific trouble with H begins with *After Many a Summer*, and it is due to Gerald Heard. "For all his in-telligence, Huxley cannot resist a dominant personality." Lawrence preceded Heard in this role. "Spandrell in *Point Counter Point* is Huxley's consequent farewell to cyni-cism and diabolism as a way to truth, beauty and de-portment; and Philip Quarles is Huxley's acceptance of Lawrence's criticism of Huxley." But H's visit to Mexico proved Lawrence's primitivism false; H's essay on Lawrence in *The Olive Tree* ironically criticizes religious en-thusiasts. H may not have recognized Lawrence's feeling for the occult, but Lawrence convinced H that religion was a cure; hence, Lawrence "had softened Huxley for Gerald Heard." The H who wrote *Crome Yellow* would have laughed at Heard's theories, but in 1935 H believed in them.

Heard, H, Bertrand Russell, and others formed the Peace
Pledge Union. H's *Ends and Means* was deeply influenced
by Heard: neo-Buddhist and neo-Lamarckian views. *Eyeless
in Gaza* tells of H's conversion to Heard's views. *After
Many a Summer* presents further propaganda for Heard's
religion. As Mr. Propter, Gerald Heard becomes coherent,
lucid, and not too redundant (qualities Tindall doesn't
find in Heard's own writing). Religious writers like
Eliot can create art, inspired by a belief which they
are under no compulsion to explain. But a private religion demands that the artist be prophet and missionary
as well as artist. This is a larger role than H can
carry off successfully.

530. Ueda, Tsutomu. "Theory and Practice: Aldous Huxley's
Ideal of Perfected Humanity." *Studies in English
Literature* (Imperial University, Tokyo), 15 (July,
1935), 372-386.

531. Ulrichsen, Erik. "Huxley, Hollywood." *Perspektiv (Det
danske magasin)*, 18, 5 (1961), 7-14.

532. Vallette, Jacques. "Aldous Huxley: esquisse d'une évolution." *Revue Anglo-Américaine*, 8 (April, 1931), 329-
340.

Vallette traces H's evolution through the early works--
Leda, the short stories, *Crome Yellow*, *Antic Hay*, to
Point Counter Point. For the first time, in *Those Barren
Leaves*, H poses a moral principle. Action is not an end
in itself; it serves the spirit; one must submit the
material to the spiritual. H lacks the means to choose
between logic and life. To close himself up in esthetic
hedonism, or other alternatives such as those of Chelifer
or Calamy or Spandrell--all are legitimate solutions.

533. Van Danzich, S. "*Adonis and the Alphabet*." *Australian
Quarterly*, 30 (1958), 113-118.

These essays have a wide range in tone and subject.
H's skill came from his intensive work as a journalist
and reviewer. The essays inform and enrich the reader's
mind, but H is sometimes glib and "new." There is still
"a certain immaturity which Huxley has never lost"--still
much muckraking about sex and other taboo topics. Despite his new turn of interest, H's "excursions into
mysticism never have the directness and sincerity of
personal experience." Language imparts knowledge, but
it also "obscures the fundamental truth it is intended

to express, and as such becomes an instrument of our undoing."

534.   Van der Volk, E.   "Huxley, Orwell en het Russische Party-
       programme." *Economische-statistische Berichten*, Summer,
       1961, pp. 976-977.

535.   Van Doren, Carl, and Mark Van Doren. *American and
       British Literature Since 1890*. New York: Century,
       1925. Pp. 210-211.

       H "has seen the established virtues practiced without
       reward and the established vices practiced without
       penalty." Always in perfect control of his fictional
       characters, H submits them to his wit, finding something
       absurd in every step they take. But H "genuinely admires
       the undeluded intelligence." He would prefer an orderly,
       just universe; not finding the universe so, he becomes
       bitter.

536.   Van Werveke, Hans.   "Aldous Huxley en de Lage Landen."
       Vlaamse Gids, 51, 7 (July, 1967), 265-272.

       H's first view of the Netherlands noted the geometrical
       arrangement of the landscape. His first wife, Maria,
       was a Belgian refugee living in England during World
       War I; they were married in Belgium in 1919. Belgium is
       the background for H's story "Uncle Spencer," and Belgium
       is referred to in Chapter 2 of *Point Counter Point*.

537.   Vedanta Society. *Vedanta in Southern California: An
       Illustrated Guide to the Vedanta Society*. Hollywood,
       Calif.: Vedanta Press, 1956.

538.   Vein, I.   "Huxley as Musical Critic." *Chesterian*, 29
       (Jan., 1955), 81-86.

       A skillful, perceptive writer is more rewarding to
       read for his account of music than the professional
       music reviewer. Not all, but many, great writers re-
       spond well to music: Nietzsche, Proust, Mann, Joyce; H
       is one of the most remarkable. He did music reviews for
       Westminster Gazette, Feb., 1922-23, then for the *Athenaeum*.
       Antic Hay contains a portrait of the composer Peter
       Heseltine (Peter Warlock). H disliked excessively
       emotional music; disliked Rimsky-Korsakoff and Scriabine,
       the latter of whom tried, in H's words, "to make art out
       of an exposed nerve." Mozart and Beethoven are his
       favorites; somewhat lesser, among the moderns, are Debussy

and Delius. De Falla and Ravel lack form. Bach is more
satisfying than Wagner, Mozart more satisfying than R.
Strauss. Beethoven's last sonatas are inexhaustible;
Tchaikovsky's *Pathétique* is not. (See also 255.)

539.   Venter, Susan. "The 'Dog Episode' in Aldous Huxley's
       Eyeless in Gaza: An Exegesis." *Standpunte*, 24 (Aug.,
       1971), 16-19.

       Though *Eyeless in Gaza* is usually accepted as a
religious novel, the sexual episodes are abhorrent to
most religious readers. Helen Amberley is Anthony
Beavis's way to his "detached sensuality," although
she's on the verge of falling in love with him and although she's married and has had other affairs. Helen
and Beavis are "purified" by the splashed blood of the
dog that fell from the airplane. Beavis ends his "detached sensuality," feels tenderness and pity for Helen.
Previously in his fiction, H used dogs to convey the
idea of base animalism in people. Now, Pavlovian re-
flexes are replaced by meaningful transcendence. H has
also renounced his "Life Worshipper's" creed--the blood
creed of animal-like purpose. The dog dies to end sym-
bolically H's attachment to D.H. Lawrence's vitalism.

540.   Vickery, John B. "Three Modes and a Myth." *Western
       Humanities Review*, 12 (Autumn, 1958), 371-378.

       A comparison of three poems on the Leda theme, by
H, W.B. Yeats, and Robert Graves. Yeats and Graves tell
only of the mating; H makes a whole story of the subject,
and is interested in "sociological aspects." Unlike Yeats,
H uses no symbolism; and unlike Yeats he is not interested in the long-term results of Leda's experience.

541.   Villard, Leonie. "Huxley et ses romans." *Revue Cours
       et Conférences*, May 30, 1935, pp. 307-316.

542.   Vines, Sherard. *Movements in Modern English Poetry and
       Prose*. London: Milford, 1927. Passim.

       H's "higher tourism" in *Jesting Pilate* discusses aphro-
disiacs in India, tigers' whiskers in Shanghai. H adapts
the "Grand Tour" of the 18th-century English gentleman to
the needs of middle-class intelligentsia of the 20th century. His *The World of Light* is a comedy about spiri-
tualism--highbrow, but not experimental. H's contributions to the Sitwell's poetry anthology *Wheels* were
"youthful, rebellious energy." The early novels were

done for the cult of the Amusing. "Wit and science
and Yoga have helped him on his way; one may believe
the best French (and no doubt Latin) prose to underlie
the decorum of his style."

543.   Vitoux, Pierre. "Aldous Huxley and D.H. Lawrence: An
       Attempt at Intellectual Sympathy." *Modern Language
       Review*, 69 (1974), 501-522.

H used Jung's psychological types in his "counterpointing" of characters in *Point Counter Point*. H and Lawrence
liked each other, but didn't refrain from criticism of
each other's works. Lawrence saw *Point Counter Point*
and H as symptoms of the evils described in the novel.
H adopted Jung's view that Western civilization was over-
extraverted. H is a much better novelist than essayist;
linking ideas to characters stimulated H's imagination.
Vitoux analyzes the characters in *Point Counter Point*
according to Jung's classifications: Quarles = extravert
intellectual; Rampion = introvert intellectual; Lord
Tantamount = intellectual introvert; Bidlake = introvert,
sexually and spiritually fastidious. H was influenced
more by Lawrence the man than by his novels, though the
"ideal balance" of *Lady Chatterley's Lover* is important
to H. "Balanced opposites" are also expressed in *Do What
You Will*. *Eyeless in Gaza* rejects Lawrence's vitalism
as an idolization of life; Beavis moves instead to
mysticism. In *Ends and Means*, H abandons Jung, uses instead Sheldon's physiological classification. But Lawrence was of far more influence on H than Jung was.

544.   ————. "Structure and Meaning in Aldous Huxley's *Eye-
       less in Gaza*." *Yearbook of English Studies*, 2 (1972),
       212-224.

Eyeless in Gaza is a "richer and better novel" than
Point Counter Point. The purpose of the discontinuous
structure in *Eyeless in Gaza* is to give the effect of
shock, the pathos of growing older in the gay and
anxious 1920's. To transcend the self, Anthony Beavis
learns, is to destroy the self. The personal does not
fit into a pattern. The structure of the novel expresses this fact; mastery of the self is an endless,
impossible task; there is no final wisdom.

545.   Vocadlo, O. "Aldous Huxley." *Rozpravy Aventina*, 7
       (1932), nos. 19, 20.

546.   Voorhes, Richard J. "The Perennial Huxley." *Prairie
       Schooner*, 23 (Summer, 1949), 189-192.

The changes in H's novels are great, but not unaccountable for. Scogan (*Crome Yellow*) anticipates some aspects of *Brave New World*. Scogan also objects to hedonism; so does Calamy in *Those Barren Leaves*, as does Mr. Propter in *After Many a Summer*. The inverted mystic appears in the novels before the true mystic does: Coleman in *Antic Hay*, Chelifer in *Those Barren Leaves*, Spandrell in *Point Counter Point*. The aging playboy is another character type whose gradations intensify as the novels succeed one another. *Eyeless in Gaza* presents Beavis's conversion to mysticism, but Mr. Propter in *After Many a Summer* is much more intensely a mystic. There are of course common displays of lechery in the later, so-called "mystical" novels: Pordage in *After Many a Summer*, as well as Virginia Maunciple in *Ape and Essence*.

547. Wagenknecht, Edward. *Cavalcade of the English Novel from Elizabeth to George VI*. New York: Henry Holt and Co., 1943.

H praised Samuel Butler's *Erewhon* as having "the sense and honesty of Chaucer." H is correct, but irrelevant, in saying that Conrad did not fathom his own creations. Of Lawrence H remarked, "different and superior in kind," but Lawrence cared nothing about the scientific evidence H presented for his consideration. Wagenknecht notes in the Appendix: "H is not interested in the 'problem' of fiction, nor is he basically a novelist; he uses the novel for the expressing of his ideas, which he has also set forth in poems, essays, books of travel, etc."

548. Wagner, Linda W. "Satiric Masks: Huxley and Waugh." *Satire Newsletter*, 3 (Spring, 1966), 160-162.

One-fifth of *After Many a Summer* is given to Mr. Propter's philosophy; the need for such "explanation" to enable the reader to understand the satire condemns H. Waugh's novel *The Loved One* was based on his visit to California; he found Forest Lawn Memorial Park "the only real thing in Hollywood." Waugh consistently wears a satirical mask; H's chameleon-like assumption of attitudes is inconsistent with satire.

549. Wain, John. "Poems of a Prosaist." *New Republic*, 165 (Sept. 11, 1971), 27-28.

Review of *The Collected Poetry of Aldous Huxley*. H had first-rate gifts that were never quite realized. *Brave New World*, in terms of the 1920's, is an interesting failure. *The Perennial Philosophy* seems like a mere

monument to work for work's sake--but it speaks for the
1940's. The essays are impressive for their vast range
of subjects, though they are no longer memorable for what
they say. H spent his career searching for some large
and luminous idea comparable to Darwinism that he could
champion. He never found the "single" idea, but he
visited with many. H wrote poetry from 1916 to 1931,
but the vast stylistic changes being made at the time in
poetry left him deviceless. He followed linguistic convention in poetry, never led it. Writing like a Georgian,
or Keats, or Verlaine, or D.H. Lawrence, he finds no way
to a major statement.

*   ————. "Tracts Against Materialism: *After Many a Summer*
           and *Brave New World*," in "A Critical Symposium on
           Aldous Huxley." See 573.

550. Wajc-Tenenbaum, Rachel. "Aesthetics and Metaphysics:
      Aldous Huxley's Last Novel." *Revue des Langues
      Vivantes* (Brussels), 37 (1971), 160-175.

      The surviving chapter of H's last novel seems to be "a
      collection of speculative self-portraits, a Shandyesque
      picture of the apparent inconsistencies of a man's mind."
      The point of view is really derived from *The Perennial
      Philosophy*. "Only after dying to the time-bound self
      and living in the timeless spirit" will man be able to
      know the divine Ground. Edward and his father in the
      story compete for his mother's attention (she writes
      novels, is often unavailable). There are three temporal
      planes: 1900 (Edward's 11th birthday, Surrey); 1899 (Ed-
      ward's tenth birthday, India); 1963 (Edward is 74). H's
      objective is to state that "time is eternally present."
      A musical, or thematic, handling of the sequence of in-
      cidents, "virtually analogous to polyphony," illuminates
      different planes of consciousness. H is imitating the
      use of the sonata-rondo by Beethoven. The central episode
      is Edward's 11th birthday: its theme is self-knowledge.
      Development and variation alternate in the 1900 and 1963
      scenes, in terms of the public Edward and the private
      one. H is searching for a truth transcending intellectual
      and physical levels: the promise of immortality.

551. ————. "Aldous Huxley and D.H. Lawrence." *Revue des
      Langues Vivantes*, 32 (1966), 598-610.

      Lawrence, when he first met H at Lady Ottoline Morrell's,
      dreamed of living with friends in an ideal community
      where "one may fulfill his own nature and deep desires."

In some ways, H's later settling in Santa Monica, and
the setting of his novel *Island*, fulfil what Lawrence
dreamed of in his Florida project. Gumbril's bravado
in *Antic Hay* shows an attempt to assume a Laurentian
pose. The "complete man" of L is familiar to all of H's
novels of the 1920's except *Those Barren Leaves*, which
defends contemplation. H was fascinated by, and ill at
ease with, Lawrence's ideas on sex: the satyrs and nympho-
maniacs in the novels show this. Kingham in "Two or Three
Graces" is an ambiguous portrait of Lawrence. Despite
his sexuality, Lawrence was prudish; he disavowed his
lower-class origins and idolized aristocrats; these traits
are shown in Kingham. From 1926 on, both H and Lawrence
traveled outside England. Rampion of *Point Counter Point*
(like Lawrence) is the balanced man at peace with himself;
other characters in the novel are foils to him. But Lawrence found Rampion a boring character--"a gas bag--
Your attempt at intellectual sympathy." Rampion is the
first positive character in H's fiction--the turning
point, after which H sought various versions of truth.
After Lawrence's death, H turned more conspicuously to mysticism. *Brave New World* no longer admires primitivism. *Beyond the Mexique Bay* is the end of H's Laurentian phase.

552. ————. "The Collected Poetry of Aldous Huxley." *Revue
     des Langues Vivantes*, 38 (1972), 438-440.

The *Collected Poems* of H, edited by Donald Watt, omits
all but two of the *Jonah* poems; from *The Defeat of Youth*
"A Little Memory" does not appear; the prose poems are
missing; as well as miscellaneous poems for *Oxford Poetry*,
Wheels, and some periodicals. Church's preface says the
poems reveal another side of H: a quality of innocence,
the spiritual side of H. H himself said the poems revealed multiple parts, but if his prose is like that of
Voltaire, the poems are like those of Shelley. The poems
are a part of H's overlong adolescence. H himself said
of his giving up the writing of poetry that men who feel
passionately about ideas don't make poets; they are men
of science or philosophers.

553. ————. "'Consider the Lilies': An Unknown Long Story
     by Aldous Huxley." *Revue des Langues Vivantes*, 44
     (1978), 45-55.

554. Walcott, C.C. "Thoreau in the Twentieth Century." *South
     Atlantic Quarterly*, 39 (April, 1940), 180-184.

Ends and Means is an elaborate application of Thoreau's
ideas to modern society. H takes over bodily ideas from

"Civil Disobedience." "War, in short, is just one manifestation of the concern with unessential externals that
characterizes people with no inner resources." Men's
lives "will be enriched more by interesting work than by
meaningless diversions and possessions." "Believers in
a personal god endow him with their own hatreds and
passions."

555.   Wallace, Mike. "Aldous Huxley on Thought Control: A
       Television Interview." *Listener*, 60 (1958), 373-374.

Overpopulation in underdeveloped countries leads to increasingly powerful governments; indirectly, this phenomenon threatens American freedom too. Over-organization
is the second threat to freedom; it is brought on by
expanded technology. The future dictatorships will win
control by using television and mind-altering drugs to
subdue the masses. There is a serious danger in political
campaigns being managed by advertising strategy. Freedom
is essential in a democracy; self-determination is essential to its citizens.

556.   Walsh, Chad. *From Utopia to Nightmare*. London: Geoffrey
       Bles, 1962. Pp. 25-26; 112-113; passim.

H loathes the society of *Brave New World*; it's a dystopia. *1984* and *Brave New World* are archetypal dystopias.
Each society is ruled by a small elite, who escape from
the grosser forms of brainwashing. Each dystopia settles
for stability, at the cost of individual freedom. *Brave
New World* assures happiness; *1984* assures sheer power.

557.   Walsh, John. "Aldous Huxley: The Late Author Felt
       Scientists Tend to Search for Truth, Ignore Consequen-
       ces." *Science*, 142 (Dec. 13, 1963), 1445-1446.

Ectogenesis perpetuates an inflexible caste system in
Brave New World. In *Brave New World Revisited*, H expressed surprise at the speed with which the prophecies
of *Brave New World* had already been fulfilled. H had an
equivocal view of scientists—their intelligence and use
of reason were admirable, but they develop intellect at
the expense of other attributes: the humane traits of
individuality, charity, sensibility. H criticized the
"specialized meaninglessness" of the sciences. He also
held that both science and art can be indulged in addic-
tively and with the "good conscience" of pursuing the
"higher life."

558.   Ward, Alfred C. "Scourgers and Scavengers of Society,"
       Chapter 5 of his *The Nineteen-Twenties: Literature and
       Ideas in the Postwar Decade*. London: Methuen, 1930.
       Pp. 115-119.

    In Dickens's novels of social justice, villains oppose
heroes, and advocacy is established through pathos, ex-
aggeration, and sentiment. H's emphasis is on the inner,
not the outer, life: the "flux of relationships among
supposedly cultured people." H uses revelation, not
condemnation, to express his views. "He is the most
shattering satirist in English literature since Swift."
But Swift uses irony more effectively. "H can be claimed
as a non-decadent and moral writer, because there is
always in the background of his books the implication
that a more desirable way of life exists and must be
found."

559.   Warnke, Frank. "Aldous Huxley's Precarious Humanism."
       New Republic, 143 (Nov. 7, 1960), 26.

    Review of *On Art and Artists*. Selections come from
nine volumes by H, from 1923 to 1956. H's favorite artists are Chaucer, Piero della Francesca, Breughel,
Bach: breadth, moderation, solidity, are their virtues.
All of them partake of "the divine equanimity, which reconciles all opposites and so transfigures the world."
H deplores the inhuman neatness of systems like that of
Hegel; he favors the good life "where efficiency is always haloed, as it were, by a tolerated aura of mess."
This describes H's own essay style: like cultivated but
casual conversation. Abstract painting for H is too nar-
row: nature is a richer source of forms. Yet despite
his love for Sir Christopher Wren's solidity, H always
comes back to the great oddballs--Dostoevsky, Baudelaire,
Swift, El Greco.

560.   Watson, David S. "*Point Counter Point*: The Modern
       Satiric Novel a Genre?" *Satire Newsletter*, 6 (Spring,
       1969), 31-35.

    Watson proposes to read *Point Counter Point* as suc-
cessful satire, which earlier critics haven't done. The
characters in satire keep the reader at a distance
(whereas in a regular novel, they engage the reader's
sympathy). *1984* is a "modern satirical novel" because
Winston and Julia are sympathetic, but live in a setting
which is satirically conceived. *Point Counter Point*
places elements of novel and satire side by side; they

sometimes even merge. The power of this novel lies in the subtle combination of both. The characters are not "mouthpieces"; they "vacillate between commitments and even interchange traits." "All the characters are not only capable of extending themselves, but equally capable of being caricatures of each other." Reading such a novel, the reader emerges empty and discomforted––he must fill the void with his own values.

561. Watt, Donald J. "The Absurdity of the Hedonist in Huxley's 'The Gioconda Smile.'" *Studies in Short Fiction*, 7 (Spring, 1970), 328-330.

Hutton in "The Gioconda Smile" is bothered by "the irrationality of his capitulation to eroticism, its frustrating nullity." Death is the purest form of absurdity: Hutton toyed with other people's lives; drove Janet to murder his wife, Emily; drove his mistress, Doris, whom he married as a joke, to attempted suicide. *Crome Yellow*, *Antic Hay*, and *Point Counter Point* all show the failure of the hedonist philosophy.

562. ––––––. "Aldous Huxley's Stereoscopic Vision." *Hartford Studies in Literature*, 2 (1970), 263-269.

Review of Meckier's *Aldous Huxley: Satire and Structure* (see 33).

Meckier's thesis is the counterpoint structure of H's fiction. This is in part the method of Crébillon the younger, whom H discusses in *Essays New and Old*. Satire and structure become fused in H, but the fusion weakens in some of the later books. Modern men are egoist-eccentrics, or else split men. "The structural technique of counterpoint thereby continually exposes the tangential egotism of the characters."

563. ––––––. "The Criminal-Victim Pattern in Huxley's *Point Counter Point*." *Studies in the Novel*, 2 (Spring, 1970), 42-51.

H often used systems to classify human beings. The idea of predators vs. victims compares with Jung's classification of extraverts and introverts. But sometimes H has a predator turn into a victim, and vice versa. The criminal-victim pattern dominates *Point Counter Point*. Walter Bidlake and Marjorie vie with each other for roles of victim and aggressor; Walter is the "murderer," but he has pangs of guilt. However, he in turn is the "victim" of Lucy Tantamount. Spandrell congratulates Lucy on her

success as a "murderer" type, with Bidlake as one of her
victims. Spandrell's directing Illidge is another part
of the pattern. Spandrell uses murder in his search for
absolute evil, whereby he can demonstrate its converse,
absolute good. But Spandrell doesn't really find any
absolutes; he only finds his own suicidal death. "Spandrell, a conscientious diabolist and murderer, becomes a
murderee of his Oedipus complex frustrations."

564. ————. "Eliot, Huxley, and 'Burnt Norton, II.'" *T.S.
Eliot Newsletter*, 1 (1974), 5-7.

"Burnt Norton II" owes something to H's "The Burning
Wheel." Eliot and H met at Garsington Manor; Eliot was
asked to read H's third volume of poetry, *Leda*, but he
didn't like it. Nevertheless, Eliot was impressed by
H's wide reading, impeccable taste, acute ear. Eliot
also criticized H's fiction; H is a "depressing life-
forcer who succeeds to some extent in elucidating how
sordid a world without any philosophy can be." "The
Burning Wheel" and "Burnt Norton II" are both meditative
poems; both describe the oscillation between Rest and
Motion; both are divided into three parts. But Eliot
reconciles the rim and hub of the wheel; H sees them as
opposites.

565. ————. "The Fugal Construction of *Point Counter Point*."
Studies in the Novel, 9 (Winter, 1977), 509-517.

H's novel moves through three interlocked stages
which parallel and imitate, as far as fiction allows,
the major parts of a fugue, but differences in the nature
of music and fiction are sufficiently great to render
too literal a reading of one in terms of the other a
gratuitous exercise. The exposition-development-conclu-
sion plan typifies many fugues and H follows such a plan
in *Point Counter Point*. In a fugue the theme is given
by the first voice before it is taken up by others; then
a second voice gives the answer which still preserves
some of the effect of the first statement. H's initial
subject in *Point Counter Point* is the trials of love,
and the countersubject is the specter of death. Walter's
early exchange with Marjorie, followed by his sense of
lust for Lucy, expresses "love"; the connective between
love and death is preoccupation with class (Walter's
disgust as he sits next to a working man on the train).
This pattern becomes the hub of the Tantamount party section (the novel's exposition) and later of the novel's
long developmental section. But in the later part of the

developmental section references to love include violence (Spandrell slashes the phallic foxgloves to shock
Connie). With Chapter 30, death becomes dominant,
figuratively and literally. Walter and Sidney Quarles
are "mortified" by disappointment in love, and Spandrell
and Illidge complete the assassination of Webley; Little
Phil dies of meningitis, Spandrell plans his own death,
old Bidlake is dying, Miss Cobbett commits suicide. "The
fugal construction gives Huxley a form which at once
assures an artistic wholeness for his composition and,
by geometrically redoubling the treatment of the themes
in each section, expansively conveys an impression of the
ubiquity of human folly."

566.   ————. "Huxley's Aesthetic Ideal." *Modern British
       Literature*, 3 (1978), 128-142.

According to H, "the business of the philosopher is to
look on reality as a whole and as it exists in all its
possible modes of being." This view is crucial to the
esthetic of his novels. He praised Pareto's *The Mind and
Society* for rejecting the hope of discovering a "sociological One." Two of H's mottoes were from Goya: "I am
still learning," and "Nothing short of everything will
really do." Most critics until recently have misread
H's aims and have complained about the "fragmentary"
nature of his fiction. Too much of the criticism of H
depends only on statements from Quarles's notebook in
Point Counter Point and from some of the essays in *Music
at Night*. But the letters and journals of H, along with
a variety of essays and interviews, give much better evidence as to how H sought to integrate his fiction. Story,
for its own sake, was not H's ideal, and although Roger
Fry and Clive Bell's esthetic theories about inner design
interested H, he did not finally accept formalism and
art-for-art's-sake. For him, the novel had the resources
of a great orchestra; or, using another figure, it was
capable of stereoscopic vision. To that end, farce and
tragedy are significantly related: "The finest comedy ...
is the most serious, the most nearly related to tragedy."
Late in life, he viewed the aim of fiction as "virtually
analogous to polyphony." In his last and fragmentary
novel, H wanted to describe "the many different human
beings that a man could be." His need to integrate
caused H to mingle literary genres: essay fragments,
playlets, or short stories crop up in the midst of his
longer fiction. The best literature and art, he felt, is
"a synthesis of cacophony and concert in human existence."

567. ————. "The Meditative Poetry of Aldous Huxley."
Modern Poetry Studies, 6 (1975), 115-128.

H's meditative voice in the poems relates to his internal struggle against doubt, as expressed in sustained
metaphors. Not until his fourth book of poems does H
discover workable metaphors. "The need for some guiding
light in the dark night of the soul becomes an enduring
theme in H's poetry." The third volume of poems, *Leda*,
contains a number of vitriolic poems, anti-biblical,
anti-love. Most of the meditative poems appear in *The
Cicadas*. "Orion" resolves the dilemma of "Arabia In-
felix"; H realizes he can dispel doubt only by cultivating
his inner resources. "The Cicadas" expresses the Laurentian theme of faith in the vitality of the universe. "The
Yellow Mustard," published in Isherwood's *Vedanta for the
Western World*, "presents with parable-like simplicity a
fundamental belief in the later Huxley's mysticism."
The field of the mind can find illumination in its own
soil. This, and "The Cicadas," are H's best meditative
poems.

568. ————. "Two Unlisted Stories by Aldous Huxley."
Renaissance and Modern Studies, 19 (1975), 5-8. ("Good
and Old-Fashioned," pp. 9-18; "Under Compulsion," pp.
19-30.)

Eschelbach and Shober's bibliography of H doesn't list
three stories: 1. "Consider the Lilies," *London Magazine*,
Nov., 1954, pp. 17-43. 2. "Good and Old-Fashioned," *The
Sphere*, Dec. 23, 1922, pp. 310-314. 3. "Under Compulsion," *The Magpie*, Summer, 1923, pp. 71-72, 74, 76, 78.
Antic Hay (1923) depicts H's infatuation with Nancy
Cunard, from the male point of view. "Under Compulsion"
deals with the same subject, but the viewpoint is that
of the besieged woman. The beautiful younger sister of
Maria Nuys, Suzanne, repeatedly rejected her persistent
lover; he committed suicide.

569. ————. "Vision and Symbol in Aldous Huxley's *Island*."
Twentieth Century Literature, 14 (Oct., 1968), 149-160;
reprinted in *Aldous Huxley: A Collection of Critical
Essays*, ed. Robert E. Kuehn (see 30), pp. 167-182.

An effective presentation of the central concepts and
symbols of *Island*. The novel uses a syncretic approach
to the problem of existence. H chose Mahayanist thought
as the best of Eastern religions because it's not escapist, but seeks to improve humanity's conditions; in

Island, it is united with Western technology. "Island"
itself symbolizes the submarine connections between all
islands; therefore, a Divine Ground connects all of
isolated humanity. Mountains are a peak of curative,
illuminating mystical experience; Jungle is the everyday
existence, chaotic and destructive. *Moksha*-medicine is
used to awaken the contemplative mind in meditation.
But both Heaven and Hell emerge in such visions. The
novel ends with ambivalence, between hope and despair.

570. Watts, Harold. "Introduction," Harper Classics edition,
      Point Counter Point. New York: Harper & Row, 1947.
      Pp. v-xxvi.

      This is among the earliest postwar attempts to under-
      stand H's works by carefully looking at his purposes
      and his conceptual basis in writing the novels. H is
      "a virtuoso able to excel in whatever form he takes up."
      Point Counter Point has enduring value that is accounted
      for by more than its flippant wit and its violation of
      accepted decencies. Techniques include the use of mul-
      tiple vision rather than a chronicle-type plot; the
      counterpoint approach has both technical and morality
      functions. The novel is H's attack on a society that
      has no morals; the fact that people are indifferent to
      one another proves that the situation is beyond despair.
      Because H had no morality that could serve to judge his
      times, he had to use counterpoint: characters and ideas
      that are set against each other to prove how incomplete
      they are individually. H is therefore a "moral essayist,"
      not simply a novelist. His own disclaimers about being
      a novelist are really understatement: he meant to be both
      a novelist and a moralist.

571. ———. "The Viability of *Point Counter Point*."
      Studies in the Novel, 9 (Winter, 1977), 406-417.

      H's characters in *Point Counter Point* are ones who
      survive, make their living, and endure, by using their
      minds, by clevernesses that impress others and please
      themselves. *Point Counter Point* still has the vitality
      of a first observation of a new phenomenon. H's technique
      is analogous to the montage method used by early films
      and to the collage method of Braque and others. The
      lack of ordinary transitions among parts gives the reader
      an extraordinary sense of closeness to the author, almost
      as if the reader shares in the author's manipulation.
      But H's mockery and admonition are not fused and do not
      accomplish the unity of disparate attitudes accomplished

by greater writers. The confident admonition offered in
Point Counter Point makes it less than fully modern.
Behind the novel is the naive conviction that its major
characters and the author are "capable of drawing up a
better--and temporarily final--agenda for a large section
of mankind."

572. Waugh, Alec. "The Neo-Georgians." *Fortnightly Review*,
      115 (Jan., 1924), 126-137.

H is the only one of his contemporaries to sustain
himself as a writer since World War I. The Georgian
poetry is too homogeneous--pastoral, without deep emotion.
In H's poems and stories, critics of the future will find
more clearly than elsewhere the mentality of the 1920's.
H seems to smile, in detachment, at the fantastic humors
of his characters.

*   Waugh, Evelyn. "Youth at the Helm and Pleasure at the
      Prow: *Antic Hay*," in "A Critical Symposium on Aldous
      Huxley." See 573.

573. ————, et al. "A Critical Symposium on Aldous Huxley."
      London Magazine, 2 (Aug., 1955), 51-64; reprinted in
      Aldous Huxley: A Collection of Critical Essays, ed.
      Robert E. Kuehn (see 30), pp. 18-32.

Contains: Waugh, Evelyn. "Youth at the Helm and Pleasure
at the Prow"; Wilson, Angus. "The House Party Novels";
Wyndham, Francis. "The Teacher Emerges"; Wain, John.
"Tracts Against Materialism"; Quennell, Peter. "Elec-
trifying the Audience."
   Waugh recalls the delightful customs memorialized in
Antic Hay--"Henry James's London possessed by carnival."
He calls it "frivolous, sentimental and perennially
delightful."
   Wilson notes that *Those Barren Leaves* follows where
Crome Yellow left off. Characters reappear, but they are
more intellectual, and more intensely the victims of H's
satire. The novels after *Crome Yellow* and *Those Barren
Leaves* had the power to delight, a quality lost in the
later novels.
   Wyndham says that H has never been an experimental
writer; he is, rather, an accomplished popularizer of
experiments recently made by others. "A certain element
in his treatment of what he thinks disgusting weakens,
in his novels, the force of his striving towards what he
thinks pure."
   Wain believes that H uses "the form of the novel for

some alien purpose." The characters in *After Many a
Summer* are not characters, they are Humours. H is too
eager to show that normal human pleasures are ugly and
degrading.

Quennell maintains that many essays republished in
Music at Night are too slight; there is charm, but im-
permanence, about them. No intermediate stage exists
in H's fiction between spiritual ecstasy and gross sensuality. Similarly in his essays, H is either deeply
stirred by his subject, or filled with flippant distaste
for it. He is more readily excited by ideas than by
things seen.

574. Weaver, Raymond. "Aldous Huxley." *Bookman* (New York),
     60 (Nov., 1924), 262-268.

H's first nine volumes include "brilliant and versatile
experiments of a serious and puritanical artist." "The
moralist in Huxley is at open war with the artist."
None of his verse is of a high order of technical ex-
cellence, passion, inspiration, or lyrical integrity.
All of H's best poetry is of the conjuring-trick variety.
Antic Hay is worthy of comparison with Gide; the *Little
Mexican* stories, by comparison, are bathetic scraps.
Gumbril in *Antic Hay* is much like H when H contributed
to the Sitwells' *Wheels*; *Antic Hay* celebrates futility
with colossal vitality.

575. Webster, H.T. "Aldous Huxley: Notes on a Moral Evolu-
     tion." *South Atlantic Quarterly*, 45 (July, 1946),
     372-383.

Webster criticizes H's partisanship in his later works
for his individualized form of mysticism. H made his own
"private utopia" thereby. Nevertheless, there is a
strong element of continuity in H's growth as an artist
and thinker.

576. Webster, Harvey Curtis. "Facing Futility: Aldous Hux-
     ley's Really Brave New World." *Sewanee Review*, 42
     (April-June, 1934), 193-208.

Those Barren Leaves has a series of characters who echo
ones found in *Antic Hay*. H's "disillusionment" is actually the matter of freeing himself and others of false
illusions: e.g., "the divine quality of physical love"--
an illusion fostered by romantic novels, of which H dis-
abuses us. "Our disillusionment may give birth to a set
of values which will be more lasting." Rampion in *Point*

Counter Point derides inordinate striving, which is typical of so many Browning characters--"an idiotic lie --all this pretending to be more than human." Shelley and St. Francis are also attacked as illusionists. Many of the essays in *Music at Night* and the selections in *Brief Candles* echo topics introduced by Rampion.

577. Weinkauf, Mary S. "The Escape from the Garden." *Texas Quarterly*, 16 (1973), 66–72.

The escape from utopia is like the Fortunate Fall. *Island* is a utopian reply to the dystopian *Brave New World*. Comparisons are also made with other utopias created by W.H. Hudson, Arthur C. Clarke, which also use the Fortunate Fall theme, and by Barjavel and Cooper.

578. Wellek, Rene. "Aldous Huxley." *Listy pro umění a kritiku*, 1 (Oct., 1933), 472–478.

579. ————. "Aldous Huxley." *English Post* (Prague), 1934, pp. 145–147; 151–152.

580. Westlake, J.H.J. "Aldous Huxley's *Brave New World* and George Orwell's *Nineteen Eighty-Four*: A Comparative Study." *Die neueren Sprachen*, 21 (1971), 94–102.

H gives a much more organized and believable account of an organized society than Orwell does in *1984*. H's view of things in *Brave New World* is much likelier to be realized than is the society described by Orwell. Orwell's world is negative, based on thought control, eliminating the past, creating power for its own sake. Society won't long tolerate such a system. H's world uses science to assure universal happiness.

581. Wickes, George, and Ray Frazer. "Aldous Huxley" (interview). *Writers at Work: The "Paris Review" Interviews*, Second Series, ed. George Plimpton. New York: Viking, 1963. Pp. 193–214.

H rewrites extensively, keeps no notebooks, works one chapter at a time rather than having a detailed overall plan. *Brave New World* was begun as a satire of H.G. Wells's *Men Like Gods*, but then it changed in focus. H doesn't read any criticism written of his works. He recommends journalism on a wide variety of subjects as apprenticeship for writers. H faults Freudian psychology because it's based solely on a study of the sick--not of the healthy. He calls *Time Must Have a Stop* his best

novel. He admires Dostoevsky, Gide, and Proust; he has
less liking for Joyce, Woolf, James, Mann; he greatly
admires Lawrence. Only a small part of Lawrence was
represented in Rampion in *Point Counter Point*. "Dostoevsky is six times as profound as Kierkegaard" because he
writes fiction. The fictional man keeps Ideas alive.

582. Wiley, Paul L. "Aldous Huxley." *Contemporary Literature*,
     15 (1974), 148-153.

        Reviews books by Birnbaum, Firchow, Woodcock (see 3,
           13, 48).
        "While assigning a limited value to art, Huxley never-
     theless depended on the art of the novel to produce its
     strongest effects, and in dramatizing his ideas to go
     beyond them, as happened in his culminating and frustrated
     effort to render supernormal states in fiction." "Birn-
     baum is driven frequently to cutting corners and slashing
     through" in his treatment of H's major ideas. Woodcock's
     is the best general study of H to date. But Woodcock
     deemphasizes the influence of Lawrence on H. Woodcock
     does treat well the neglected area of H's short fiction.
     Firchow discusses only novels, in their true role as
     satire rather than as realistic novels. He succeeds
     best with the close structural analysis of works hereto-
     fore judged defective. After *Point Counter Point*, H
     turns from destructive to constructive satire.

*   Wilson, Angus. "The House Party Novels: *Crome Yellow*
        and *Those Barren Leaves*," in "A Critical Symposium on
        Aldous Huxley." See 573.

583. ————. "The Naive Emancipator." *Encounter*, 5 (July,
     1955), 73-76.

        Review of *The Genius and the Goddess*.
        This novel recalls the innocence and absurdity of the
     time of H's own youth, which he first depicted in *Crome
     Yellow*. But it's ultimately a religious tract on the
     vanity of human life, the need to prepare for death.
     In fact, H has never valued earthly life in adult terms.
     "Lawrence's genius almost awoke Huxley from the adoles-
     cent dream that has gradually turned into a Yogi trance."

584. Wilson, Colin. "Existential Criticism and the Work of
        Aldous Huxley." *London Magazine*, 5 (Sept., 1958),
        46-59.

        The existentialist asks whether man should trust his
     emotions when they tell him life is, or is not, worth

living. Self-analysis and a sense of frivolity and
worthlessness give negative verdicts in H's early novels.
Both Philip Quarles and Spandrell in *Point Counter Point*
are examples of unauthentic existence. H himself recognized that *Point Counter Point* is "superficial, bloodless,
observed"--but he understood this only intellectually.
Though H criticizes Swift, St. Francis, and Dostoevsky
in *Do What You Will* for bodiless character, H himself
exhibits the same bodilessness in *Point Counter Point*.
"Though Huxley is so expert at exposing the meaningless and
boring, the un-vital and futile, he has no *creative*
power to express the vital, the heroic." In *Eyeless in
Gaza* the need for stern spiritual discipline is shown;
intellect is not enough. But judged from the existential
viewpoint, H has stood still as a creator. He aimed at
a synthesis, but it turns out to be an intellectual
synthesis, not an existential one.

585. Wilson, Edmund. "Aldous Huxley in the World Beyond Time."
    New Yorker, 20 (Sept. 2, 1944), 64-66; reprinted in his
    Classics and Commercials, New York: Farrar, Straus,
    1950.

    Time Must Have a Stop is a better novel than *After
    Many a Summer* because H returns to the material he handles
    best--London and Florence of the 1920's. *After Many a
    Summer* was an obvious, purely external caricature of
    fantastic California life. *Time Must Have a Stop* drama-
    tizes more effectively H's new interest in mysticism.
    Wilson objects to H's presenting a moral experience which,
    though exalted, is also "a reaction from an incomplete
    experience of what the life of human beings, in their
    relationships on earth, may hold." H's satire is always
    related to his distaste for humanity and his inability to
    understand what other people were aroused about. He is
    not, like Swift or Flaubert, complete and self-sufficient
    as a satirist. The satire in *Time Must Have a Stop* mixes
    oddly with a fable about the most serious questions of
    human destiny.

586. Wilson, Robert. "*Brave New World* as Shakespeare Criti-
    cism." *Shakespeare Association Bulletin*, 21 (July,
    1946), 99-107.

    This is the first of the Shakespeare-H studies. *Brave
    New World* is notable for the extent and variety of its
    Shakespeare allusions. Chapters 16 and 17 contain the
    debate between Mond's Fordian values and Savage's Shake-
    spearean values. Chapter 12 shows Dr. Watson, the

"emotional engineer," praising Savage's rendition of
Shakespeare. Eleven other chapters also cite Shakespeare; in addition to those to *The Tempest*, there are
60 other allusions to 13 other plays. Some are conscious
quotations, and others are unconsciously embedded in
ordinary conversation. H shows the "universality" of
Shakespeare by having Savage so attracted to the plays;
even so, the world of Shakespeare is not shown as being
ideal. In *Those Barren Leaves*, Shakespeare's values
are shown to be confused and archaic, as in their attitudes toward feminine chastity or masculine domination.
Thus, neither the Savage/Shakespeare argument in *Brave
New World* nor the Fordian view takes full precedence.
H seems to mean that Shakespeare ranks as an esthetic
premium, but he is not (as Savage misreads him) an ir-
refutable moral guide.

587. ————. "Versions of *Brave New World*." *Library Chronicle
of the University of Texas*, 8 (Spring, 1968), 28-41.

Wilson describes H's typed copy of *Brave New World*,
theorizes on H's mode of composition, though the revisions
on the manuscript are mostly minor ones.

588. Wing, George. "The Shakespearean Voice of Conscience in
Brave New World." *Dalhousie Review*, 51 (1971), 153-
164.

The Savage's understanding of Shakespeare represents
not only his having read the plays, but also his inborn
moral scruples. His dilemma shows that even the best-
conceived utopia has its weaknesses. The juxtaposition
of a "savage" and Shakespeare forms a double-edged weapon
with which H attacks the Utilitarianism of the Brave New
World.

589. Witschel, Gunter. *Rausch und Rauschgift bei Baudelaire,
Huxley, Benn und Burroughs*. Bonn: Bouvier, 1968.

This is a brief survey of H's theoretical and practical
involvement with drugs.

590. [Wjlden-Raethinge, Anne.] *Ninka & Bendix: 33 portraetter*.
Illus. Hans Bendix. Copenhagen: Rhodos, 1969.

591. Woodcock, George. "Aldous Huxley: The Man and His
Work." *World Review* (London), 4 (June, 1949), 52-54.

H's career as a novelist peaked with *Antic Hay* and
Point Counter Point. The last decade of his life has not

been given to literary work, but to the search for
ethical and religious truth. An increased interest in
moral problems has destroyed the formal quality of his
novels. H turned more successfully to parable and satire,
recognizing he couldn't succeed with the novel. Up
through *Point Counter Point*, personalities and play of
ideas are well integrated, though in Rampion the moraliz-
ing element becomes very strong. Thereafter, H produces
awkward hybrids of sermon and novel. *Ape and Essence* is
deliberately awkward, but for shock value. It has the
anger of satire, but behind it is a real love and respect
for humanity.

592. ————. "Five Who Fear the Future." *New Republic*, 134
        (April 16, 1956), 17-19.

Discusses Shaw, Wells, H, Orwell, Koestler.
H and Orwell are anti-utopians; Wells, Shaw, and
Koestler are ex-utopians. Ex-utopians present a modern
liberal and radical pessimism that rejects man as we
have known him. Anti-utopians are "advocates of the
human race against the distortion of progress"--they
express parables of warning. They are not anti-progres-
sive in an absolute sense.

593. ————. "Mexico and the English Novelist." *Western
        Review*, 21 (Autumn, 1956), 21-32.

Lawrence, H, Waugh, and Greene all went to Mexico in
the 1930's; all but Waugh wrote important books on their
experiences. Each author projected on Mexico the state
of mind he dreads most; then from the horror is extracted
the opposing and consoling virtue. H went to Mexico in
late 1933. *Those Barren Leaves* moves past the brilliance
and cynicism of the earlier novels; with Calamy, it turns
to introspection and self. H was in Mexico after he wrote
Brave New World; seeing the country itself made him re-
ject the primitivism of the native Indians, which he had
partially defended in the person of Savage in *Brave New
World*. H saw a "reptilian glitter" in the eyes of these
natives, but this is characteristic of his quick, dilettante judgment. *Eyeless in Gaza* was written after the
trip to Mexico; it recounts the conversion of the cold
hedonist Anthony Beavis. Beavis's travels in Mexico
parallel H's. Miller, an anthropologist, converts Beavis
to pacifism. Seeing how crude and primitive life was, H
turned to a philosophy of responsibility and love--though
he went on to further stages of mysticism not directly
involving Mexico.

594. Woods, Richard D. *"Sangre patricia* and *The Doors of Perception." Romance Notes*, 12 (Spring, 1971), 302-306.

Manuel Díaz Rodríguez' *Sangre patricia* (1902) presents the hero, Tulio Arcos, taking drugs; he "fantasizes a sensually evocative environment that in many ways conformed to Modernist goals." In both *Sangre patricia* and *The Doors of Perception*, "the participant seems to lose sense of self so that the outer world might be recreated and reexperienced." H said his thinking ability was unimpaired during the drug experience; Tulio's state fluctuated between clarity and haziness. For both, "commonplace objects take on a pristine beauty ... for the first time." Both experience "the destruction of normal spatial relationships." Time also becomes unimportant, unmeasured, for both authors. Neither Tulio nor H experienced aftereffects--though Tulio later drowns himself in the sea to "rejoin" his beloved, who was drowned earlier.

595. Woolf, G. "Prophet and Preacher." *Newsweek*, 75 (May 4, 1970), 101.

Review of H's *Letters*, ed. Grover Smith.
H wrote to Sybille Bedford, "I was born wandering between two worlds, one dead, the other powerless to be born, and have made, in a curious way, the worst of both." These "worlds" were those of the informed skeptic and the mystic. Thus H fixes himself in the traditional dilemma of Matthew Arnold, from whom the quotation is taken. Smith estimates that H wrote at least 10,000 letters; 943 were selected for this edition. The letters have no great literary distinction, save for those written in the 1920's, when H was at his creative peak. They show that H "was a very good and generous man ... that his mind was very rare, very intimidating, very valuable."

*   Wyndham, Francis. "The Teacher Emerges: *Point Counter Point, Eyeless in Gaza, Mortal Coils*," in "A Critical Symposium on Aldous Huxley." See 573.

596. Yeats, W.B. *The Letters of W.B. Yeats*, ed. Alan Wade. New York: Macmillan, 1955. Pp. 849-852.

Yeats remarks of H's *Those Barren Leaves* that it "has the pessimism of modern philosophy." It has historical significance, but is not a lasting work. The style of the book belongs to a previous movement. It has precision but no rhythms, "not a single sentence anybody will ever murmur to himself." Yeats admires H immensely but dislikes him. H "seems unaware how badly his people are behaving. I sympathize however with his sadistic hatred of life."

597. Yoder, Edwin M., Jr. "Aldous Huxley and His Mystics." *Virginia Quarterly Review*, 42 (Spring, 1966), 290-294.

H is "both a writer rebellious against the barrier of the senses and a man much involved in the concrete world of politics and history." He wrote more about mystics than about mysticism. H was haunted by the truth that mysticism is often ethically neuter--as shown in *Grey Eminence*, and more strongly in *The Devils of Loudun*, in which fanaticism makes idolatry of "belief." Saints are disinterested men who achieve indifference to the sensate world; they're least likely to become fanatics. But Father Surin, monk and mystic, betrays this theory too.

598. Young, G.M. "The Emotions and Mr. Huxley." *Life and Letters*, 10 (June, 1934), 280-289.

Young responds to a commentary by H written in the April issue of *Life and Letters*. H, he argues, doesn't use philosophic terms with precision. For example, H uses the word "lust" sometimes in the philosophical sense of sensual appetite, and sometimes in the sense of sexual appetite illicitly indulged. H conceives of Nationalism as if it existed in the light of Orgy, as a part of Hate and Vanity; Young disagrees.

599. Zaehner, R.C. "The Menace of Mescalin." *Blackfriars*, 35 (July-Aug., 1954), 310-323.

H has often written on mysticism, but not until *The Doors of Perception* had he undergone any sort of mystical experience. But what is described isn't any different from what could be experienced by any normally sensitive, cultivated person. There are many parallels to H's experience--as in William James's *The Varieties of Religious Experience*. H confusedly assumes an equation of the Beatific Vision of Christian mysticism with the Dharma-body of the Buddha. The various stages of H's mescalin experience are: (1) transfiguration of natural objects to unimagined beauty; (2) feeling that one is the transfigured things; (3) sudden panic at the overpowering realism of the vision. H's report has interest for physiological reasons, but it has no value for philosophy or theology. H came closer to the gates of hell in this experience than he did to the Beatific Vision.

600. ———. "Mescalin and Mr. Aldous Huxley." *Listener*, 55 (April 26, 1956), 506-507.

In this account of *Heaven and Hell*, Zaehner repeats the claims of his earlier review of *The Doors of Perception*. Zaehner asserts that the effects of mescalin vary with individuals. Zaehner himself tried the drug, but found no increase of color intensity (an effect H experienced); nor did any other of H's "patterns" emerge in Zaehner's experience. Zaehner's experiences were incongruous; mescalin produces an artificially manic condition. H claimed to be merged with his environment--he "was" the chair--but the mystic is totally detached from his environment. H's main failure was not to discriminate among the various kinds of mysticism.

601. ———. *Mysticism Sacred and Profane*. London: Oxford University Press, 1957. Pp. 1-29.

H equates preternatural experience (via mescalin) with religious experience. Eastern religions, however, constitute something to be experienced, not something to be professed (which is the Western way). H's *The Doors of Perception* presents a valid case study. He believes that: (1) Thinking and remembering are not impaired by mescalin. (2) Visual impressions are intensified; space and time are unimportant. (3) Will is impaired, at least in normally accepted causes and beliefs. (4) "Better things," both inner and outer, are experienced. Therefore, H sees salvation as an escape from the self, as the annihilation of the ego and the merging into a greater entity which he calls Mind at Large. As in his earlier essays, Zaehner questions whether what H experienced was really the Beatific Vision. Later in *The Doors of Perception*, H calls the mescalin experience "gratuitous grace." But H is incoherent and contradictory on the use of mescalin for sacramental purposes. If H's definition of mysticism is accepted, then the experiences of manic-depressives must be included also.

602. Zeitlin, Jake. "A Note on Aldous Huxley." *Southwestern Review*, 49 (Spring, 1964), 136-139.

H is unique among English men of letters--he has vast areas of interest and expertise; he is exempt from C.P. Snow's "Two World" categories. A stylistic virtuoso, he is also a compassionate philosopher. Zeitlin introduced H to some Hollywood producers, whereby H got several writing assignments. Zeitlin commissioned H's essays to accompany the edition of Piranesi's "Prisons" published by Zeitlin.

603. Zolla, Elemire. "Aldous Huxley and the Doom of Reason." *Letterature Moderne*, 5 (Sept.-Dec., 1954), 523-530.

H is stylistically cold and cynical, like his philosophical view toward life. Unlike Joyce's *Stephen Hero*, in which the objects have radiance, H's world is opaque. Zolla analyzes a passage from *Time Must Have a Stop* (Sebastian's disappointment following his first sexual experience with Mary Esdaile); the passage shows an unlyrical view of sex; in fact, H's puritanical dislike of the body is shown by his colorless style. But conversely, H is precise and clear where such writers as Conrad and James are vague and evocative. H excels in the quasi-scientific calculation of juxtaposition. (The latter part of this article is fragmented and not greatly supportive of the thesis.)

III

DISSERTATIONS

604. Aninger, Thomas. "The Essay Element in the Fiction of Aldous Huxley." *DA*, 29 (1968), 892A-893A (UCLA).

605. Bentley, Joseph Goldridge. "Aldous Huxley and the Anatomical Vision." *DA*, 22 (1962), 3655-3656 (Ohio State).

606. Birnbaum, Milton. "Aldous Huxley: A Study of His Quest for Values." *DA*, 16 (1957), 360 (NYU).

607. Bowersox, Herman Clay. "Aldous Huxley: The Defeat of Youth." Chicago, 1943.

608. Browning, William Gordon. "Anti-Utopian Fiction: Definition and Standards of Evaluation." *DA*, 27 (1966), 1360A-1361A (Louisiana State).

609. Caylor, Ruth Anita. "The Modern Spanish Novel of the Multiple Protagonist." *DA*, 37 (1976), 2915A-2916A (Wayne State). [Mann, Dos Passos, H as antecedents of the modern Spanish novel.]

610. Cottrell, Beekman Waldron. "Conversation Piece: Four Twentieth Century English Dialogue Novelists." *DA*, 16 (1956), 2159 (Columbia). [On H, Firbank, Green, Compton-Burnett.]

611. Dooley, David Joseph. "The Impact of Satire on Fiction: Studies of Norman Douglas, Sinclair Lewis, Aldous Huxley, Evelyn Waugh, and George Orwell." *DA*, 15 (1955), 2203-2204 (State U. of Iowa).

612. Dykstra, Emmanuel David. "Aldous Huxley: The Development of a Mystic." *DA*, 17 (1957), 3013 (State U. of Iowa).

613. Enroth, Clyde Adolph. "The Movement Toward Mysticism in
      the Novels of Aldous Huxley." *DA*, 16 (1956), 1905
      (Minnesota).

614. Firchow, Peter Edgerly. "Aldous Huxley and the Art of
      Satire: A Study of His Prose Fiction to *Brave New
      World*." *DA*, 26 (1966), 5433 (Wisconsin).

615. Gottwald, Johannes. "Die Erzahlformen der Romane von
      Aldous Huxley und David Herbert Lawrence." München,
      1964 (Inaugural dissertation, München).

616. Gurtoff, Stanley Arthur. "The Impact of D.H. Lawrence
      on His Contemporaries." *DA*, 26 (1966), 5412-5413
      (Minnesota).

617. Hammond, Evelyn B. "Aldous Huxley: Syncretic Synthesist."
      DA, 35 (1974), 3741A-3742A (Southern California).

618. Heckathorn, John Gene. "The Early Novels of Aldous Hux-
      ley." *DA*, 36 (1976), 5316A-5317A (Pennsylvania).

619. Heintz-Friedrich, Suzanne. "Aldous Huxley: Entwicklung
      seiner Metaphysik." Zurich, 1948.

620. Heller, Pamela. "The Spiritual Quest in the Writings
      of Aldous Huxley." Witwatersrand, 1969.

621. Herzog, Ronald M. "From Castle to Commune: A Study of
      Expanding Consciousness in the Novels of Aldous Huxley."
      DA, 35 (1974), 1657A (CUNY).

622. Hines, Father Bede. "The Social World of Aldous Huxley."
      Montreal, 1954.

623. Holmes, Charles Mason. "The Novels of Aldous Huxley."
      DA, 20 (1960), 3743 (Columbia).

624. Holz, Ludwig. "Methoden der Meinungsbeeinflussung bei
      Orwell und Aldous Huxley." Hamburg, 1963.

625. Horwath, William E. "The Ache of Modernism: Thomas Hardy,
      Time, and the Modern Novel." *DA*, 31 (1971), 4164A-
      4165A (Michigan).

626. Jyoti, Dev Datta. "Mystical and Transcendental Elements
      in Some Modern English and American Writers in Relation
      to Indian Thought: R.W. Emerson, H.D. Thoreau, E.M. For-

ster, T.S. Eliot, A. Huxley." King's College, U. of
London, 1957.

627. Krishnan, Bharati. "Aspects of Structure, Technique
and Quest in Aldous Huxley's Major Novels." Uppsala,
1977.

628. Kumar, Prem. "Aldous Huxley's Voyage of Discovery into
Otherness: A Study of His Later Novels." *DA*, 32 (1978),
2955A–2956A (Washington State).

629. Kumler, Alden Dale. "Aldous Huxley's Novel of Ideas."
DA, 18 (1957), 1432 (Michigan).

630. LeGates, Charlotte Jane. "Aldous Huxley and Visual Art."
DA, 35 (1975), 6144A–6145A (Michigan State).

631. Lockridge, Ernest Hugh. "Aldous Huxley and the Novel of
Diversity." *DA*, 25 (1965), 4703 (Yale).

632. Lowry, Wilson McNeil. "Aldous Huxley: Humanist and
Mystic." Illinois, 1941.

633. Lyngstad, Sverre. "Time in the Modern British Novel:
Conrad, Woolf, Joyce and Huxley." *DA*, 27 (1966),
1374A–1375A (NYU).

634. Matter, William Ward. "Aldous Huxley and the Utopian
Tradition." *DA*, 33 (1972), 279A–280A (Texas Tech).

635. Muhawi, Ibrahim M. "A Study of Self and Other in the
Novels of Aldous Huxley." *DA*, 31 (1969), 2394A
(California, Davis).

636. Murray, Donald Charles. "A Study of the Novels of Aldous
Huxley." *DA*, 27 (1967), 4261A (Syracuse).

637. Noonan, Gerald Andrew. "Idea and Technique in the Novels
of Aldous Huxley." *DA*, 32 (1970), 3320A (Toronto).

638. Pandey, Nand Kumar. "The Influence of Hindu and Buddhist
Thought on Aldous Huxley." *DA*, 25 (1964), 1921 (Stan-
ford).

639. Poschmann, Wilhelm. "Das kritische Weltbild bei Aldous
Huxley. Eine Untersuchung über Bedeutung, Grenzen und
Mittel seiner Kritik." Friedrich-Wilhelms Universität,
1937.

640. Powell, Judith A. "Three Vanishing Values--Huxley's
      Permutations of *The Tempest*." *DA*, 34 (1973), 1930A
      (Utah).

641. Sadler, Jeffrey A. "The Politics of the Margin: Aldous
      Huxley's Quest for Peace." *DA*, 35 (1974), 415A (Wis-
      consin, Madison).

642. Schmerl, Rudolf B. "Reason's Dream: Anti-Totalitarian
      Themes and Techniques of Fantasy." *DA*, 21 (1961),
      2298-2299 (Michigan). [On H, C.S. Lewis, Orwell, Rex
      Warner.]

643. Selck, Maren. "Der Kontrapunkt als Strukturpinzip bei
      Aldous Huxley." Cologne, 1954.

644. Shepard, Leslie A. "The Implosion of Personality in the
      Modern European Novel." *DA*, 30 (1969), 340A (NYU).

645. Tomshany, Robert Aladar, II. "Counterpoint in Modern
      British Fiction: A Study of Norman Douglas, Aldous
      Huxley and Lawrence Durrell." *DA*, 36 (1976), 7448A
      (Louisville).

646. Vinocur, Jacob. "Aldous Huxley: Themes and Variations."
      DA, 19 (1958), 1392-1393 (Wisconsin).

647. Watt, Donald James. "The Human Fugue: Thought and Tech-
      nique in Four Novels of Aldous Huxley." *DA*, 29 (1968),
      2728A (Connecticut).

648. Whitesel, George E. "Evolutionary Metaphor: Patterns of
      Continuity in the Thought and Aesthetic of Aldous Hux-
      ley." *DA*, 31 (1971), 6027A (Michigan State).

649. Wigston, Nancy Lee. "Unity and Diversity in the Novels
      of Aldous Huxley." *DA*, 39 (1978), 2267A (Toronto).

IV

BIBLIOGRAPHIES

650. Clareson, Thomas D., and Carolyn S. Andrews. "Aldous Huxley: A Bibliography, 1960-64," *Extrapolation*, 6 (1964), 2-21.

Published by the Department of English, College of Wooster, Wooster, Ohio.
This work continues the Eschelbach and Shober bibliography (see 653).

651. Davis, Dennis D. "Aldous Huxley: A Bibliography, 1965-1973," *Bulletin of Bibliography*, 31 (1973), 67-70.

652. Duval, H.R. *Aldous Huxley: A Bibliography*. New York: Arrow Edition, 1939. 205 pp.

Includes contributions to periodicals.

653. Eschelbach, Claire John, and Joyce Lee Shober. *Aldous Huxley: A Bibliography, 1916-1959*. Foreword by Aldous Huxley. Berkeley: University of California Press, 1961. 150 pp.

Review:
Roberts, R.J. *Library*, 18 (1963), 159-160.

This bibliography includes full lists of original publication of essays, articles, etc.; newspaper contributions and reviews; also a section of secondary material, including unpublished dissertations. Continued by 650 and 654.

654. Eschelbach, Claire John, and Joyce S. Marthaler. "Aldous Huxley: A Bibliography, 1914-1964 (A Supplementary Listing)," *Bulletin of Bibliography*, 28 (1971), 114-117.

This item continues 653.

655. Lash, Barry. *By and About Aldous Huxley: A Bibliography
      of the Aldous Huxley Collection at Milne Library.*
      Foreword by Donald Watt. Milne Library, State Univer-
      sity of New York, College of Arts & Sciences at Geneseo,
      1973. 34 pp.

656. Millett, Fred B.; John M. Manly; and Edith Rickert. *Con-
      temporary British Literature: A Critical Survey and 232
      Author-Bibliographies.* New York: Harcourt, Brace and
      Co., 1944. Pp. 287-288.

      Contains a brief survey of factual notes, including a
      bibliography to date of H's works and studies about H.

657. Muir, P.H., and B. Van Thal. *Bibliographies of the First
      Editions of Books by Huxley and T.F. Powys.* London:
      Dulau, 1927. 61 pp.

      Includes contributions to periodicals.

658. Powell, Lawrence C. *The Writings of Aldous Huxley, 1916-
      1943; an Exhibition of the Collection of Jacob I.
      Zeitlin at the Library of the University of California,
      Los Angeles, July 1 to August 15, 1943.* Los Angeles:
      G. Dahlstrom, 1943. 16 pp.

659. University of California, Santa Barbara. Announcement of
      forthcoming Huxley lecture series and partial checklist
      of Huxley collection. Santa Barbara, 1959. 4 pp.

660. Vitoux, Pierre. "Aldous Huxley at Texas: A Checklist of
      Manuscripts." *Library Chronicle of the University of
      Texas*, 9 (n.d.), 41-58.

      The checklist is divided into four parts: (1) Plays;
      (2) Novels and books of essays; (3) Poems; (4) Separate
      essays. Items previously unrecorded in bibliographies
      are: (1) Now More Than Ever (1932), an unpublished play;
      (3) Myrrhine, The Lady and the Pug, On the Road to Gar-
      sington; (4) The separate essays done mostly for the
      Hearst newspapers: Cars and Babies, The Best Hundred
      Books, The Importance of Being Stupid, Jonah and Politics,
      Leisure, A New Deal Education, Old Age in a Changing
      World, On Living through History, Pea-Nuts and Landscape
      Painters, Political Murder, Population and Politics,
      Racial History, Religion, Science and Man, Talk versus
      Print, A Theory of Buses, The Unscientific Spirit, An
      Afternoon at Cholula, Modern Amusements, Untitled article,
      Abroad in England....

661. Wickes, G. *Aldous Huxley at UCLA: A Catalogue of the Mss in the Aldous Huxley Collection, with the Texts of Three Unpublished Letters.* Los Angeles: University of California, 1964.

AUTHOR INDEX

TITLE INDEX